BEGINNING GERMAN

THE MACMILLAN COMPANY
NEW YORK · CHICAGO
DALLAS · ATLANTA · SAN FRANCISCO
LONDON · MANILA

IN CANADA
BRETT-MACMILLAN LTD.
GALT, ONTARIO

BEGINNING GERMAN

by

The late Otto P. Schinnerer
COLUMBIA UNIVERSITY

Revised by Barbara Schinnerer Tovey

THE MACMILLAN COMPANY, New York

PREFACE TO THE REVISED EDITION

The chief reason for a revised edition of *Beginning German* is to provide an up-to-date description of present-day Germany and Austria in the supplementary readings. This meets an urgent need, since many locales described in the original edition were destroyed by war-time bombing. Whereas the original supplementary readings described the major cities of all Germany, the new text confines itself to locales in West Germany on the ground that East Germany has not been accessible to the American visitor. On the other hand, the readings have been augmented by descriptions of several places in Austria, including Vienna. Large cities are no longer the exclusive objects of attention; the revised readings place equal stress upon the countryside, small towns and villages, and isolated spots of unusual interest. Completely new illustrations have been provided.

A second important innovation is the resetting of the book in Roman type throughout. This change is in conformity with postwar German printing practice and, moreover, is expected to facilitate the task of the student in mastering the fundamentals of the language.

The pedagogical aims of the original edition, as set forth in the author's preface, have been retained in entirety. The initial reading selections, the active vocabulary and the exercises remain unchanged. As far as the grammar is concerned, the only alteration has been a slight amplification, and it is hoped a clarification, of the treatment of prepositions.

The reviser wishes in particular to thank Professor Frederick Sell of Mount Holyoke College, whose collaboration in the writing of the new readings and whose constant advice and assistance have made this edition possible. Thanks are also due to Mr. Henry B. McCurdy and Mr. J. G. Case of The Macmillan Company. Their unfailing courtesy and cooperation have facilitated every aspect of the revision. In conclusion, grateful acknowledgment is made to the German Tourist Information Office and the Austrian State Tourist Department, both of New York City, for the photographs which they so generously made available for the purpose of illustrating this book.

B. S. T.

South Hadley

FROM THE PREFACE
TO THE FIRST EDITION

The outstanding feature of this beginners' book in German is its differentiation between *active* and *passive* vocabulary and the limitation of the former to 500 words.

In recent years there has been an increasing tendency to reduce the vocabularies in elementary grammars and to bring them in line with approved word lists. Some of these books have vocabularies of 1000 to 1200 words, while others exceed this number. No one, it seems, has attempted to reduce the vocabulary below 1000 items. And good reasons have been advanced for not going below this minimum. It is claimed, and generally admitted, that a book with a vocabulary much below 1000 words would become so dry and stilted that it would entail a serious loss of interest on the part of students.

But what is the practical result? The majority of teachers treat these vocabularies as active and require students to memorize them, to learn genders of nouns, declensions, conjugations, spelling, etc. As a consequence the beginning student is confronted with words such as the following, selected at random from a number of recent grammars: **sich auszeichnen, Bergbau, bestätigen, büßen, Eichelsaat, Heugabel, Kabinentür, Kachelofen, Kubikwurzel, Mannigfaltigkeit, Mäuseplage, Nachwelt, Schulzwang, Verfassung, Volksvertreter, Weizenfeld, Zentralheizung.** There would be no very serious objection to the introduction of words like the above if they remained limited in number and were clearly designated as passive words, merely to be recognized by the student in the given passages but not actually made part and parcel of his elementary vocabulary.

Competent authorities in the field of modern language teaching believe that 1000 *active* words constitute about the maximum number that students can reasonably be expected to master in two years of high school or two college semesters. It has been the author's own experience over a period of years that one of the chief difficulties encountered by students in elementary German has been the excessive number of words they were expected to memorize and produce at will with all the grammatical variations involved. In view of the relatively large number of grammatical forms which the student must acquire and control, and in view of the further fact that some students are so deficient in a knowledge of general grammar that frequently they must first be taught the difference between an indirect and a direct object, transitive and intransitive verbs, personal and reflexive pronouns, active and passive voice, etc., it has seemed but reasonable to reduce the load by limiting the active vocabulary without, however, sacrificing the student's interest by curtailing the passive vocabulary. It is with this primary purpose that the preparation of the present book was undertaken.

As this book is planned to be completed in one college semester or one year of high school, the number of active words has been limited to 500. If the student really masters these words and can recognize a considerably large number of passive words, he should have no great difficulty in adding another 500 words to his active vocabulary and a proportionately larger number to his passive vocabulary in the second year of high school or the second college semester, especially as the essential grammatical forms have already been acquired.

These 500 active words were selected from the Schinnerer-Wendt list of 1000 suggested active words.[1] It is not contended that these words necessarily constitute the 500 most frequent or most common active words. While the author has constantly striven to include what seemed to him the most frequent or common words, the exigencies of telling a connected story occasionally required one set of words rather than another. However, even if there should be no general agreement as to the 500 most important active words, this does not constitute any grave difficulty. Practically all students take at least two years of high school German or two college semesters, and by the end of these terms all the other active words will have been introduced.

The author firmly believes in the reading objective, but he also believes that this can best be attained by a reasonable amount of oral and aural practice in the initial stages of modern language teaching. He has attempted to restrict all the exercises (questions, grammatical exercises, and translation exercises) to the limited list of 500 active words. On the other hand, he has felt that because of this very limitation the student should experience no difficulty in

---

[1] Cf. *The German Quarterly*, VI, 2 (March, 1933), pp. 77–90.

acquiring a passive knowledge of the additional words employed in the reading selections proper and in the supplementary reading selections.

The question has been raised why it should be necessary to produce another textbook with the emphasis on active vocabulary when any teacher could designate a limited number of active words in any of the existing texts. The answer is that even if teachers would take the trouble to do so, many obviously passive words are used indiscriminately in the various exercises supplied, and that students would therefore be required to have active control over them.

Idioms

Eighty idioms, an average of three and one-third per lesson, are introduced in the reading selections and designated as active in the vocabulary. These were selected from Hauch's Idiom List.[1] Here too an attempt was made to select only those idioms which might properly be regarded as active.

Reading Selections

The reading selections are connected prose passages, mostly of the anecdotal type. In the author's experience this type has always seemed superior to *realia* for purposes of oral drill. Anecdotes in a foreign language arouse the student's interest as he looks forward to the point of the story. They present a concrete situation which the student easily remembers. They lend themselves readily to the introduction of the common everyday words which the student is to learn. Finally, they can be more easily reproduced in German.

No effort was made to present original stories not hitherto used, although all of them were rewritten and modified. Suitability for the specific purpose was the only criterion. Many of these anecdotes have repeatedly proved their worth in previous textbooks.

Grammar

In each reading selection the new grammatical elements to be introduced are inductively developed and printed in blackface type. Only so much grammar as is essential for a full comprehension of the reading selections is presented as precisely and concisely as possible. Numerous points that many other grammars include for the

[1] *German Idiom List.* Compiled by Edward F. Hauch. The Macmillan Company, New York, 1929.

sake of completeness have been omitted, as such supplementary grammatical information can be more profitably supplied in the succeeding stage of the study of German.

Questions

Most teachers prefer to formulate their own questions. Those supplied here are intended as an aid to the student in preparing his lesson. By writing out the answers or formulating oral responses, the student will be better prepared for the oral drill in class. In a few rare cases the questions themselves contain passive words which the student need merely recognize, but all words required to supply the answers are limited to active words.

Grammatical Exercises

These exercises on the whole follow the conventional patterns. Here again all the words to be supplied by the student are active.

Translation Exercises

Some teachers believe strongly in translation exercises, while others abhor them. They are presented here for the benefit of those who approve. Since these sentences are restricted to the active words, they should not cause insurmountable obstacles.

Vocabulary Building

Each lesson contains a section on vocabulary building. Most of these point out the relationship between German and English and some show the formation of derivatives and compounds. These exercises are intended as an aid to the student's memory, once this relationship or derivation has been established. For this reason English equivalents for the German words are given, as the author does not wish to encourage the dangerous habit of indiscriminately jumping at conclusions of etymological affinity. There was no intention of exhausting the subject. It is believed that the meanings of inseparable prefixes, of suffixes such as **heit, keit, ei, nis, sal, schaft, tum,** etc., can be more profitably introduced at a later stage.

The words employed in these sections as illustrations are not listed in the vocabularies unless they were actually introduced in the reading selections.

Supplementary Reading

These readings deal with German geography and a trip through Germany touching upon the more important cities.

They have a twofold purpose. First, they are to provide facilities for practice in rapid reading without the close analysis of the text required in the regular reading selections at the beginning of each lesson. Secondly, they are to familiarize the student with some of the elementary facts about Germany.

As there seems to be no special virtue in thumbing the vocabulary at the end of the book, the new words used are listed after each selection in order to facilitate more rapid reading.

Teachers who may desire to postpone or omit these readings may do so without inconvenience. All the words employed here are listed again in the vocabulary when first introduced in the regular reading selections.

Poems

Many teachers follow the commendable practice of having students even in the elementary stage memorize a few poems. It is hoped that those supplied as a supplement will offer sufficient range and variety.

In conclusion, the author takes pleasure in expressing his great indebtedness to his colleagues Mr. H. G. Wendt, who not only collaborated with the author in drawing up the list of active words but who also discussed with him in detail the general plan of the book, to Professor Henry H. L. Schulze, who went over the manuscript with meticulous care and made innumerable valuable suggestions, and to Professor F. W. J. Heuser, who generously gave his assistance in reading the proof. It goes without saying that the author has also derived incalculable benefit from his numerous predecessors in the field.

The task of seeing the book through publication was rendered exceedingly pleasant by the invariable courtesy of all the members of The Macmillan Company with whom the author came in contact. He is especially grateful to Mr. Joseph C. Palamountain, whose persuasive powers induced the author to undertake the preparation of this book, to Mr. Henry B. McCurdy, and to Mr. F. T. Sutphen for their sincere cooperation in meeting the author's wishes.

O. P. S.

New York City, March 1, 1935

CONTENTS

xi

ILLUSTRATIONS

Beginning German

In printing and writing German, either German type and script or Roman type and script may be used. German script is now almost wholly obsolete. In print German type predominated until the end of World War II, but today nearly all German publishers are employing Roman type. Therefore Roman type exclusively is used in this book. The student who wishes to familiarize himself with German type will find the German equivalents of Roman letters on pages 260–261 of the appendix.

I. THE GERMAN ALPHABET

ROMAN LETTER		GERMAN NAME	ROMAN LETTER		GERMAN NAME
A	a	ah	N	n	enn
B	b	bay	O	o	oh
C	c	tsay	P	p	pay
D	d	day	Q	q	koo
E	e	ay	R	r	err
F	f	eff	S	s	ess
G	g	gay	T	t	tay
H	h	hah	U	u	oo
I	i	ee	V	v	fow
J	j	yut	W	w	vay
K	k	kah	X	x	iks
L	l	ell	Y	y	ipsilon
M	m	emm	Z	z	tset

Double s has the symbol ß at the end of words and syllables, after long vowels and diphthongs, and before consonants.

II. PRONUNCIATION

German is pronounced with more energy, more precision, and greater distinctness than English.

The only silent letters in German are **h** to indicate length of the preceding vowel, and **e** in **ie** to render long **i** (*ee*).

The representations of German sounds given below are only approximate. The most satisfactory way of acquiring a good pronunciation is to imitate a good living model.

1. *Vowels*

German vowels may be long or short. A vowel is long
- (a) when doubled: **Paar, See, Boot**
- (b) when followed by silent **h: Bahn, geht, ihn**
- (c) generally when followed by a single consonant: **Glas, los, Hut**
- (d) at the end of an accented syllable: **Na′me, le′ben, Blu′me**
- (e) a long stem vowel remains long in inflected forms before two or more consonants: **sagen, sag-st, sag-t.**

A vowel is always short before a double consonant and generally before two or more consonants: **denn, offen, finden, singen.**

Before **ch** and **ß** a vowel may be long or short.

German vowels differ from English vowels in that they are pure, not diphthongs, i.e., they preserve the same sound from beginning to end.

ā	Long as in *father:* **Bahn, Glas, Name, Paar.**
ă	Short as in *what:* **arm, dann, fallen, Mann.**
ē	Long as in *gate:* **geht, leben, nehmen, See.**
ĕ	Short as in *set:* **Bett, Ende, es, messen.**
ī, ie	Long as in *thief:* **die, ihn, Kino, liegen.**
ĭ	Short as in *in:* **bin, finden, immer, Tinte.**
ō	Long as in *no:* **Boot, holen, los, wo.**
ŏ	Short as in *son:* **Gott, offen, Onkel, Sommer.**
ū	Long as in *rule:* **Blume, du, Hut, tun.**
ŭ	Short as in *full:* **Butter, dumm, Mutter, unser.**
y	Like long or short **ü** (see below).

2. Umlaut (Modified Vowels)

The vowels **a**, **o**, **u**, and the diphthong **au** may undergo a change of sound and are then written **ä**, **ö**, **ü**, **äu**. This is called Umlaut or modification of the vowel. A few similar changes are preserved in English.

foot—feet; goose—geese; man—men; mouse—mice.

ā   Long as in *air:* **sähe, spät, Väter, wäre.**

ă   Short as in *let:* **Bänke, Gäste, hängen, Männer.**

ō   Long as in French long *eu.* To produce this sound prepare to pronounce German **ē** and then round your lips while making the sound: **mögen, schön, Söhne, Töne.**

ŏ   Prepare to pronounce *e* as in *let* and round your lips while making the sound: **Dörfer, Göttin, können, öffnen.**

ū   Long as in French long *u.* Prepare to pronounce German **ie** (*ee*) and round your lips while making the sound: **für, müde, Süden, Tür.**

ŭ   Prepare to pronounce short *i* as in *pin* and round your lips while making the sound: **füllen, fünf, Hütte, Mütter.**

3. Diphthongs

ei, ai   Pronounced like *i* in *mine:* **ein, kein, Mai, Kaiser.**

au   Pronounced like *ou* in *mouse:* **Baum, braun, Haus, Maus.**

eu, äu   Pronounced like *oi* in *toil:* **heute, Leute, Bäume, Mäuse.**

4. Consonants

b   At the beginning of a word or syllable as in English: **Ball, bis, blau, Butter.**
At the end of a word or syllable and before consonants like English *p*: **ab, gab, liebt, ob.**

c   Occurs only in words of foreign origin, or in proper names. Before **a, o, u, au, ou,** and consonants, like English *k*: **Café, Cato, Cranach, Crusoe.**
Elsewhere like *ts* in *cats:* **Cäsar, Celsius, Cent, Cicero.**

ch   Has four different sounds, for two of which there are no English equivalents. Front **ch** or **ich**-sound occurs after the front vowels **e, i, ei (ai), eu (äu), ö, ü,** and consonants. The air is made to escape between the tongue and the roof of the mouth. Practice by whispering the *y* of *yes:* **ich, dich, Licht, mich.**

Back **ch** or **ach**-sound occurs after the back vowels **a, o, u,** and **au: auch, Buch, Dach, Loch.**

Before **a, o,** or a consonant, in words derived from Greek or Latin, like English *k:* **Charak'ter, Chor, Christ, Chronik.**

Before other vowels it has the **ich**-sound: **Chemie', China.**

In words derived from the French like *sh:* **Champa'gner, Chef, Chauffeur'.**

chs	When the **s** is not an inflectional ending, or the beginning of a suffix, like English *x:* **Achse, Ochs, sechs, Wachs.**
ck	Like English *ck:* **Acker, backen, stecken, Stück.**
d	At the beginning of a word or before vowels like English *d:* **da, dumm, finden, reden.**
	At the end of a word or syllable and before consonants like English *t:* **Band, Hand, Land, Lied.**
dt	Like English *t:* **sandte, Stadt, Städte, wandte.**
f	Like English *f:* **fallen, Feder, Fenster, folgen.**
g	At the beginning of a word or syllable like English *g* in *get:* **Garten, gut, legen, sagen.**
	At the end of a word or syllable and before consonants like *k:* **Berg, lag, sagt, Tag.** This is the official stage pronunciation, but many Germans pronounce final **g** like **ch.**
	The ending **-ig** is always pronounced like **ich: König, wenig.**
gn	Both letters are pronounced: **Gnade, Gnom, Vergnü'gen.**
h	At the beginning of a word or syllable like English *h:* **haben, halten, hart, Haus.**
	After a consonant (except **c** or **s**) and after a vowel it is silent, but indicates that the vowel is long: **geht, ihn, Lehrer, nehmen.**
j	Like English *y:* **ja, Jahr, jeder, Ju'li.**
k	Like English *k:* **kalt, Karte, Katze, Kind.**
kn	Both letters are pronounced: **Knabe, kneten, Knie, Knopf.**
l	Pronounced farther forward than in English. The tip of the tongue touches the back of the upper teeth: **laut, lernen, liegen, sollen.**

m	Like English *m*: **Mann, mehr, mein, morgen; Dame, Dom, Heim, um.**
n	Like English *n*: **Name, neben, nein, Nummer; Bahn, Ende, in, tun.**
ng	Always like English *ng* in *singer* (not as in *finger*): **Finger, lang, sang, singen.**
nk	Like English *nk*: **Bank, Funke, sinken, trinken.**
p	Like English *p*: **Paar, Park, Post, Preis; Lippe, Oper, Papst, Suppe.**
pf	Both letters are pronounced: **Pfeife, Pferd, Pflanze, Pfund; Apfel, Kupfer, Opfer, stampfen.**
ph	Like English *ph*: **Phantasie′, Phili′ster, Philosoph′, Phrase.**
ps	Both letters are pronounced: **Psalm, Psychologie′.**
qu	Like English *kv*: **Qual, Quelle, quer, Quinta.**
r	Either is trilled by vibrating the tip of the tongue against the upper gum, or it is guttural, i.e., the uvula is vibrated. American students generally find the trilled **r** easier: **reden, reisen, Ring, rund; fahren, Erde, Ohr, Uhr.**
s	At the end of a word or syllable, when doubled, or before a consonant and not at the beginning of a word, like English *s* in *see:* **das, Haus, ist, Post.**
	At the beginning of a word or syllable, before a vowel, like English *z* in *zeal:* **lesen, Rose, sehen, sein.**
	Before **p** or **t**, but only at the beginning of a word, like English *sh*: **spät, spielen, Stein, still.**
ss, ß	Like English *s* in *see:* **Fluß, lassen, messen, Straße.**
sch	Like English *sh*: **schade, scheinen, Schiff, Schule; Busch, frisch, Tasche, waschen.**
t	Like English *t*: **Tafel, Tee, tief, Tisch; Hut, rot, Luft, weit.**
	Before the endings **-ian, -ion, -ient** in words of Latin origin like English *ts* in *cats:* **Nation′, Patient′, Portion′, Station′.**
th	Now found only in words of foreign origin and in proper nouns. Pronounced like English *t.* The English *th* sound does not exist in German: **Thea′ter, Theodor, Theorie′, Thron.**
tz	Like English *ts* in *cats:* **jetzt, Netz, Platz, sitzen.**
v	Like English *f*: **Vater, viel, Vogel, von.**

In words still felt as foreign, like English *v*: **Novel'le, Novem'ber, Universität', Vene'dig.**

w   Like English *v*: **Wagen, waschen, wer, Wind.**

x   Always like English final *x* (*ks*): **Axt, Hexe, lax, Max.**

z   Like English *ts* in *cats:* **Zahl, zehn, Zimmer, zwei; Herz, Holz, kurz, tanzen.**

III. CAPITAL AND SMALL LETTERS

All nouns, or words used as nouns, are capitalized: **das Haus** *the house;* **der Alte** *the old man;* **das Interessanteste** *the most interesting thing.*

The conventional pronoun of address **Sie** *you* and the corresponding possessive adjective **Ihr** *your* always begin with a capital letter.

The personal pronoun **ich** *I* is not capitalized except when it begins a sentence.

Proper adjectives denoting nationality are not usually capitalized: **deutsch** *German;* **englisch** *English.* However, indeclinable proper adjectives ending in **-er** begin with a capital letter: **die Leipziger Messe** *the Leipzig Fair.*

IV. DIVISION INTO SYLLABLES

A single consonant between two vowels goes with the following vowel: **sa-gen, le-sen, ha-ben.**

Of two or more consonants, the last one usually goes with the following vowel: **fin-den, Gar-ten, Was-ser.**

ch, sch, ß, ph, th, st are not separated but go with the following vowel: **Bü-cher, Hä-scher, Bu-ße, So-phie, katholisch, be-ste.** **ck** is resolved into **k-k, tz** is divided **t-z.**

Compounds are divided into their component parts when the last element is a distinct word: **Schul-zimmer, Blei-stift.**

V. PUNCTUATION

In English commas are used to indicate speech-pauses; in German they indicate syntactical relations.

All subordinate clauses are set off by commas.

Er lernte die Aufgabe, als er nach Hause kam.
He learned the lesson when he came home.

All infinitive phrases containing modifiers are set off by commas.

Er ging nach Hause, um die Aufgabe zu lernen.
He went home to learn the lesson.

A comma is NOT used before **und** *and* introducing the last of a series.

Vater, Mutter und Kind
father, mother, and child

The exclamation point is used after imperatives.

Lernen Sie die Aufgabe!
Learn the lesson.

The colon (:) is used before a direct quotation, and the quotation marks are printed ,,-".

Er sagte: ,,Ich habe kein Buch."

The apostrophe indicates the omission of one or more letters. It is NOT used to indicate the possessive case except in the case of proper names ending in an **s**-sound: **Strauß' Musik.**

Aufgabe Eins

Gender of Nouns. *Pronouns.* *Present Tense of Verbs*

I. READING SELECTION

Die Familie

Karl ist ein Junge. Anna ist ein Mädchen. Karl geht in
die Schule. Er ist ein Schüler und hat ein Buch. Es ist grün
und schwarz. Karl hat eine Schwester. Sie ist ein Mädchen
und heißt Anna. Sie geht auch in die Schule und hat auch
ein Buch. Es ist auch grün und schwarz. Anna ist eine
Schülerin. Karl ist Annas Bruder. Anna ist Karls Schwester. Sie sind Schüler.

Karl und Anna haben auch einen Vater und eine Mutter.
Der Vater heißt Herr Braun. Die Mutter heißt Frau Braun.
Der Vater ist kein Junge. Er ist ein Mann. Er ist auch kein
Schüler. Er geht nicht in die Schule. Die Mutter ist kein
Mädchen. Sie ist eine Frau. Sie ist auch keine Schülerin
und geht nicht in die Schule. Nur der Bruder und die Schwe-
ster gehen in die Schule. Sie heißen Karl und Anna.

Karl hat einen Vater, eine Mutter und eine Schwester.
Anna hat keine Schwester. Sie hat einen Bruder.

II. VOCABULARY

Words marked with an asterisk are to be considered *active*
words, i.e., they are to be so thoroughly memorized that you
can produce them in German instantaneously. You must also
be able to spell them correctly, you must know the corresponding article with each noun, and later the principal parts
of both nouns and verbs.

Words not marked with an asterisk are *passive* words, i.e.,

9

it will be sufficient for the purposes of this book if you recognize their meaning when they appear in German.

With the object of reducing to a minimum the effort involved in learning vocabulary, the active words in each lesson, beginning with the third, will be limited to twenty. The first lesson contains thirty-five, the second lesson twenty-five active words, making a total of five hundred for the entire book. However, words will frequently be introduced in an earlier lesson as passive words and in a later lesson will be reintroduced as active words. All the idioms listed are to be considered active and should be memorized.

Naturally it is much easier to recognize the meaning of words when they appear in German than to know them actively. You are therefore advised to concentrate on the active list. The passive words will cause you much less trouble than the active words.

*Idioms
- **in die Schule**   to school
- **er heißt**   he is called, his name is
- **wie heißt er?**   what is his name?

*auch   also, too
*die Aufgabe   the lesson, task
*der Bruder   the brother
*das Buch   the book
*das   the (neuter article)
*der   the (masculine article)
*die   the (feminine article)
*ein   a, one; eins   one (used in counting)
*er   he; it
*es   it; she
  die Fami'lie   the family
*die Frau   the woman; Mrs.; wife
*gehen   to go
  grün   green
*haben   to have
*heißen   to be called
*der Herr   the gentleman; Mr.
*in   in, into, to
*ja   yes

*der Junge   the boy
*kein   not a, no
*das Mädchen   the girl
*der Mann   the man; husband
*die Mutter   the mother
*nein   no
*nicht   not
*nur   only
*die Schule   the school
*der Schüler   the pupil
*die Schülerin (fem.)   the pupil
  schwarz   black
*die Schwester   the sister
*sein   to be
*sie   she; they; it
*und   and
*der Vater   the father
*was   what
*wohin   where (whither, to what place)

III. GRAMMAR

A. *Nouns and Pronouns*

	MASCULINE	FEMININE	NEUTER
Nominative	der ein kein ⎱Vater Bruder Mann Schüler	die eine keine ⎱Mutter Schwester Frau Schülerin	das ein kein ⎱Mädchen Buch
Accusative	den einen keinen ⎱Vater Bruder Mann Schüler	Always the same as the Nominative	Always the same as the Nominative
Nominative case of corresponding pronouns	**er** *he*	**sie** *she*	**es** *it, she*
Plural	**sie** *they*		

1. In German all nouns are capitalized.
2. Nouns denoting living beings usually have their natural gender. **Das Mädchen** and a few others are exceptions. Lifeless objects may be either masculine, feminine, or neuter. *The only satisfactory way of knowing the gender of a noun is to memorize the definite article with it.*
3. The accusative case differs from the nominative only in the masculine. Even here the noun forms are generally identical with those of the nominative. The article **der** is changed to **den**, whereas **ein** and **kein** add the ending -en in the masculine accusative.
4. The feminine singular forms of **ein** and **kein** are **eine** and **keine** in both the nominative and accusative cases.
5. Pronouns must correspond in gender and number with the nouns for which they stand.

	MASCULINE	FEMININE	NEUTER
Nominative	der Stuhl *the chair* der Tisch *the table*	die Tür *the door* die Feder *the pen*	das Zimmer *the room* das Heft *the notebook*
Corresponding pronouns	er *it*	sie *it*	es *it*
Plural	sie *they*		

B. *Verbs*

PRESENT TENSE

THIRD PERSON SINGULAR	THIRD PERSON PLURAL
er sie es $\Big\{$ ist *is* geht *goes* hat *has* heißt *is called*	sie $\Big\{$ sind *are* gehen *go* haben *have* heißen *are called*

1. Most German verbs have the infinitive ending **-en.** The third person singular of the present indicative is usually formed by adding **-t** to the stem, i.e., to the infinitive form minus the ending **-en. Ist** and **hat** are exceptions. The third person plural is identical with the infinitive. **Sie sind** is an exception. The infinitive is **sein.**

2. In German there is no emphatic or progressive form corresponding to the English *he does go* or *he is going.*

$$\textbf{Er geht} = \begin{cases} \textit{He goes} \\ \textit{He does go} \\ \textit{He is going} \end{cases}$$

C. *Word Order*

Adverbs cannot ordinarily stand between the subject and the verb in simple declarative statements.

Er geht **auch** in die Schule. *He also goes to school.*

IV. QUESTIONS

1. Was ist Karl? 2. Was ist Anna? 3. Wohin geht Karl?
4. Was hat er? 5. Hat Karl eine Schwester? 6. Wie heißt
die Schwester? 7. Ist sie ein Junge? 8. Ist sie auch ein
Schüler? 9. Wohin geht sie auch? 10. Wie heißt Annas
Bruder? 11. Wie heißt der Vater? 12. Wie heißt die Mutter? 13. Ist der Vater ein Junge? 14. Ist er ein Schüler?
15. Wohin geht er nicht? 16. Ist die Mutter ein Mädchen?
17. Geht sie auch in die Schule? 18. Wohin gehen der Bruder und die Schwester? 19. Wie heißen der Schüler und die
Schülerin?

V. GRAMMATICAL EXERCISES

(a) Supply the proper forms of **ein** or **kein**:

1. Der Vater ist ——— Schüler. 2. Anna hat ——— Bru-
der. 3. Karl ist ——— Mädchen. 4. Die Mutter ist ———
Frau. 5. Karl hat ——— Vater. 6. Der Vater ist ———
Junge. 7. Anna hat ——— Buch. 8. Karl hat ——— Mut-
ter. 9. Die Mutter ist ——— Mädchen. 10. Karl hat
——— Schwester. 11. Der Vater ist ——— Mann. 12.
Anna ist ——— Schülerin. 13. Anna ist ——— Junge. 14.
Karl hat ——— Bruder. 15. Karl ist ——— Mann. 16.
Anna ist ——— Frau.

(b) Supply the definite article:

1. ——— Schüler hat ——— Buch. 2. ——— Mutter
heißt Frau Braun. 3. ——— Bruder und ——— Schwester
gehen in ——— Schule. 4. ——— Frau ist ——— Mutter.
5. ——— Mann ist ——— Vater. 6. ——— Mädchen ist
——— Schülerin. 7. ——— Junge ist ——— Schüler. 8.
——— Schwester heißt Anna.

(c) Substitute the correct pronoun for each noun in black-
face type:

1. **Der Junge** heißt Karl. 2. **Das Mädchen** heißt Anna.
3. **Die Mutter** heißt Frau Braun. 4. **Der Vater** heißt Herr

Braun. 5. **Karl** hat **das Buch.** 6. **Karl und Anna** sind Schüler. 7. **Die Mutter** ist keine Schülerin. 8. **Der Vater** ist ein Mann. 9. **Der Bruder und die Schwester** gehen in die Schule. 10. **Der Schüler** hat ein Buch. 11. **Die Schülerin** hat einen Bruder.

VI. TRANSLATION EXERCISES

1. Anna is a girl. 2. She has a book and goes to school. 3. She also has a brother. 4. The brother is called Karl. 5. Karl is a boy. 6. He is a pupil and goes to school. 7. Anna has no sister. 8. Karl has no brother. 9. Karl and Anna are pupils. 10. They have a father and a mother. 11. What is the father's name? 12. He is not a pupil. 13. He is a man. 14. The mother's name is Mrs. Braun. 15. She is not a pupil. 16. She is a woman. 17. Does the father go to school? 18. The mother is not going to school. 19. Only the brother and the sister go to school. 20. Karl has a father and a mother.

VII. VOCABULARY BUILDING

Under this heading succeeding lessons will contain illustrations showing how the German vocabulary resembles English and how it is further built up by the formation of compounds and derivatives from simple stems. This should be of great help in increasing your passive knowledge of words. At the same time it will aid you in memorizing many active words. In this first lesson, however, it may be helpful to show the historical relationship existing between German and English.

Several thousand years before the birth of Christ, there was one of many other languages which philologists now call the Indo-Germanic or the Indo-European language. No records of this language exist, but on the basis of comparative philology we are assured that such a language must have existed. In the course of time, roughly speaking about a thousand years before Christ, this language began to split into a number of different recognizable branches. We may roughly present the growth of these languages by means of the following language tree.

In this diagram we have indicated the growth of only the Italic and the Germanic Languages. The other branches had a similar development.

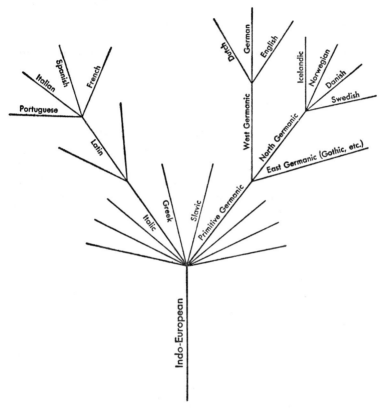

Primitive Germanic eventually split into three additional branches: East Germanic, North Germanic, and West Germanic. East Germanic or Gothic has become extinct. Our knowledge of it is practically limited to the fragments of the biblical translation made in the fourth century by Ulfilas, the bishop of the West Goths. North Germanic eventually branched out into Swedish, Norwegian, Danish, and Icelandic.

West Germanic developed into English, German, and Dutch. It is apparent from the diagram that German and English are more closely related than either German and French or English and French. The numerous French or Latin elements in English date from the time of the Norman conquest of England in 1066. German, English, and French have a common ancestor in the Indo-European language, but German and English are like brother and sister, whereas the close relationship between English and French is one by marriage, as it were.

VIII. SUPPLEMENTARY READING

The words employed in these supplementary reading selections are to be regarded as passive. It will be sufficient to recognize their meaning. With the aid of the Supplementary Vocabulary given below, you will be able to read these passages almost at sight. The most important words used here will be reintroduced as active words in subsequent lessons.

Geographie

Deutschland ist ein Land in Europa. Es ist in der Mitte Europas. Im Norden von Deutschland sind die Nordsee, Dänemark und die Ostsee oder das Baltische Meer. Im Osten ist Polen. Im Südosten sind die Tschechoslowakei und Österreich. Im Süden sind Österreich und die Schweiz. Im Westen sind Frankreich, Belgien und Holland. Im Westen von Europa ist der Atlantische Ozean. Im Osten von Europa ist Asien. Rußland, China, Japan und Indien sind in Asien. Andere Kontinente sind Nordamerika, Südamerika, Afrika und Australien.

Ein Mann in Europa ist ein Europäer. Ein Mann in Deutschland ist ein Deutscher. Ein Mann in England ist ein Engländer. Ein Mann in Amerika ist ein Amerikaner. Eine Frau in Europa ist eine Europäerin. Eine Frau in Deutschland ist eine Deutsche. Eine Frau in England ist eine Engländerin. Eine Frau in Amerika ist eine Amerikanerin.

IX. SUPPLEMENTARY VOCABULARY

(das) **Afrika** Africa
(das) **Amē'rika** America
der **Amērika'ner** the American
die **Amērika'nerin** the American (woman)
ander other
(das) **Asien** Asia
der **Atlantische Ozean** the Atlantic Ocean
(das) **Austra'lien** Australia
das **Baltische Meer** the Baltic Sea
(das) **Belgien** Belgium
(das) **China** China
(das) **Dänemark** Denmark
eine **Deutsche** a German (woman)
ein **Deutscher** a German
(das) **Deutschland** Germany
(das) **England** England
der **Engländer** the Englishman
die **Engländerin** the English woman
(das) **Euro'pa** Europe
der **Europä'er** the European
die **Europä'erin** the European (woman)

(das) **Frankreich** France
die **Geographie'** the geography
(das) **Holland** Holland
im = in dem in the
(das) **Indien** India
(das) **Ja'pan** Japan
der **Kontinent'** the continent
das **Land** the land, country
die **Mitte** the middle, center
(das) **Nord'amē'rika** North America
der **Norden** the north
die **Nordsee** the North Sea
oder or
der **Osten** the east
(das) **Österreich** Austria
die **Ostsee** the Baltic Sea
(das) **Polen** Poland
(das) **Rußland** Russia
die **Schweiz** Switzerland
(das) **Süd'amē'rika** South America
der **Süden** the south
der **Südosten** the southeast
die **Tschechoslowakei'** Czechoslovakia
von of
der **Westen** the west

Aufgabe Zwei

Present Tense of Verbs

I. READING SELECTION

Die Schule

Heute ist Montag. Der Vater fragt Karl und Anna: „Geht ihr heute in die Schule?" Sie antworten: „Ja, wir gehen heute in die Schule." Der Vater und die Mutter gehen nicht in die Schule. Sie bleiben zu Hause. Der Vater fragt Karl: „Hast du das Buch?" Karl antwortet: „Ja, ich habe das Buch, und Anna hat auch ein Buch." Anna sagt: „ Ich habe auch einen Bleistift und eine Feder."
Ein Lehrer ist ein Mann. Eine Lehrerin ist eine Frau. Ein Schüler ist ein Junge. Eine Schülerin ist ein Mädchen. Der Lehrer lehrt. Der Schüler lernt.
Der Lehrer fragt Anna: „Wie heißt du?" Sie antwortet: „Ich heiße Anna Braun." Der Lehrer fragt auch Karl: „Wie heißt du?" Er antwortet: „Ich heiße Karl Braun." Der Lehrer fragt Anna: „Bist du Karls Schwester?" Sie antwortet: „Ja, ich bin Karls Schwester."
Der Lehrer lehrt Deutsch. Der Schüler und die Schülerin lernen Deutsch. Karl fragt den Lehrer: „Wie heißen Sie?" Er antwortet: „Ich heiße Herr Meyer." Anna fragt: „Sind Sie der Lehrer?" Herr Meyer antwortet: „Ja, ich bin der Lehrer. Was seid ihr?" Karl und Anna antworten: „Wir sind Schüler und haben ein Buch."
Der Lehrer fragt: „Habt ihr auch einen Bleistift und eine Feder?" Die Klasse antwortet: „Ja, wir haben einen Bleistift und eine Feder." Der Lehrer sagt: „Ich schreibe die Aufgabe an die Tafel. Ihr schreibt sie in das Heft." Die Schule ist aus. Karl und Anna gehen nach Hause.

II. VOCABULARY

*Idioms {
zu Hause   home, at home
nach Hause   home (*direction*)
die Schule ist aus   school is over
}

*an   on; at; to
*antworten   to answer
 aus   out
*bleiben   to remain, to stay
*der Bleistift   the lead pencil
*deutsch   German (*adjective*)
 (das) Deutsch   the German
 language
*du   you (*familiar sing.*)
*die Feder   the pen; the
 feather
*fragen   to ask
*das Haus   the house
*das Heft   the notebook
*heute   today
*ich   I
*ihr   you (*familiar pl.*)

*die Klasse   the class
 lehren   to teach
*der Lehrer   the teacher
*die Lehrerin   the teacher
 (*fem.*)
*lernen   to learn
*der Montag   Monday
 nach   toward, to
*sagen   to say
*schreiben   to write
*die Tafel   the blackboard
*wer   who
*wir   we
*wo   where
 zu   at; to
*zwei   two

III. GRAMMAR

A. *Present Tense of Verbs*

Infinitive	fragen	lernen
Stem	frag-	lern-
Singular	1. ich frag-**e**	1. ich lern-**e**
	2. du frag-**st** Sie frag-**en**	2. du lern-**st** Sie lern-**en**
	3. er ⎫ sie ⎬ frag-**t** es ⎭	3. er ⎫ sie ⎬ lern-**t** es ⎭
Plural	1. wir frag-**en**	1. wir lern-**en**
	2. ihr frag-**t** Sie frag-**en**	2. ihr lern-**t** Sie lern-**en**
	3. sie frag-**en**	3. sie lern-**en**
Infinitive	antworten	heißen
Stem	antwort-	heiß-
Singular	1. ich antwort-**e**	1. ich heiß-**e**
	2. du antwort-**est** Sie antwort-**en**	2. du heiß-**t** Sie heiß-**en**
	3. er ⎫ sie ⎬ antwort-**et** es ⎭	3. er ⎫ sie ⎬ heiß-**t** es ⎭
Plural	1. wir antwort-**en**	1. wir heiß-**en**
	2. ihr antwort-**et** Sie antwort-**en**	2. ihr heiß-**t** Sie heiß-**en**
	3. sie antwort-**en**	3. sie heiß-**en**

Infinitive	haben	sein
Stem	hab-	

Singular	1. ich hab-**e**
	
	2. du **hast**
	Sie hab-**en**
	
	3. er
	  sie } **hat**
	  es
		1. ich **bin**
		
		2. du **bist**
		Sie **sind**
		
		3. er
		  sie } **ist**
		  es

Plural	1. wir hab-**en** 2. ihr hab-**t** Sie hab-**en** 3. sie hab-**en**	1. wir **sind** 2. ihr **seid** Sie **sind** 3. sie **sind**

1. Note the endings in black-face type in the conjugation of **fragen** and **lernen**. These are the regular endings for the present indicative. When the stem ends in a **d** or **t,** as in **antworten,** an **e** is inserted before the regular endings in the second person singular and plural familiar and in the third person singular. **Haben** is regular except in the second person singular familiar and the third person singular where the **b** of the stem **hab-** has been lost. The conjugation of **sein** is quite irregular and must be memorized as such. In the second person singular familiar **heißen** adds -t instead of -st: **du heißt.**

2. The second person singular and plural has two forms, the familiar and the conventional (or polite) forms. The familiar forms, with the pronouns **du** and **ihr,** are used to address near relatives, intimate friends, and children up to the age of about fifteen. As a general rule the familiar form is used in addressing people whom you call by their first names. In most other cases the conventional form is used. This is always identical with the third person plural except that the pronoun **Sie** is capitalized.

3. A simple question in German is usually rendered in English by the progressive or emphatic form.

Schreibt er die Aufgabe? $\begin{cases} \textit{Is he writing the lesson?} \\ \textit{Does he write the lesson?} \end{cases}$

B. Word Order

Adverbs or adverbial phrases of time precede adverbs or adverbial phrases of place.

Er geht heute in die Schule. *He goes to school today.*
Er ist heute hier. *He is here today.*

IV. QUESTIONS

1. Was ist heute? 2. Was fragt der Vater? 3. Was antworten Karl und Anna? 4. Gehen der Vater und die Mutter auch in die Schule? 5. Wo bleiben sie? 6. Hat Karl ein Buch? 7. Wer hat auch ein Buch? 8. Was hat Anna auch? 9. Was ist ein Lehrer? 10. Was ist eine Lehrerin? 11. Was ist ein Schüler? 12. Was ist eine Schülerin? 13. Wer lernt? 14. Was lernt der Schüler? 15. Lernt die Schülerin auch Deutsch? 16. Wer schreibt die Aufgabe an die Tafel? 17. Wer schreibt die Aufgabe in das Heft? 18. Wohin geht Karl?

V. GRAMMATICAL EXERCISES

(a) Conjugate in the present tense:

1. I remain at home.
2. I learn the lesson.
3. What do I say?
4. I write the lesson.

(b) Supply the correct verb forms:

1. Wir (gehen) in die Schule. 2. (Gehen) du auch in die Schule? 3. Nein, ich (bleiben) zu Hause. 4. Der Lehrer (fragen) die Klasse: „(Haben) ihr einen Bleistift?" 5. Der

Schüler (antworten): „Ja, ich (haben) einen Bleistift." 6. (Sein) du ein Schüler, Karl? 7. Ja, ich (sein) ein Schüler. 8. (Sein) Sie ein Lehrer, Herr Braun? 9. Anna (lernen) die Aufgabe. 10. Der Lehrer (schreiben) sie an die Tafel. 11. Ich (heißen) Karl. 12. (Sein) ihr Schüler oder Lehrer?

(c) Give the German forms of the words in parentheses:

1. Ich habe (a) Feder und (a) Bleistift. 2. Er schreibt an (the) Tafel. 3. Er geht (home). 4. Sie ist (a) Lehrerin. 5. Er hat (no) Bruder. 6. Sie bleiben (at home). 7. Der Lehrer fragt (the) Schüler: „Hast du (a) Buch?" 8. (A) Schülerin ist (a) Mädchen. 9. Wie heißt (the) Lehrerin?

VI. TRANSLATION EXERCISES

1. Karl asks the teacher: What is your name? 2. He answers: My name is Mr. Meyer. 3. The pupil (*masc.*) learns the lesson. 4. Where are Karl and Anna going? 5. Who is staying at home? 6. Does the mother go to school? 7. We have no pencil. 8. Are you a pupil, Anna? 9. Karl and Anna are learning German. 10. They go to school today. 11. Karl and Anna, are you writing the lesson in the notebook? 12. The brother and the sister are called Karl and Anna. 13. What is the teacher's name? 14. Anna has a pencil and a pen. 15. School is over and Anna goes home.

VII. VOCABULARY BUILDING

Many words in German and English are cognates, i.e., they have a common ancestor, as explained in the preceding lesson. In some cases this is very striking as they are identical in spelling and meaning, though differing in pronunciation. The following list is only a partial selection from a much larger number available.

der Arm	die Hand	die Rose
der Ball	das Land	der Sand
die Butter	das Nest	der Wind
der Finger	der Ring	der Winter

Many words of foreign origin are likewise identical in spelling and meaning, but not in pronunciation.

der April'	das Auto	das Muse'um
der August'	der Meter	der Profes'sor
der Septem'ber	der Kilometer	das Restaurant'
der Novem'ber	die Million'	das Thea'ter

VIII. SUPPLEMENTARY READING

Mehr Geographie

Deutschland ist ungefähr so weit nördlich wie der Süden von Kanada. England ist noch weiter nördlich als Deutschland. Aber das Klima in England und Deutschland ist mild wegen des Golfstroms. Im Winter ist es in Deutschland nicht so kalt wie im Norden der Vereinigten Staaten und im Sommer ist es nicht so heiß. Am Nordpol ist es sehr kalt. Am Äquator ist es sehr heiß.

Deutschland hat ungefähr 68 (achtundsechzig) Millionen Einwohner, die Vereinigten Staaten ungefähr 150 (hundertundfünfzig) Millionen. Die Vereinigten Staaten haben mehr als doppelt so viele Einwohner wie Deutschland. Aber Deutschland ist nicht so groß wie die Vereinigten Staaten von Nordamerika. Deutschland hat ungefähr 350 000 (dreihundertfünfzigtausend) Quadratkilometer oder 145 000 (hundertfünfundvierzigtausend) englische Quadratmeilen. Der Staat Texas allein hat beinahe 700 000 (siebenhunderttausend) Quadratkilometer oder 265 000 (zweihundertfünfundsechzigtausend) englische Quadratmeilen. Deutschland ist also nicht so groß wie der Staat Texas. Aber Texas hat nur ungefähr 8 000 000 (acht Millionen) Einwohner. Westdeutschland hat 250 000 (zweihundertfünfzigtausend) Quadratkilometer oder 95 000 (fünfundneunzigtausend) englische Quadratmeilen und ungefähr 49 000 000 (neunundvierzig Millionen) Einwohner. Ostdeutschland hat nur 100 000 (hunderttausend) Quadratkilometer oder 40 000 (vierzigtausend) englische Quadratmeilen und ungefähr 18 000 000 (achtzehn Millionen) Einwohner.

Von Norden nach Süden in Deutschland ist es ungefähr 850 (achthundertundfünfzig) Kilometer oder 530 (fünfhundertunddreißig) englische Meilen. Ein Kilometer ist ungefähr 5/8 (fünf Achtel) Meilen. Ein Meter ist ungefähr 39 (neununddreißig) Zoll. Ein Kilometer ist tausend Meter.

IX. SUPPLEMENTARY VOCABULARY

aber but
allein alone
als than
also therefore
am = an dem at the
der Äqua'tor the equator
beinahe almost
doppelt double; twice
der Einwohner the inhabitant
englisch English
der Golfstrom the Gulf Stream
groß large
heiß hot
kalt cold
(das) Kanada Canada
das (or **der**) **Kilometer** the kilometer
das Klima the climate
mehr more
die Meile the mile
das (or **der**) **Meter** the meter
mild mild
die Million' the million
noch still
nördlich north
der Nordpol the North Pole

(das) Ostdeutschland East Germany
das (or **der**) **Quadrat'kilometer** the square kilometer
die Quadrat'meile the square mile
sehr very
so so, as
der Sommer the summer
der Staat the state
der Südwesten the southwest
tausend thousand
(das) Texas Texas
ungefähr about, approximately
die Verei'nigten Staaten the United States
viel much; *pl.* many
wegen on account of
weit far; **weiter** farther
(das) Westdeutschland West Germany
wie as
der Winter the winter
der Zoll the inch

Aufgabe Drei

Singular Declension of Nouns.   Use of Cases.
Prepositions

I. READING SELECTION

Das Schulzimmer

Das Schulzimmer ist ein Zimmer in **der** Schule.   Das Zimmer hat zwei Fenster und eine Tür.   Das Fenster **des** Zimmers ist groß und breit.   Die Tür **des** Zimmers ist auch groß und breit, aber sie ist nicht so groß und breit wie das Fenster.   In **dem** Zimmer sind auch ein Tisch und ein Stuhl.   Die Farbe **des** Tisches ist braun.   Die Farbe **des** Stuhles ist auch braun. An **der** Wand ist eine Karte von Deutschland.   In **dem** Buche ist auch eine Karte von Deutschland.   Die Karte an **der** Wand ist groß, aber die Karte in **dem** Buche ist klein.   Die Farben **des** Buches sind rot und schwarz.   Der Lehrer schreibt die Aufgabe an die Tafel.   Er schreibt mit **der** Kreide.   Die Farbe **der** Kreide ist weiß.   Der Schüler und die Schülerin schreiben die Aufgabe in das Heft.   Sie schreiben mit **der** Feder und **dem** Bleistift.   Die Farbe **der** Feder ist schwarz. Die Farbe **des** Bleistifts ist gelb.

Herr und Frau Braun gehen nicht in die Schule.   Sie bleiben zu Hause.   Der Bruder und die Schwester gehen gern in die Schule.   Sie haben ein Buch, einen Bleistift und eine Feder.   Der Lehrer ist ein Mann und heißt Herr Meyer.   Er lehrt Deutsch, aber Karl und Anna lernen Deutsch.   Sie lernen gern Deutsch.

Die Schule ist aus.   Der Schüler und die Schülerin gehen nach Hause.   Sie lernen die Aufgabe und schreiben sie in das Heft.   Karl schreibt gern mit **dem** Bleistift, Anna schreibt gern mit **der** Feder.

II. VOCABULARY

*Idioms $\begin{cases} \text{so groß wie} \quad \text{as large as} \\ \text{er schreibt (etc.) gern} \quad \text{he likes to write (etc.)} \\ \text{wie ist . . . ?} \quad \text{how is . . . ?} \end{cases}$

*aber but
*braun brown
breit wide, broad
*(das) Deutschland Germany
drei three
*die Farbe the color; *pl.* die Farben
*das Fenster the window
*gelb yellow
gern(e) gladly
*groß big, large
*die Karte the card; map
*klein small
*die Kreide the chalk

*mit (+ *dat.*) with
*rot red
das Schulzimmer the school-room
*schwarz black
so so, as
*der Stuhl the chair
*der Tisch the table
*die Tür the door
von (+ *dat.*) of; from
*die Wand the wall
*weiß white
*wie as; how
*das Zimmer the room

III. GRAMMAR

A. The Definite Article in the Singular

	MASCULINE	FEMININE	NEUTER
Nominative	der	die	das
Genitive	des	der	des
Dative	dem	der	dem
Accusative	den	die	das

B. Singular Declension of Nouns

	MASCULINE	FEMININE	NEUTER
Nominative	der Mann	die Frau	das Buch
Genitive	des Mannes	der Frau	des Buches
Dative	dem Mann(e)	der Frau	dem Buch(e)
Accusative	den Mann	die Frau	das Buch
Nominative	der Bruder	die Schule	das Fenster
Genitive	des Bruders	der Schule	des Fensters
Dative	dem Bruder	der Schule	dem Fenster
Accusative	den Bruder	die Schule	das Fenster

1. Feminine nouns, except for the article, do not change in the singular.

2. Masculine and neuter nouns of one syllable generally add **-es** in the genitive and **-e** in the dative, whereas nouns of more than one syllable merely add **-s** in the genitive.   In colloquial speech the **-e** in the genitive and dative is usually dropped.

C. Use of Cases

1. The nominative is used as the subject of a sentence.

Der Vater geht nach Hause.

It is also the case of the predicate noun, used with verbs such as **sein, heißen, bleiben,** and **werden** (*to become*).

Herr Meyer ist **der Lehrer.**
Er heißt **Herr Meyer.**

2. The genitive denotes possession or relation.

Das Buch **des Schülers** ist rot und schwarz.
Die Mutter **der Schülerin** heißt Frau Braun.
Die Farbe **des Zimmers** ist gelb.

The genitive is also used after certain prepositions.

wegen **des Golfstroms**   *on account of the Gulf Stream*

3. The dative is the case of the indirect object.

Die Schwester schreibt **dem Bruder** einen Brief (*letter*).

The dative is also used after certain prepositions.

Der Lehrer schreibt mit **der Kreide.**
Der Tisch ist in **dem Zimmer.**
Die Karte ist an **der Wand.**

4. The accusative is the case of the direct object.

Karl und Anna haben **einen Vater** und eine Mutter.
Sie schreiben **die Aufgabe.**

The accusative is also used after certain prepositions.

Der Lehrer schreibt an **die Tafel.**
Der Schüler schreibt in **das Heft.**
Der Junge geht in **die Schule.**
Das Mädchen geht in **das Zimmer.**

D. *Prepositions*

Certain prepositions always take the genitive, others always the dative, and still others always the accusative. A fourth group, however, such as **in** and **an,** may govern either the dative or the accusative. These prepositions require the dative when the verb expresses rest or action not directed towards somebody or something. They are generally used in answer to the question **wo?** (*where, in what place?*). They govern the accusative when the verb expresses action directed towards somebody or something. They are generally used in answer to the question **wohin?** (*whither, to what place?*).

In time expressions these prepositions require the dative in answer to the question *when?* the accusative in answer to the question *how long?*

The following prepositions have already been employed. Only those marked with an asterisk have so far been designated as active.

1. Prepositions governing the genitive:

wegen   *on account of*

2. Prepositions governing the dative:

aus   *out, of, from*
*__mit__   *with, by, at*
nach   *toward, to, for, after, according to*
von   *from, of, by*
zu   *to, at, for, in, with*

3. Prepositions governing either the dative or the accusative:

*__an__   *on, at, by, along, in, to, near*
*__in__   *in, at, into, to, within*

A complete list of all prepositions used in this book will be found on pages 176–177 (Lesson XX) and on pages 246–247 of the appendix.

IV. QUESTIONS

1. Was ist ein Schulzimmer? 2. Wo ist das Schulzimmer?
3. Wer ist in dem Schulzimmer? 4. Wie ist das Fenster des
Zimmers? 5. Was ist in dem Zimmer? 6. Was ist die Farbe
des Tisches? 7. Wo ist der Stuhl? 8. Was ist die Farbe des
Stuhles? 9. Was ist an der Wand? 10. Wo ist auch eine
Karte? 11. Wie ist die Karte an der Wand? 12. Wie ist die
Karte in dem Buche? 13. Was sind die Farben des Buches?
14. Wer schreibt die Aufgabe an die Tafel? 15. Wer schreibt
die Aufgabe in das Heft? 16. Schreibt der Lehrer mit dem
Bleistift an die Tafel? 17. Wer schreibt mit dem Bleistift?
18. Ist die Farbe der Kreide schwarz oder weiß? 19. Was ist
schwarz? 20. Was ist gelb?

V. GRAMMATICAL EXERCISES

(a) Supply the genitive of the definite article:

1. Die Farbe ———— Bleistifts ist gelb. 2. Die Tür ————
Zimmers ist groß. 3. Das Buch ———— Schülers ist rot und
schwarz. 4. Die Farbe ———— Tisches ist braun. 5. Die
Feder ———— Schülerin ist schwarz. 6. Der Bleistift ————
Bruders ist gelb. 7. Die Farbe ———— Tafel ist schwarz. 8.
Die Farben ———— Buches sind rot und schwarz.

(b) Supply the dative of the definite article:

1. Der Lehrer schreibt mit ———— Kreide. 2. In ————
Zimmer ist ein Stuhl. 3. Die Karte in ———— Buche ist klein.
4. Der Schüler schreibt mit ———— Feder. 5. An ————
Wand ist eine Karte von Deutschland. 6. Anna geht mit
———— Bruder in die Schule. 7. Karl schreibt ———— Lehrer
einen Brief. 8. Anna ist in ———— Schule.

(c) Supply the correct form of the definite article:

1. ———— Mädchen fragt ———— Bruder: „Wo ist ————
Buch?" 2. Er antwortet: „Es ist in ———— Schule." 3.
- ———— Schwester ———— Schülers geht heute nicht in ————

Schule. 4. Herr Meyer ist ——— Lehrer. 5. ——— Schülerin schreibt ——— Aufgabe in ——— Heft. 6. ———
Tisch ist in ——— Zimmer. 7. ——— Karte ist an ———
Wand. 8. ——— Farbe ——— Stuhles ist braun.

VI. TRANSLATION EXERCISES

1. I have a book, a pencil, and a pen. 2. On the wall is a map of Germany. 3. Anna likes to go to school. 4. How is the door of the room? 5. Karl remains home today. 6. What is the color of the chalk? 7. A chair is in the room. 8. The color of the pen is black. 9. The map in the book is not so large as the map on the wall. 10. The teacher writes the lesson on the blackboard. 11. We are going to school today. 12. The teacher asks the pupil: Have you the notebook? 13. The pupil answers: No, it is at home. 14. Karl likes to write with the pencil. 15. Are you (*pl. fam.*) learning the lesson?

VII. VOCABULARY BUILDING

Some words in German closely resemble the English in pronunciation, but differ in spelling.

der Bär	das Eis	der Pudel
das Bier	das Haus	sauer
das Boot	hier	der Schuh
braun	der Onkel	der Ton

VIII. SUPPLEMENTARY READING

Berlin und Hamburg

Berlin ist die größte Stadt in Deutschland. Es liegt ungefähr in der Mitte Deutschlands und hat mehr als 3 (drei) Millionen Einwohner. Berlin ist jetzt zwischen Westen und Osten geteilt.

Neuyork ist die größte Stadt in Amerika, aber es ist nicht die Hauptstadt der Vereinigten Staaten. Neuyork ist auch nicht die Hauptstadt des Staates Neuyork. Die Hauptstadt der Vereinigten Staaten ist Washington im Columbia-Distrikt. Die Hauptstadt des Staates Neuyork ist Albany am Hudson. Berlin liegt nicht an dem Ozean wie Neuyork und ist keine Hafenstadt. Es liegt im Inland wie Chikago in den Vereinigten Staaten. Die größte Hafenstadt des europäischen Kontinentes ist Hamburg. Hamburg hat mehr als eine Million Einwohner. Aber Hamburg liegt auch nicht direkt an dem Ozean. Es liegt an einem großen Fluß. Der Fluß heißt die Elbe. Hamburg ist ungefähr 110 (hundertzehn) Kilometer von dem Ozean. Aber die Elbe bei Hamburg ist sehr breit und sehr tief, und viele große Dampfer landen direkt in der Mitte der Stadt. Die größten Dampfer landen in Cuxhaven.

IX. SUPPLEMENTARY VOCABULARY

(das) **Albany** Albany
bei at
(das) **Berlin'** Berlin
(das) **Chikago** Chicago
der **Columbia-Distrikt** the District of Columbia
(das) **Cuxhaven** Cuxhaven
der **Dampfer** the steamer
direkt direct(ly)
die **Elbe** the Elbe (river)
europä'isch European
der **Fluß** the river
geteilt divided
größt largest
die **Hafenstadt** the seaport

(das) **Hamburg** Hamburg
die **Hauptstadt** the capital
der **Hudson** the Hudson (river)
das **Inland** the interior
jetzt now
landen to land
liegen to lie, be situated
(das) **Neuyork** New York
der **Ozean** the ocean
die **Stadt** the city
tief deep
(das) **Washington** Washington
zwíschen between

Aufgabe Vier

Strong and Weak Verbs. *Past Tense*

I. READING SELECTION

Ein Spaziergang

Karl und Anna wohnen nicht auf dem Lande, sondern in einer Stadt. Sie **wohnten** früher auf dem Lande, aber sie wohnen jetzt in der Stadt. Der Vater und die Mutter wohnen auch in der Stadt. Die Stadt ist groß. Es ist eine Großstadt.

Herr und Frau Braun haben eine Wohnung in der Stadt. Die Wohnung ist in der Parkstraße. Die Straße ist groß und breit. Die Familie ist in dem Wohnzimmer. Das Wohnzimmer ist ein Zimmer in der Wohnung.

Der Vater **sagte**: „Heute ist Sonntag. Ihr geht heute nicht in die Schule." Karl **antwortete**: „Ja, wir haben keine Schule, aber wir bleiben auch nicht zu Hause, sondern wir machen einen Spaziergang. Aber wir gehen nicht in den Park, sondern wir machen einen Spaziergang auf das Land." Anna **fragte** den Bruder: „Gehen wir zu Fuß oder fahren wir mit der Straßenbahn?" Der Bruder **antwortete**: „Wir fahren zuerst mit der Straßenbahn. Wir gehen dann zu Fuß."

Sie **fuhren** also zuerst mit der Straßenbahn und **gingen** dann zu Fuß. Sie **lösen** Fahrkarten in der Straßenbahn. Sie **kamen** in einen Wald. Sie **blieben** eine Stunde in dem Walde und **gingen** dann nach Hause. Sie **sangen** ein Lied auf dem Wege nach Hause.

33

II. VOCABULARY

*Idioms
{
zu Fuß   on foot, afoot
auf dem Lande   in the country
auf das Land   to the country
einen Spaziergang machen   to take a walk
}

also   so, therefore
auf (+ *dat.* or *acc.*)   on, upon, at, in, to, for
*dann   then
*fahren, fuhr   to ride, to travel
*die Fahrkarte   the ticket; *pl.* die Fahrkarten
*früh   early; früher   earlier, formerly
*der Fuß   the foot
die Großstadt   the metropolis, metropolitan city
*jetzt   now
*kaufen, kaufte   to buy
*kommen, kam   to come
*das Land   the land, country
*das Lied   the song
lösen   to buy
machen, machte   to make
*oder   or
der Park   the park
die Parkstraße   Park Street

*singen, sang   to sing
*sondern   but
der Sonntag   the Sunday
der Spazier'gang   the walk
*die Stadt   the city
*die Straße   the street
*die Straßenbahn   the street car, trolley
*die Stunde   the hour
vier   four
*der Wald   the forest, wood
*der Weg   the way, road, path
*wohnen, wohnte   to live, dwell, reside
die Wohnung   the dwelling, apartment, house
das Wohnzimmer   the living room
zu (+ *dat.*)   to, at, for, in, with; *adv.*   too
zuerst   first, at first

NOTE: The past tense of verbs is listed after the infinitive.

III. GRAMMAR

A. Verbs

1. In German there are two kinds of verbs, weak and strong, corresponding to the regular and irregular verbs in English. The principal parts of a German weak verb and an English regular verb are:

INFINITIVE	PAST TENSE	PAST PARTICIPLE
frag-en	frag-te	ge-frag-t
ask	*ask-ed*	*ask-ed*

Weak verbs in German and regular verbs in English do not
change the stem vowel, but add **-te** and *-ed* respectively to
form the past tense, and **-t** and *-ed* respectively to form the
past participle. In addition the past participle in German
has the prefix **ge-**.

2. Strong verbs in German and irregular verbs in English
change the stem vowel to form the past tense and the past
participle.

INFINITIVE	PAST TENSE	PAST PARTICIPLE
sing-en	**sang**	**ge-sung-en**
sing	*sang*	*sung*

The first and third persons singular of the past tense in both
German and English have no additional ending. The past
participle in German has the prefix **ge-** and the ending **-en.**

NOTE: The strong verbs in German corresponding to the irregular verbs
in English are the more primitive, extending back to Primitive Germanic.
The weak verbs in German corresponding to the regular verbs in English
are for the most part later derivatives.

3. With the knowledge of these principal parts you can
form all six tenses of the verb in accordance with the following
synopsis in the third person singular:

WEAK VERB

Present: **er fragt** *he asks*
Past: **er fragte** *he asked*
Future: **er wird fragen** *he will ask*
Present Perfect: **er hat gefragt** *he has asked*
Past Perfect: **er hatte gefragt** *he had asked*
Future Perfect: **er wird gefragt haben** *he will have asked*

STRONG VERB

Present: **er singt** *he sings*
Past: **er sang** *he sang*
Future: **er wird singen** *he will sing*
Present Perfect: **er hat gesungen** *he has sung*
Past Perfect: **er hatte gesungen** *he had sung*
Future Perfect: **er wird gesungen haben** *he will have sung*

4. The complete conjugation of a weak and strong verb in the past tense is as follows:

	WEAK	STRONG
Infinitive	frag-**en**	sing-**en**
Singular	1. ich frag-**te** 2. du frag-**test** Sie frag-**ten** 3. er sie } frag-**te** es	1. ich sang 2. du sang-**st** Sie sang-**en** 3. er sie } sang es
Plural	1. wir frag-**ten** 2. ihr frag-**tet** Sie frag-**ten** 3. sie frag-**ten**	1. wir sang-**en** 2. ihr sang-**t** Sie sang-**en** 3. sie sang-**en**
Infinitive	antwort-**en**	fahr-**en**
Singular	1. ich antwort-**ete** 2. du antwort-**etest** Sie antwort-**eten** 3. er sie } antwort-**ete** es	1. ich fuhr 2. du fuhr-**st** Sie fuhr-**en** 3. er sie } fuhr es
Plural	1. wir antwort-**eten** 2. ihr antwort-**etet** Sie antwort-**eten** 3. sie antwort-**eten**	1. wir fuhr-**en** 2. ihr fuhr-**t** Sie fuhr-**en** 3. sie fuhr-**en**

The endings in black-face type added to the stem of **fragen** are the regular endings of a weak verb in the past tense. When, however, the stem of a verb, such as **antworten**, ends in a **d** or **t**, an additional **-e** is inserted before the endings. The endings in black-face type added to the stem of the past tense of **singen** and **fahren** are the regular endings of a strong verb in the past tense. Note that the first and third persons singular have no endings.

5. The strong and weak verbs used up to this point are as follows:

STRONG		WEAK	
Infinitive	Past Tense	Infinitive	Past Tense
*bleiben	blieb	*antworten	antwortete
*fahren	fuhr	*fragen	fragte
*gehen	ging	*haben	hatte
*heißen	hieß	*kaufen	kaufte
*kommen	kam	lehren	lehrte
*schreiben	schrieb	*lernen	lernte
*singen	sang	machen	machte
		*sagen	sagte
		*wohnen	wohnte

B. Aber *and* sondern

Both **aber** and **sondern** mean *but*. **Aber** is used after either an affirmative or negative statement. It concedes the preceding statement and introduces a limitation.

Sie wohnten früher auf dem Lande, aber sie wohnen jetzt in der Stadt.

Sondern is used only after a negative. It introduces a positive statement which excludes what goes before. Its implication is *but on the contrary.*

Sie wohnen nicht auf dem Lande, sondern in der Stadt.

IV. QUESTIONS

1. Wo wohnen Karl und Anna? 2. Wo wohnten sie früher? 3. Wer wohnt auch in der Stadt? 4. Wie ist die

Stadt? 5. Was haben Herr und Frau Braun in der Stadt?
6. Wo ist die Wohnung? 7. Wie ist die Straße? 8. Wo ist
die Familie? 9. Was ist ein Wohnzimmer? 10. Was sagte
der Vater? 11. Gehen Karl und Anna heute in die Schule?
12. Bleiben sie zu Hause? 13. Gehen sie in den Park? 14.
Gehen sie zu Fuß oder fahren sie mit der Straßenbahn? 15.
Was kauften sie in der Straßenbahn? 16. Wohin kamen sie?
17. Wo blieben sie eine Stunde? 18. Wohin gingen sie dann?
19. Was sangen sie auf dem Wege nach Hause?

V. GRAMMATICAL EXERCISES

(a) Supply the correct form of the definite article:

1. ——— Wohnung ist in ——— Parkstraße. 2. Karl und
Anna wohnen in ——— Stadt. 3. ——— Stadt ist groß.
4. ——— Familie ist in ——— Wohnzimmer. 5. Sie gehen
nicht in ——— Park, sondern auf ——— Land. 6. Sie fuh-
ren mit ——— Straßenbahn. 7. Sie kauften Fahrkarten in
——— Straßenbahn. 8. Sie gingen in ——— Wald. 9.
Sie blieben eine Stunde in ——— Wald. 10. Sie sangen
——— Lied.

(b) Supply the correct past tense forms of the verbs in
parentheses:

1. Der Vater (sagen): „Heute ist Sonntag." 2. Anna (fragen) den Bruder: „Gehen wir zu Fuß?" 3. Karl (antworten):
„Ja." 4. Sie (wohnen) früher auf dem Lande. 5. Sie (fahren) zuerst mit der Straßenbahn. 6. Sie (kaufen) Fahrkarten.
7. Sie (gehen) zu Fuß. 8. Karl (singen) ein Lied. 9. Er
(kommen) in einen Wald. 10. Anna (gehen) zu Fuß.

(c) Conjugate in the past indicative:

1. I lived in the country.
2. I wrote the lesson.
3. I took a walk.
4. I went home.

VI. TRANSLATION EXERCISES

1. Karl does not go to school today. 2. He does not stay at home, but takes a walk. 3. He first rode in the street car. 4. He then went on foot. 5. Anna sang a song. 6. Anna, do you like to sing? 7. Do you live in the city, Mr. Braun? 8. Karl formerly lived in the country. 9. He now lives in the city. 10. Anna said: I am not going to school today. 11. Anna asked Karl: Are you staying home today? 12. Karl answered: No, I am going to take a walk. 13. He bought a ticket in the street car. 14. Karl, do you live in the country? 15. She remained in the forest for an hour. 16. They sang a song on the way home.

VII. VOCABULARY BUILDING

Some words are so nearly identical in German and English despite slight differences in spelling and pronunciation that they are easily recognized.

blau blue		**neu** new	
frei free		**sitzen** to sit	
der Freund the friend		**setzen** to set	
das Haar the hair		**der Sohn** the son	
die Lippe the lip		**die Sonne** the sun	
liegen to lie		**der Sommer** the summer	

VIII. SUPPLEMENTARY READING

Deutsche Flüsse

Deutschland hat ungefähr 90 (neunzig) Flüsse. Die meisten fließen von Süden nach Norden. Der größte Fluß in Deutschland ist der Rhein. Sie finden ihn auf der Karte von Deutschland. Der Rhein beginnt nicht in Deutschland, sondern in der Schweiz. Er bildet zuerst die Grenze zwischen Deutschland und der Schweiz. Dann fließt er nach Norden und bildet die Grenze zwischen Deutschland und Frankreich, aber nur ungefähr 120 (hundertzwanzig) amerikanische

Meilen oder 200 (zweihundert) Kilometer weit. Dann fließt er weiter nach Norden und nach Nordwesten durch Deutschland und dann durch Holland in die Nordsee.

Der zweitgrößte Fluß in Deutschland ist die Elbe. Sie beginnt auch nicht in Deutschland, sondern in der Tschechoslowakei. Sie fließt dann nordwestlich durch Deutschland in die Nordsee. Hamburg, die größte Hafenstadt in Deutschland, liegt an der Elbe.

Die Weser beginnt in Deutschland und fließt auch in die Nordsee. An diesem Fluß liegt Bremen, die zweitgrößte Hafenstadt Deutschlands.

Die Oder beginnt in Polen und fließt auch von Süden nach Norden, aber sie fließt in die Ostsee oder das Baltische Meer.

Die Donau beginnt in Deutschland. Sie fließt dann durch Österreich und Ungarn, bildet dann teilweise die Grenze zwischen Rumänien und Bulgarien und fließt dann in das Schwarze Meer. Wien in Österreich und Budapest in Ungarn liegen an der Donau.

IX. SUPPLEMENTARY VOCABULARY

amerika'nisch (*adj.*)   American
beginnen   to begin
bilden   to form
(das) Bremen   (city of) Bremen
(das) Budapest   (city of) Budapest
(das) Bulga'rien   Bulgaria
dies-   this
die Donau   the Danube (river)
durch   through
finden   to find
fließen   to flow
der Fluß   the river; *pl.* **die Flüsse**

die Grenze   the boundary
ihn (*acc.* of **er**)   him, it
meist   most
die Oder   the Oder (river)
der Rhein   the Rhine (river)
(das) Rumä'nien   Rumania
das Schwarze Meer   the Black Sea
teilweise   partly, partially
(das) Ungarn   Hungary
weit   far, for a distance
die Weser   the Weser (river)
(das) Wien   Vienna
zweitgrößt   second largest

Aufgabe Fünf

*Possessive Adjectives.   Word Order.   Use of Tenses
and Articles*

I. READING SELECTION

Eine Reise nach Deutschland

Herr Braun lebt in Amerika.   Er ist Amerikaner.   Frau
Braun ist Amerikanerin.   Früher lebte Herr Braun in
Deutschland.   Dort studierte er Medizin.   Jetzt lebt er in
Amerika.   Er ist Arzt oder Doktor der Medizin.
Herr Braun hat einen Vater und eine Mutter in Deutsch-
land.   **Sein** Vater ist Karls und Annas Großvater, **seine**
Mutter ist **ihre** Großmutter.   Der Vater sagte zu Karl und
Anna: „Jetzt ist es Sommer.   Im Sommer habt ihr keine
Schule.   Wir machen eine Reise nach Deutschland und
besuchen **meinen** Vater und **meine** Mutter, d.h. **euren** Groß-
vater und **eure** Großmutter.   Im Herbst kommt ihr wieder
nach Amerika und geht wieder in die Schule."   Die Mutter
fragte: „Geht ihr gern nach Deutschland?"   Karl antwor-
tete: „Ja, wir besuchen gern **unseren** Großvater und **unsere**
Großmutter."   Anna fragte **ihre** Mutter: „Lebte **dein** Vater
früher auch in Deutschland?"   Die Mutter antwortete:
„Nein, **mein** Vater lebte immer in Amerika."
Der Vater ging in die Stadt und kaufte Fahrkarten für die
Familie.   Dann machten sie die Reise nach Deutschland.
Aber sie fuhren nicht mit der Straßenbahn, sie gingen auch
nicht zu Fuß, sondern sie fuhren mit einem Dampfer.   Die
Reise dauerte eine Woche.   Nach einer Woche kamen sie
nach Hamburg.   Hamburg ist eine Stadt in Deutschland.
Hamburg ist eine Großstadt, aber es ist nicht so groß wie
Berlin.

II. VOCABULARY

*Idioms { **eine Reise machen**   to take a trip
in die Stadt gehen   to go down town
d.h. (das heißt)   i.e. (that is)

*(das) **Amē′rika**   America
*der **Amērika′ner**   the American
*die **Amērika′nerin**   the American (woman)
*der **Arzt**   the doctor, physician
*besuchen, **besuchte**   to visit
der **Dampfer**   the steamer
dauern, **dauerte**   to last
*dein   your (*fam. sing.*)
der **Doktor**   the doctor
*dort   there
*euer   your (*fam. pl.*)
fünf   five
*für (+ *acc.*)   for
*die **Großmutter**   the grandmother

*der **Großvater**   the grandfather
*der **Herbst**   the fall, autumn
immer   always
*ihr   her, their; **Ihr**   your (*polite*)
*leben, **lebte**   to live
die **Medizin′**   the medicine
*mein   my
nach (+ *dat.*)   to, after
*die **Reise**   the journey, trip
*sein   his, its
*der **Sommer**   the summer
studie′ren, **studierte**   to study
*unser   our
wieder   again
*die **Woche**   the week

III. GRAMMAR

A. *Possessive Adjectives*

1. The nominative case of the possessive adjectives corresponding to the personal pronouns is as shown in the table on page 43.

The possessive adjectives take the same endings as **ein** and **kein**. The forms **unsere** and **euere,** used with feminine singular nouns, are usually shortened to **unsre** and **eure.**

2. The accusative singular forms differ from the nominative only when used with masculine nouns, and then they always add **-en,** like **ein** and **kein.** The forms **unseren** and **eueren** are usually shortened to **unsern** and **euern,** and sometimes to **unsren** and **euren.** In other words, one of the last two **e**'s is generally dropped:

1. Ich habe meinen Bleistift.
2. Du hast deinen Bleistift.
   Sie haben Ihren Bleistift.
3. Er hat seinen Bleistift.
   Sie hat ihren Bleistift.
   Es hat seinen Bleistift.
1. Wir haben unsern Bleistift.
2. Ihr habt euern Bleistift.
   Sie haben Ihren Bleistift.
3. Sie haben ihren Bleistift.

PERSONAL PRONOUNS	WITH MASCULINE NOUN	WITH FEMININE NOUN	WITH NEUTER NOUN
1. ich	mein ⎫	meine ⎫	mein ⎫
2. du	dein	deine	dein
Sie	Ihr ⎬ Bleistift	Ihre ⎬ Feder	Ihr ⎬ Buch
3. er	sein	seine	sein
sie	ihr	ihre	ihr
es	sein ⎭	seine ⎭	sein ⎭
1. wir	unser ⎫	uns(e)re ⎫	unser ⎫
2. ihr	euer ⎬ Bleistift	eu(e)re ⎬ Feder	euer ⎬ Buch
Sie	Ihr	Ihre	Ihr
3. sie	ihr ⎭	ihre ⎭	ihr ⎭

B. Word Order

1. In normal word order the verb follows the subject.

Der Schüler schreibt die Aufgabe.

2. In inverted word order the verb precedes the subject. This is used in questions.

Schreibt der Schüler die Aufgabe?

It is also used when any part of the predicate begins the sentence. This may be either a single word, usually an adverb, or it may be a phrase, or even an entire clause.

Früher lebte er in Deutschland.
Im Sommer gehen sie nach Deutschland.

C. Use of Tenses

In German the present tense is more frequently used in place of the future than in English, especially when the future is either expressed by some adverb or phrase, or is distinctly understood.

Im Sommer machen wir eine Reise nach Deutschland.
In summer we shall take a trip to Germany.

D. Use of the Definite Article

In German the definite article must be used with the seasons.

In dem Sommer, in dem Herbst.

In dem is usually contracted to **im**.

E. Omission of the Indefinite Article

Before predicate nouns denoting vocation or nationality, and used without a modifying adjective, the indefinite article is commonly omitted.

Herr Braun ist Amerikaner.
Er ist Arzt.

F. Wohnen *and* leben

Wohnen denotes specific location, **leben** general existence.

IV. QUESTIONS

1. Wie heißt die Aufgabe für heute? 2. Wo lebt Herr Braun? 3. Was ist er? 4. Was ist Frau Braun? 5. Wo lebte Herr Braun früher? 6. Wo leben sein Vater und seine Mutter? 7. Lebt Frau Brauns Vater auch in Deutschland? 8. Wohin gehen Karl und Anna im Sommer nicht? 9. Wohin machen sie eine Reise? 10. Gehen sie gern nach Deutschland? 11. Wohin gehen sie wieder im Herbst? 12. Was kaufte der Vater für die Familie? 13. Wo kaufte der Vater die Fahrkarten? 14. Gingen Karl und Anna zu Fuß nach Deutschland? 15. Wohin kamen sie nach einer Woche? 16. Ist Hamburg so groß wie Berlin? 17. Wer ging mit dem Vater nach Deutschland? 18. Lebt Ihr Vater in Deutschland oder in Amerika? 19. Was ist die Mutter Ihres Vaters? 20. Lebt Ihr Großvater in Deutschland?

V. GRAMMATICAL EXERCISES

(a) Supply the German equivalents of the English words in parentheses:

1. Anna hat (my) Feder. 2. Karl, hast du (your) Bleistift? 3. Wo ist (your) Buch, Herr Meyer? 4. Karl und Anna, wo wohnt (your) Vater? 5. Der Schüler lernt (his) Aufgabe. 6. Wir besuchen (our) Großvater und (our) Großmutter. 7. Die Schülerin schreibt in (her) Heft. 8. (My) Schwester geht in (our) Schule. 9. Karl und Anna besuchen (their) Lehrer. 10. (Our) Zimmer in der Schule ist gelb. 11. Karl, wo ist (your) Feder? 12. (My) Vater und (my) Mutter besuchen (our) Lehrer.

(b) Conjugate:

1. Ich besuche meinen Großvater, du besuchst deinen Großvater, etc.
2. Ich schreibe in mein Heft.
3. Ich kaufe meine Fahrkarte.

(c) Begin each of the following sentences with the under-scored words or phrases:

1. Sie fahren <u>im Herbst</u> nach Hause.
2. Er studierte Medizin <u>in Deutschland.</u>
3. Sie kaufte <u>dann</u> eine Fahrkarte.
4. Er wohnt <u>jetzt</u> in der Parkstraße.
5. Ich mache <u>im Sommer</u> eine Reise nach Deutschland.
6. Wir besuchten unseren Großvater <u>nach einer Woche.</u>
7. Er lebte <u>früher</u> in Amerika.
8. Du gehst <u>jetzt</u> in die Schule.

VI. TRANSLATION EXERCISES

1. In summer we shall take a trip to Germany. **2.** We shall visit our grandfather and our grandmother. 3. Does your grandfather also live in Germany, Mr. Meyer? 4. She bought her ticket in the city. 5. Formerly his father lived in Germany. 6. Our teacher likes to go to the country. 7. Anna, is your brother writing his lesson? 8. No, he is taking a walk. 9. My brother and my sister like to learn German. 10. The brother of the teacher is also a teacher. 11. Is your father an American, Mr. Braun? 12. He and his sister went down town. 13. What is your teacher's name, Karl? 14. Her brother is living in the country. 15. On the way home her sister sang a song.

VII. VOCABULARY BUILDING

A German medial or final **b** frequently corresponds to an English *v*.

eben even		**der Rabe** the raven	
das Grab the grave		**die Salbe** the salve	
haben to have		**das Sieb** the sieve	
heben to heave		**das Silber** the silver	
leben to live		**streben** to strive	
die Leber the liver		**weben** to weave	

In some cases the German **b** is replaced by an *f*, but the plural of nouns again has *v*.

> **der Dieb**   the thief
> **das Kalb**   the calf
> **taub**   deaf
> **das Weib**   the wife

VIII. SUPPLEMENTARY READING

Deutsche Gebirge

Im Norden von Deutschland ist das Land eben oder flach. Norddeutschland ist eine Ebene. Eine Ebene ist ebenes Land. Im Süden ist das Land gebirgig, d.h. dort sind Gebirge. Die Gebirge in der Schweiz heißen die Alpen. Sie sind die höchsten Gebirge in Europa. Die Alpen in Deutschland heißen die Bayrischen Alpen, denn sie sind in dem Staate Bayern. In Österreich sind auch Alpen. Sie heißen die Österreichischen Alpen. Der höchste Berg der Bayrischen Alpen heißt die Zugspitze. Sie ist ungefähr 3000 (dreitausend) Meter hoch, d.h. mehr als 9000 (neuntausend) Fuß. Sie ist nicht weit von der österreichischen Grenze. Im Sommer und im Winter besuchen viele Deutsche die Zugspitze.

Im Südwesten von Deutschland ist der Schwarzwald. Dieser Wald heißt der Schwarzwald, denn auf dem Gebirge sind viele Tannenbäume und die Tannenbäume sehen aus der Ferne dunkel oder schwarz aus. Der Schwarzwald ist ungefähr 160 (hundertundsechzig) Kilometer lang und 50–60 (fünfzig bis sechzig) Kilometer breit. Der höchste Berg des Schwarzwaldes ist ungefähr 1500 (fünfzehnhundert) Meter, d.h. beinahe 5000 (fünftausend) Fuß hoch. In dem Schwarzwald sind viele Seen und Mineralquellen.

Der Böhmer Wald und das Erzgebirge sind im Osten Deutschlands. Sie bilden die Grenze zwischen Deutschland und der Tschechoslowakei.

In der Mitte Deutschlands ist der Thüringer Wald. Das höchste Gebirge in Norddeutschland ist der Harz. Der höchste Berg des Harzes ist der Brocken.

IX. SUPPLEMENTARY VOCABULARY

die **Alpen**   the Alps
aus, sehen . . . aus   look, appear
(das) **Bayern**   Bavaria
bayrisch   Bavarian
der **Berg**   the mountain
der **Böhmer Wald**   the Bohemian Forest
der **Brocken**   the Brocken
denn   for
dunkel   dark
eben   even, flat, level
die **Ebene**   the plain
das **Erzgebirge**   the Ore Mountains
die **Ferne**   the distance
flach   flat
das **Gebirge**   the mountain range

gebirgig   mountainous
der **Harz**   the Harz Mountains
hoch   high
höchst   highest
lang   long
die **Mineral'quelle**   the mineral spring
(das) **Norddeutschland**   Northern Germany
österreichisch   Austrian
schwarz   black
der **Schwarzwald**   the Black Forest
der **See** (pl. die **Seen**)   the lake
sehen . . . aus   look, appear
der **Tannenbaum**   the fir tree
der **Thüringer Wald**   the Thuringian Forest
die **Zugspitze**   the Zugspitze

Courtesy of the German Tourist Information Office

Berlin: Blick in den Ostsektor

Die Ruine der Kaiser-Wilhelm-Gedächtniskirche in Berlin

Courtesy of the German Tourist Information Office

Courtesy of the German Tourist Information Office

Die Alsterbecken in Hamburg

Die Theatinerkirche in München

Courtesy of the German Tourist Information Office

Aufgabe Sechs

Past Tense of **haben** *and* **sein.** *Strong and Weak Verbs*

I. READING SELECTION

In der Schule

Es **war** Montag. Karl und Anna **waren** in der Schule.
Der Lehrer fragte Karl und Anna: „Wo **wart** ihr gestern?"
Karl antwortete: „Gestern **waren** wir auf dem Lande." Der
Lehrer sagte zu Anna: „Du **warst** auch auf dem Lande, nicht
wahr?" Anna antwortete: „Ja, ich **war** auch auf dem Lande,
aber der Vater und die Mutter **blieben** zu Hause. Wo
waren Sie gestern, Herr Lehrer?" Er antwortete: „Gestern
war Sonntag und ich machte einen Spaziergang."
Die Schule beginnt. Der Lehrer sagte: „Freitag **hatten**
wir Aufgabe fünf, nicht wahr? Heute haben wir Aufgabe
sechs. Wo ist dein Buch, Karl?" Karl antwortete: „Gestern
hatte ich mein Buch, aber Anna **hatte** es heute morgen. Sie
schrieb ihre Aufgabe in ihr Heft. Anna, **hattest** du nicht
heute morgen mein Buch?" Anna sagte: „Es tut mir leid,
aber ich **hatte** dein Buch nicht, ich **hatte** mein Buch."

Eine Anekdote

Herr Braun **hatte** einen Freund. Der Freund **hieß** Herr
Müller. Herr Braun **ging** zu der Wohnung des Freundes und
klopfte an die Tür. Ein Dienstmädchen öffnete die Tür.
Herr Braun fragte: „Ist Herr Müller zu Hause?" Das Dienstmädchen antwortete: „Nein, Herr Müller ist ausgegangen."
Dann fragte Herr Braun: „Ist Frau Müller zu Hause?" Die
Antwort des Dienstmädchens **war:** „Nein, Frau Müller ist
auch ausgegangen, aber sie kommt bald nach Hause." Herr
Braun sagte: „Dann warte ich bei dem Feuer." Das Dienstmädchen antwortete: „Es tut mir leid, aber das Feuer ist auch
ausgegangen."

II. VOCABULARY

*Idioms {
nicht wahr?   is it not so, isn't it true?
heute morgen   this morning
es tut mir leid   I am sorry
}

die Anekdo'te   the anecdote
*die Antwort   the answer
*auf (+ *dat.* or *acc.*)   on, upon, at, in, to, for
(ist) ausgegangen   (has) gone out
*bald   soon
beginnen, begann   to begin
*bei (+ *dat.*)   by, at, near, with, at the house of
*das Dienstmädchen   the maid
*drei   three
*das Feuer   the fire
*der Freitag   Friday
*der Freund   the friend

*fünf   five
*gestern   yesterday
*klopfen, klopfte   to knock
*machen, machte   to make
öffnen, öffnete   to open
*sechs   six
*der Sonntag   Sunday
*vier   four
*wahr   true
*warten, wartete   to wait
*die Wohnung   the house, apartment, residence, dwelling
*zu (+ *dat.*)   to, at, for, in, with; *adv.* too

III. GRAMMAR

A. *Past Tense of* haben *and* sein

	haben	sein
Singular	1. ich hatte	1. ich war
	2. du hattest / Sie hatten	2. du warst / Sie waren
	3. er sie } hatte es	3. er sie } war es
Plural	1. wir hatten	1. wir waren
	2. ihr hattet / Sie hatten	2. ihr wart / Sie waren
	3. sie hatten	3. sie waren

1. The past tense of **haben** is formed by adding the regular past tense endings of the weak verb. In addition the **b** of the stem **hab-** has been assimilated to the **t** of the ending. 2. The stem of the past tense of **sein** is **war.** To this are added the regular past tense endings of the strong verb.

B. *Strong and Weak Verbs*

1. There is no way of telling from the infinitive of a verb whether it is strong or weak. Once you have learned that a given verb is weak, it follows the models of weak verbs given in Lesson IV. In the case of strong verbs the principal parts must be memorized. 2. The vowel change that takes place in the past tense and the past participle of strong verbs is called Ablaut in contradistinction to the Umlaut which is only a modified vowel. Again there is no way of telling what series of vowel changes a given strong verb may require. The following Ablaut series may satisfy your curiosity as to the various possibilities:

1. ei —ie—ie: **bleiben, blieb, geblieben**   to remain
2. ei —ie—ei: **heißen, hieß, geheißen**   to be called
3. ei —i —i: **schneiden, schnitt, geschnitten**   to cut
4. ē —ō —ō: **heben, hob, gehoben**   to lift
5. ie —ō —ō: **fliegen, flog, geflogen**   to fly
6. ü —ō —ō: **lügen, log, gelogen**   to lie, tell a falsehood
7. ie —ŏ—ŏ: **fließen, floß, geflossen**   to flow
8. i —a —u: **singen, sang, gesungen**   to sing
9. i —a —o: **beginnen, begann, begonnen**   to begin
10. ĕ —ă—ŏ: **helfen, half, geholfen**   to help
11. ĕ —ā —ŏ: **sprechen, sprach, gesprochen**   to speak
12. ē —ā —ō: **stehlen, stahl, gestohlen**   to steal
13. ē —ā —ē: **sehen, sah, gesehen**   to see
14. ĕ —ā—ĕ: **essen, aß, gegessen**   to eat
15. ā —ū —ā: **fahren, fuhr, gefahren**   to ride, travel
16. ă —ū —ă: **schaffen, schuf, geschaffen**   to create
17. ā —ie —ā: **schlafen, schlief, geschlafen**   to sleep
18. au—ie—au: **laufen, lief, gelaufen**   to run
19. ō —ie—ō: **stoßen, stieß, gestoßen**   to strike, push
20. ū —ie—ū: **rufen, rief, gerufen**   to call

In addition there are a limited number of irregular verbs
which do not fit in with any of the above classifications.

3. Of the verbs so far employed, the following are weak:

*antworten	*klopfen	*sagen
*besuchen	lehren	studieren
dauern	*lernen	*warten
*fragen	*machen	*wohnen
*kaufen	öffnen	

4. The following verbs used up to and including this lesson
are strong:

> beginnen, begann, begonnen
> *bleiben, blieb, geblieben
> *fahren, fuhr, gefahren
> *heißen, hieß, geheißen
> *kommen, kam, gekommen
> *schreiben, schrieb, geschrieben
> *singen, sang, gesungen

5. The following verbs are irregular:

> *haben, hatte, gehabt
> *sein, war, gewesen
> *gehen, ging, gegangen

6. Hereafter the principal parts of all strong and irregular
verbs will be given in the vocabulary. When these are not
given, the verb is weak.

IV. QUESTIONS

1. Wie heißt die Aufgabe für heute?   2. Wie hieß die Auf-
gabe für gestern?   3. Wo waren Karl und Anna Montag?   4.
Wo waren sie Sonntag?   5. Wo waren Sie gestern?   6.
Waren der Vater und die Mutter auch auf dem Lande?   7.
Wo blieben der Vater und die Mutter?   8. Blieb der Lehrer
auch zu Hause?   9. Hatten wir gestern Aufgabe fünf oder
sechs?   10. Was hatte Karl nicht in der Schule?   11. Hatte
Anna das Buch des Bruders?

12. Wer hatte einen Freund? 13. Wie hieß der Freund?
14. Wohin ging Herr Braun? 15. Wer klopfte an die Tür?
16. Wer antwortete? 17. Was fragte Herr Braun? 18. War
Frau Müller zu Hause? 19. Wer kommt bald nach Hause?

V. GRAMMATICAL EXERCISES

Change the verbs in the following sentences to the past tense:

1. Herr Braun bleibt zu Hause. 2. Ich habe einen Freund.
3. Sie sind in der Schule. 4. Anna hat sein Buch nicht. 5.
Wir gehen auf das Land. 6. Der Lehrer fragt: „Hast du dein
Buch?" 7. Ich bin in der Schule. 8. Sie fahren mit der
Straßenbahn. 9. Er singt ein Lied. 10. Herr Müller ist
nicht zu Hause. 11. Er geht in die Stadt. 12. Sie wohnen
auf dem Lande. 13. Wir haben Aufgabe fünf. 14. Er heißt
Herr Müller. 15. Sie kommen in einen Wald. 16. Anna
schreibt ihre Aufgabe. 17. Ich kaufe eine Fahrkarte. 18.
Wir lernen unsere Aufgabe. 19. Du besuchst deinen Großvater. 20. Ich mache einen Spaziergang. 21. Der Lehrer
fragt und ich antworte. 22. Herr Braun klopft an die Tür.
23. Wohin gehen Sie im Sommer? 24. Wir schreiben in
unser Heft.

VI. TRANSLATION EXERCISES

1. The teacher asked Karl: Where were you yesterday?
2. Karl answered: I was in the country. 3. The teacher had
no school Sunday. 4. He took a walk. 5. Anna was also in
the country. 6. The father stayed at home. 7. Were you
also in the country, Anna? 8. Friday we went to school,
didn't we? 9. Karl did not have his book. 10. The teacher
asked Karl: Have you your book? 11. Karl had his book
yesterday. 12. This morning he did not have it. 13. Anna
had her book. 14. Mr. Braun went to the apartment of his
friend and knocked on the door. 15. He was not at home.

VII. VOCABULARY BUILDING

A German medial or final **f** frequently corresponds to a *p* in English, with possible vowel changes in addition.

der Affe	the ape	**offen**	open
auf	up	**reif**	ripe
der Bischof	the bishop	**das Schaf**	the sheep
die Harfe	the harp	**scharf**	sharp
helfen	to help	**das Schiff**	the ship
hoffen	to hope	**schlafen**	to sleep

VIII. SUPPLEMENTARY READING

Die Staaten des Deutschen Reiches

Im 18. (achtzehnten) Jahrhundert hatte das Deutsche Reich 318 (dreihundertachtzehn) Staaten. Das Deutsche Reich hieß damals das Heilige Römische Reich Deutscher Nation. Einige Staaten, wie Österreich und Preußen, waren sehr groß, aber die meisten waren sehr klein. Einige hatten nur wenige Quadratkilometer und auch sehr wenige Einwohner. Am Anfang des 19. (neunzehnten) Jahrhunderts wurde die Zahl der Staaten durch Napoleons Einfluß auf ungefähr 100 (hundert) reduziert. Bei der Gründung des neuen Deutschen Reiches im Jahre 1871 (achtzehnhunderteinundsiebzig) wurde die Zahl der Staaten auf 25 (fünfundzwanzig) reduziert. Vier dieser Staaten waren Königreiche: Preußen, Bayern, Württemberg und Sachsen. Der König von Preußen war auch der deutsche Kaiser. Sechs Staaten waren Großherzogtümer, fünf Staaten waren Herzogtümer, sieben waren Fürstentümer, und drei waren Freie Städte. Die drei Freien Städte waren Bremen, Hamburg und Lübeck im Norden Deutschlands.

Nach der Revolution im Jahre 1918 (neunzehnhundertachtzehn) wurde die Zahl der Staaten auf 18 (achtzehn) reduziert. Sie heißen jetzt nicht mehr Staaten, sondern Länder. Nach dem zweiten Weltkrieg entstanden in Deutschland zwei Republiken, die Bundesrepublik Deutschland im Westen und die Deutsche Demokratische Republik im Osten. In der

Bundesrepublik sind neun Länder, in der Demokratischen Republik fünf. Preußen, einst das größte Land, existiert nicht mehr. Die Länder der Bundesrepublik sind Bayern, Württemberg-Baden, Rheinland-Pfalz, Hessen, Nordrhein-Westfalen, Niedersachsen, Schleswig-Holstein. Auch die Städte Bremen und Hamburg sind jetzt Länder der Bundesrepublik. Die Hauptstadt der Bundesrepublik ist Bonn, die Hauptstadt von Bayern ist München, die Hauptstadt von Württemberg-Baden ist Stuttgart. München liegt im Süden von Bayern und ist nicht weit von den Bayrischen Alpen. Die größten Industriestädte sind Düsseldorf, Essen und Dortmund, sie liegen in dem Ruhrgebiet.

IX. SUPPLEMENTARY VOCABULARY

am = an dem at the
der Anfang the beginning
(das) Bayern Bavaria
(das) Bonn (city of) Bonn
die Bundesrepublik the federal republic
damals at that time
demokratisch democratic
(das) Dortmund (city of) Dortmund
(das) Dresden (city of) Dresden
(das) Düsseldorf (city of) Düsseldorf
der Einfluß the influence
einige some, a few
einst once, at one time
entstehen to arise; **entstanden** arose, there arose
(das) Essen (city of) Essen
existieren to exist
frei free
das Fürstentum the principality

das Großherzogtum the grand duchy
die Gründung the founding
heilig holy
das Herzogtum the duchy
(das) Hessen Hesse
die Industrie'stadt the manufacturing city
das Jahr the year
das Jahrhun'dert the century
der Kaiser the emperor
klein little, small
der König the king
das Königreich the kingdom
die Länder (*plural of* **das Land**) the states
liegen to lie, be situated
(das) Lübeck (city of) Lübeck
(das) München (city of) Munich
nach after
die Nation' the nation
neu new
nicht mehr no longer

(das) **Niedersachsen** Lower Saxony
(das) **Nord'rhein-Westfalen** North Westphalia
(das) **Preußen** Prussia
das **Reich** the Reich, the empire
die **Republik'** the republic
die **Revolution'** the revolution
(die) **Rheinland-Pfalz** the Rhineland Palatinate
römisch Roman
das **Ruhrgebiet** the Ruhr district
(das) **Sachsen** Saxony
(das) **Schleswig-Holstein** Schleswig-Holstein

sieben seven
die **Städte** (*plural of* die **Stadt**) the cities
(das) **Stuttgart** (city of) Stuttgart
teilen to divide; **geteilt** divided
unter under
der **Weltkreig** the world war
wenig little; **wenige** few
wurde . . . reduziert was reduced
(das) **Württemberg** Württemberg
(das) **Württemberg-Baden** Württemberg-Baden
die **Zahl** the number
zweit second

Aufgabe Sieben

Present Perfect and Past Perfect Tenses

I. READING SELECTION

Der Hund und der Bauer

Ein Mann **hat** einmal in der Stadt **gewohnt.** Er **hat** Herr Becker **geheißen.** Einmal **hat** Herr Becker einen Freund **besucht.** Der Freund **hat** ein Haus auf dem Lande **gehabt.** Herr Becker **hatte** dem Freunde am Dienstag einen Brief **geschrieben.** In dem Briefe **hatte** er **gesagt:** ,,Ich komme morgen.''

Aber Herr Becker **ist** nicht zu Fuß **gegangen,** er **ist** auch nicht mit der Straßenbahn **gefahren,** denn er **ist** reich **gewesen** und **hatte** ein Automobil **gekauft.** Er **ist** immer mit dem Auto zu dem Freunde auf das Land **gefahren.**

Am Mittwoch Morgen **ist** Herr Becker in dem Automobil auf das Land **gefahren.** Er **ist** sehr schnell **gefahren,** ungefähr 70 (siebzig) Kilometer die Stunde. Auf einmal **ist** ein Hund vor das Automobil **gelaufen.** Herr Becker **hatte** den Hund nicht schnell genug **gesehen** und **hatte** den Hund **getötet.**

Ein Bauer **ist** nicht weit von dem Automobil **gewesen.** Herr Becker **hat** die Tür des Automobils **geöffnet** und zu dem Bauer **gesagt:** ,,Guten Morgen! Es tut mir leid, aber ich **habe** den Hund **getötet.''** Dann **hat** er den Mann **gefragt:** ,,Sind 40 (vierzig) Mark genug für den Hund?'' Der Bauer **hat geantwortet:** ,,Ja, vierzig Mark sind genug.'' Dann **hat** Herr Becker dem Mann die vierzig Mark **gegeben, hat gesagt** ,,Auf Wiedersehen!'' und **ist** mit dem Automobil zu dem Freunde **gefahren.** Der Bauer war sehr erstaunt, denn es war nicht sein Hund.

57

II. VOCABULARY

*Idioms {
auf einmal   all at once, suddenly
guten Morgen (Abend, Tag)   good morning (evening, day)
auf Wiederseh(e)n   goodbye, au revoir
}

*das **Auto(mobil')**   the automobile
*der **Bauer**   the peasant, farmer
*der **Brief**   the letter
*denn   for
*der **Dienstag**   Tuesday
*einmal   once
erstaunt'   astonished
*geben, gab, hat gegeben   to give
*der **Hund**   the dog
*immer   always
das (*or* der) **Kilometer**   the kilometer
*laufen, lief, ist gelaufen   to run
die **Mark**   the mark (*normal rate of exchange about 24 cts.*)

*der **Mittwoch**   Wednesday
*der **Morgen**   the morning
*morgen   tomorrow
*reich   rich
schnell   quick, fast
*sehen, sah, hat gesehen   to see
*sehr   very
*sieben   seven
töten   to kill
*ungefähr   about, approximately
*vor (+ *dat.* or *acc.*)   before, in front of; ago (*with numerical time expressions*)
*wann   when (*in questions*)
weit   far
wiedersehen   to see again

III. GRAMMAR

A. *Present Perfect and Past Perfect Tenses*

PRESENT PERFECT TENSE

	haben		sein	
Singular	1. ich habe 2. du hast Sie haben 3. er sie ⎱hat es	⎱das Buch ⎰gehabt	1. ich bin 2. du bist Sie sind 3. er sie ⎱ist es	⎱in der Stadt ⎰gewesen
Plural	1. wir haben 2. ihr habt Sie haben 3. sie haben	⎱das Buch ⎰gehabt	1. wir sind 2. ihr seid Sie sind 3. sie sind	⎱in der Stadt ⎰gewesen

PAST PERFECT TENSE

	haben		sein	
Singular	1. ich hatte 2. du hattest Sie hatten 3. er sie ⎱hatte es	⎱das Buch ⎰gehabt	1. ich war 2. du warst Sie waren 3. er sie ⎱war es	⎱in der Stadt ⎰gewesen
Plural	1. wir hatten 2. ihr hattet Sie hatten 3. sie hatten	⎱das Buch ⎰gehabt	1. wir waren 2. ihr wart Sie waren 3. sie waren	⎱in der Stadt ⎰gewesen

PRESENT PERFECT TENSE

schreiben   kommen

Singular	1. ich habe 2. du hast Sie haben 3. er sie } hat es	den Brief geschrieben	1. ich bin 2. du bist Sie sind 3. er sie } ist es	nach Hause gekommen
Plural	1. wir haben 2. ihr habt Sie haben 3. sie haben	den Brief geschrieben	1. wir sind 2. ihr seid Sie sind 3. sie sind	nach Hause gekommen

PAST PERFECT TENSE

Singular	1. ich hatte 2. du hattest Sie hatten 3. er sie } hatte es	den Brief geschrieben	1. ich war 2. du warst Sie waren 3. er sie } war es	nach Hause gekommen
Plural	1. wir hatten 2. ihr hattet Sie hatten 3. sie hatten	den Brief geschrieben	1. wir waren 2. ihr wart Sie waren 3. sie waren	nach Hause gekommen

1. The present perfect and past perfect tenses are ordinarily formed by conjugating the present and past tenses of **haben** with the past participle of the given verb. In German, however, the past participle comes at the end of a normal sentence. Both strong and weak verbs have the prefix **ge-** in the past participle, but weak verbs add the ending **-t** and strong verbs the ending **-en** to the stem of the verb. Except for the word order and the prefix and suffix in the past participle, English and German are very similar.

WEAK VERB

Present Perfect: **Ich habe die Aufgabe gelernt.**
I have learned the lesson.
Past Perfect: **Ich hatte die Aufgabe gelernt.**
I had learned the lesson.

STRONG VERB

Present Perfect: **Ich habe das Lied gesungen.**
I have sung the song.
Past Perfect: **Ich hatte das Lied gesungen.**
I had sung the song.

2. Certain verbs require the auxiliary **sein** to form the present perfect and past perfect tenses, i.e., the present and past tenses of the verb **sein** are conjugated with the past participle of the given verb. Such verbs must fulfil *two* conditions. First, they must be intransitive, i.e., verbs that do not take a direct (accusative) object. Secondly, they must denote motion or change of condition. In addition, **sein** and **bleiben,** which do not fulfill above conditions, require **sein** as the auxiliary. The following verbs hitherto used require **sein:**

ausgehen — ist ausgegangen	kommen — ist gekommen
bleiben — ist geblieben	laufen — ist gelaufen
fahren — ist gefahren	sein — ist gewesen
gehen — ist gegangen	

3. Hereafter the auxiliary of the perfect tenses will be listed with the principal parts of strong verbs as follows: **bleiben, blieb, ist geblieben.** Weak verbs requiring **sein** will be listed as follows: **reisen (sein)** *to travel.*
4. In general the past perfect tense in German is used very much the same as in English. The present perfect tense, however, is commonly used in disconnected statements, especially in conversation, where English would use the imperfect or past tense. This is particularly true in the English emphatic form of a question: *Did you buy the book?* **Haben Sie das Buch gekauft?**

B. Use of the Definite Article

After the preposition **an** the dative form of the definite article is used with the days of the week:

Am (an dem) Sonntag. *On Sunday.*

IV. QUESTIONS

1. Wie heißt die Aufgabe für heute?   2. Wo hat ein Mann gewohnt?   3. Wie hat er geheißen?   4. Wer hat einen Freund besucht?   5. Wo hat der Freund ein Haus gehabt?   6. Wann hat Herr Becker einen Brief geschrieben?   7. Was hatte er in dem Brief gesagt?   8. Ist Herr Becker zu Fuß gegangen?   9. Ist er mit der Straßenbahn gefahren?   10. Was hatte er gekauft?   11. Wie war Herr Becker?   12. Wohin ist er mit dem Auto gefahren?   13. Wann ist er auf das Land gefahren?   14. Was ist vor das Automobil gelaufen?   15. Was hatte Herr Becker nicht gesehen?   16. Wer ist nicht weit von dem Auto gewesen?   17. Was hat Herr Becker zu dem Bauer gesagt?

V. GRAMMATICAL EXERCISES

(a) Change the following sentences (1) to the present perfect tense, (2) to the past perfect tense:

1. Er macht einen Spaziergang. 2. Wir besuchen unseren
Großvater. 3. Sie singt ein Lied. 4. Er bleibt zu Hause.
5. Ich lerne die Aufgabe. 6. Ich schreibe sie in das Heft.
7. Der Lehrer fragt und der Schüler antwortet. 8. Du
klopfst an die Tür. 9. Ich fahre in dem Automobil. 10. Er
heißt Herr Becker. 11. Sie kommen nach Hause. 12. Wir
wohnen in der Stadt. 13. Karl ist nicht in der Schule.

(b) Change the following sentences (1) to the present tense,
(2) to the past tense:

1. Er hat einen Brief geschrieben. 2. Ich habe ein Haus
auf dem Lande gekauft. 3. Wir sind mit der Straßenbahn
gefahren. 4. Karl hat sein Buch nicht gehabt. 5. Sie haben
ein Auto gekauft. 6. Er ist in die Stadt gegangen. 7. Ihr
habt eure Großmutter besucht. 8. Hast du den Brief
geschrieben? 9. Wann ist er nach Hause gekommen? 10.
Im Sommer habe ich in Deutschland gelebt. 11. Wo bist du
gewesen? 12. Was hat er zu dem Mann gesagt?

VI. TRANSLATION EXERCISES

In the following sentences use the present perfect or past
perfect tenses:

1. Where were you this morning, Mr. Braun? 2. I visited
a friend in the country. 3. Mr. Becker was very rich. 4. He
had bought an automobile. 5. The peasant said: Good
morning. 6. Did you go to school yesterday, Karl? 7.
Anna stayed at home. 8. On Sunday I took a walk. 9.
Yesterday we had no school. 10. He had written the letter
on Tuesday. 11. On Wednesday he drove to his friend. 12.
I knocked on the door. 13. In summer we lived in the country. 14. Have you learned your lesson, Anna? 15. I am
sorry, but I did not see the dog.

VII. VOCABULARY BUILDING

A German medial or final **s** often corresponds to an English *t*.

aus out
beißen to bite
besser better
daß that
das Faß the vat
der Fuß the foot
grüßen to greet
hassen to hate

der Kessel the kettle
lassen to let
das Los the lot
die Nuß the nut
rasseln to rattle
der Schweiß the sweat
das Wasser the water
weiß white

VIII. SUPPLEMENTARY READING

Die Reise nach Deutschland

Die Familie war endlich auf einem Dampfer. Der Dampfer war sehr groß und hatte drei Klassen: erste, Kabinen- und Touristen Klasse. Herr Braun war reich und so reisten sie erster Klasse. Die erste Klasse ist sehr teuer und kostet viel Geld. Die meisten Studenten und auch viele Lehrer reisen in der Touristen Klasse. Sie ist auch sehr gut und ist viel billiger als die erste oder Kabinen Klasse. Hunderte von Passagieren waren an Bord und Hunderte von Freunden der Passagiere waren an dem Landungsplatz. Der Dampfer fuhr am Vormittag bei klarem Wetter aus dem Neuyorker Hafen. Nach einigen Stunden waren sie auf dem Ozean.

Die Reise von Neuyork nach Hamburg dauerte sieben Tage, aber das Wetter war schön und der Ozean war ruhig. Herr Braun sagte zu Karl und Anna: ,,Ich bin einmal im Winter nach Deutschland gereist. Damals war das Wetter sehr stürmisch und viele Passagiere waren seekrank. Auch dauerte die Reise damals 10 (zehn) Tage und ich war nicht in der ersten, sondern in der dritten Klasse. Aber im Sommer ist eine Reise nach Europa sehr angenehm und in der ersten Klasse lebt man so gut wie in einem großen, feinen Hotel.''

Anna und Karl machten jeden Tag einen Spaziergang auf

dem Deck. Auch hatten sie guten Appetit und das Essen war sehr gut. Anna hatte eine Freundin an Bord. Sie hieß Barbara und war eine Schülerin in ihrer Schule. In Amerika hatte Anna ihre Freundin oft besucht und jetzt machten sie beide die Reise nach Europa. Barbaras Vater und Mutter waren auch auf dem Dampfer. Barbaras Vater war Professor an einer Universität in Amerika und fuhr oft nach Europa. Nach sieben Tagen kamen sie endlich nach Hamburg. Aber sie landeten nicht in Hamburg, sondern in Cuxhaven. Sie fuhren dann mit der Eisenbahn nach Hamburg. Das dauerte ungefähr zwei Stunden. In Hamburg gingen sie in ein großes Hotel. Dort blieben sie einige Tage.

IX. SUPPLEMENTARY VOCABULARY

angenehm pleasant, agreeable
der Appetit' the appetite
beide both
billiger cheaper
(an) Bord (on) board
das Deck the deck
dritt third
die Eisenbahn the railroad
endlich finally
erst first
das Essen the food
fein fine
die Freundin the friend (*fem.*)
das Geld the money
gut good
der Hafen the harbor
das Hotel the hotel
Hunderte hundreds
jeder each, every
die Kabine the cabin

klar clear
kosten to cost
der Landungsplatz the landing place, pier, dock
man one
oft often
der Passagier' the passenger
der Profes'sor the professor
reisen (sein) to travel
ruhig quiet, calm
schön beautiful, fine
seekrank seasick
stürmisch stormy
der Student' the student
der Tag the day
teuer dear, expensive
der Tourist' the tourist
die Universität' the university
der Vormittag the forenoon
das Wetter the weather

Aufgabe Acht

Plural of Strong Nouns

I. READING SELECTION

Allerlei

In den **Städten** sind **Häuser**. In den **Häusern** sind **Zimmer**. Die **Zimmer** haben **Wände** und **Fenster** und eine Tür. In den **Zimmern** sind **Tische** und **Stühle**. Karl und Anna sind **Schüler**. Die **Schüler** haben **Bücher, Bleistifte** und **Hefte**. Die **Väter** und die **Mütter** der **Schüler** bleiben zu Hause, aber die **Brüder** der **Schüler** gehen auch in die Schule. Die **Lehrer** sind **Männer**. Anna und Barbara sind **Mädchen**. Karl hat viele **Freunde** in der Schule. In den **Sommern** schreibt er den **Freunden** Briefe. An den **Sonntagen** machen die **Freunde Spaziergänge** in die **Wälder**. In den **Wäldern** sind **Wege**. Auf dem Wege nach Hause singen sie **Lieder**.

In Deutschland haben viele Leute **Dienstmädchen,** aber keine[1] **Automobile**. Viele **Amerikaner** haben **Automobile,** aber keine **Dienstmädchen**.

Eine Anekdote

Ein Junge ist einmal zu dem Arzt gelaufen. Ein Arzt ist ein Doktor der Medizin. Der Arzt war erstaunt und fragte: „Was ist los, mein Junge?" Der Junge sagte: „Herr Doktor, haben Sie Medizin gegen Kopfweh? Aber machen Sie schnell, bitte!" Der Arzt gab dem Jungen schnell eine bittere Medizin zu trinken. Dann fragte er den Jungen: „Hast du noch Kopfweh?" Der Junge sagte: „Aber Herr Doktor, ich habe kein Kopfweh, meine Mutter hat das Kopfweh."

[1] Accusative plural of **kein**.

II. VOCABULARY

*Idioms {
bitte please
was ist los? what is the matter?
machen Sie schnell (*fam.* mach' schnell) make haste, hurry (up)
}

*acht eight
das Allerlei, -s, -s all kinds of things; miscellany
bitter bitter
*breit broad, wide
*der Dampfer, -s, - the steamer
*der Doktor, -s the doctor
*erstaunt' astonished
*die Fami'lie the family
gegen (+ *acc.*) against; for
*gern(e) gladly
das Kopfweh the headache
*die Leute (*pl. only*) people
*die Mark, - the mark

*die Medizin', - the medicine
*noch still
*der Park, -(e)s, -e the park
*schnell fast, quick
*so so
*der Spazier'gang, -(e)s, ⁻e the walk
*studie'ren, studierte, hat studiert to study
*trinken, trank, hat getrunken to drink
*viel much; **viele** many
*weit far
*zuerst' first, at first

III. GRAMMAR

A. The Definite Article in the Plural

Nominative	**die**
Genitive	**der**
Dative	**den**
Accusative	**die**

1. There is only one plural form of the definite article for all three genders.

2. The definite article in the plural is the same as the definite article in the feminine singular, except that the dative in the plural is **den** instead of **der**.

B. Plural of Nouns

1. Nouns in German are classified as strong, weak, and mixed. Strong nouns are declined in the singular as explained

in Lesson III, i.e., the genitive of masculine and neuter nouns ends in -(e)s. Feminine nouns take no endings in the singular.

2. In the plural, however, strong nouns are divided into three classes. In the following lists the plurals of all active nouns hitherto employed are given. Parentheses indicate that the plural forms of these nouns are relatively rare.

I	II	III
No endings added to form plural, but sometimes Umlaut	-e added to form plural. Umlaut frequent	-er added to form plural. Umlaut whenever possible
die Amerikaner	die Ärzte	die Bücher
die Brüder	die Automobile	die Häuser
die Dampfer	die Bleistifte	die Länder
die Dienstmädchen	die Briefe	die Lieder
die Fenster	(die Dienstage)	die Männer
(die Feuer)	(die Freitage)	die Wälder
die Großmütter	die Freunde	
die Großväter	die Füße	
die Lehrer	die Hefte	
die Mädchen	(die Herbste)	
(die Morgen)	die Hunde	
die Mütter	(die Mittwoche)	
die Schüler	(die Montage)	
(die Sommer)	(die Parke)	
die Väter	(die Sonntage)	
die Zimmer	(die Spaziergänge)	
	die Städte	
	die Stühle	
	die Tische	
	die Wände	
	die Wege	

3. Except for the article the nominative, genitive, and accusative plural are always alike.

4. Every dative plural ends in -n or -en.

5. Certain classifications could be given to help you determine whether a noun is strong, weak, or mixed, and if strong,

to what class of strong nouns it belongs. Such classifications, however, become very extensive and are subject to numerous exceptions. As the number of nouns to be learned actively in this book is greatly restricted, it will be found easier and more helpful in the long run to simply memorize the principal parts of each active noun. These principal parts are the nominative and genitive singular and the nominative plural. With the aid of these three principal parts you can form the remaining five cases. Hereafter the principal parts of nouns will always be indicated in the vocabulary as follows: **der Bruder, -s, ̈,** which stands for **der Bruder, des Bruders, die Brüder.**

6. The complete declension in the plural of the three classes of strong nouns is as follows:

	I	II	III
Nominative	**die Brüder**	**die Stühle**	**die Bücher**
Genitive	**der Brüder**	**der Stühle**	**der Bücher**
Dative	**den Brüdern**	**den Stühlen**	**den Büchern**
Accusative	**die Brüder**	**die Stühle**	**die Bücher**

C. Past Participles of Verbs Ending in **-ieren**

Verbs of foreign origin ending in **-ieren,** such as **studieren,** do not have the prefix **ge-** in the past participle.

IV. QUESTIONS

In answering the following questions use the plural forms of nouns whenever possible.

1. Wo sind Häuser? 2. Was ist in den Häusern? 3. Was haben die Zimmer? 4. Was ist in den Zimmern? 5. Was sind Karl und Anna? 6. Was haben die Schüler? 7. Wer bleibt zu Hause? 8. Wer geht auch in die Schule? 9. Wer hat Freunde in der Schule? 10. Was schreibt Karl den Freunden? 11. Wann schreibt Karl den Freunden Briefe? 12. Was machen die Freunde an den Sonntagen? 13. Wann machen sie Spaziergänge? 14. Wohin machen sie Spazier-

gänge? 15. Was singen sie auf dem Wege nach Hause? 16. Was haben viele Leute in Deutschland? 17. Was haben viele Leute in Deutschland nicht? 18. Was haben viele Amerikaner? 19. Was haben viele Amerikaner nicht? 20. Was ist ein Arzt? 21. Wer ist einmal zu dem Arzt gelaufen? 22. Was fragte der Arzt? 23. Was antwortete der Junge? 24. Was gab der Arzt dem Jungen?

V. GRAMMATICAL EXERCISES

(a) Whenever possible, change nouns and verbs to the plural:

1. Das Mädchen schreibt den Brief. 2. Der Schüler singt ein Lied. 3. In dem Zimmer ist ein Tisch. 4. Der Lehrer ist mit dem Dampfer gefahren. 5. Der Schüler hat ein Buch. 6. Das Haus ist in der Stadt. 7. In dem Wald ist ein Weg. 8. Das Dienstmädchen hat kein Automobil. 9. Der Amerikaner hat kein Dienstmädchen. 10. Der Lehrer ist ein Mann. 11. Die Mutter geht nicht in die Schule. 12. Der Vater bleibt auch zu Hause. 13. Der Stuhl ist braun. 14. In der Wand ist ein Fenster. 15. Der Schüler schreibt mit dem Bleistift. 16. Der Bruder des Schülers macht einen Spaziergang. 17. Karl schreibt dem Freunde einen Brief. 18. Der Lehrer wohnt in der Stadt. 19. Der Hund ist in dem Wald.

(b) Change plural nouns and verbs to the singular:

1. An den Sonntagen machen die Schüler Spaziergänge. 2. In den Sommern gehen die Lehrer nach Deutschland. 3. Die Wege sind in den Wäldern. 4. Die Freunde schreiben Briefe. 5. Die Amerikaner haben Automobile. 6. Die Dampfer sind nach Europa gefahren. 7. Die Lehrer sind Männer. 8. Die Schüler haben Bleistifte und Hefte. 9. Die Häuser sind in den Städten. 10. Die Brüder der Schüler haben Bücher. 11. Die Zimmer haben Wände. 12. Die Mädchen haben Lieder gesungen. 13. Die Schüler haben Väter und Mütter. 14. Die Dienstmädchen haben keine

Bücher. 15. In den Wänden sind Fenster. 16. Die Tische sind in den Zimmern. 17. In den Wäldern sind keine Stühle gewesen. 18. Die Hunde sind schnell gelaufen.

VI. TRANSLATION EXERCISES

Use the present perfect tense whenever possible.

1. Mr. Braun once visited friends. 2. First he wrote letters. 3. The friends had houses in the country. 4. The automobiles went (fahren) very fast. 5. The pupils sang songs. 6. The men did not see the dogs. 7. The girls wrote with pencils. 8. In the living rooms were chairs and tables. 9. The dogs ran in front of the automobiles. 10. The windows of the rooms are wide. 11. Do you like to take walks, Mr. Braun? 12. Did the father of the pupils also go to school? 13. The brothers stayed at home. 14. The teachers had books. 15. The pupils wrote in the notebooks.

VII. VOCABULARY BUILDING

A t in German frequently corresponds to an English d.

das Bett	the bed	der Spaten	the spade
der Garten	the garden	der Tag	the day
der Gott	God	das Tal	the dale, valley
hart	hard	der Tanz	the dance
die Karte	the card	tief	deep
laut	loud	trinken	to drink
reiten	to ride	waten	to wade
die Seite	the side	das Wort	the word

VIII. SUPPLEMENTARY READING

In Hamburg

Die Familie Braun war jetzt in einem Hotel in Hamburg. Hamburg ist eine Großstadt und hat viele große Hotels. Das Hotel lag in der Mitte der Stadt. Es hatte mehr als 200 (zweihundert) Zimmer und die Zimmer waren alle groß und rein. Die Familie hatte drei Zimmer: ein Wohnzimmer, zwei Schlafzimmer und ein Badezimmer. Es war gerade Mittag und sie waren alle sehr hungrig, aber sie waren auch neugierig, etwas von Hamburg zu sehen. Der Vater sagte: „Wir machen zuerst einen Spaziergang, dann essen wir unser Mittagessen in einem Restaurant in der Stadt." Auf den Straßen sahen sie viele Leute und Automobile. Vor den Restaurants standen viele Tische und Stühle. Hier saßen Damen und Herren, tranken Wein oder Bier, Kaffee, Tee oder Limonade, lasen die Zeitung oder plauderten. Später kamen sie an die Elbe. Die Elbe fließt in mehreren Armen durch Hamburg und bildet viele Kanäle. Ein kleiner Fluß, die Alster, fließt hier in die Elbe und bildet zwei große Wasserbecken, d.h. kleine Seen. Auf den Becken der Alster waren viele kleine Dampfer und Boote. Um die Becken sind breite Straßen und große Häuser und viele Leute machten dort Spaziergänge.

Endlich wurden sie müde und hungrig und gingen in ein Restaurant. Das Restaurant war sehr groß und hatte viele Tische und Stühle. An den Tischen saßen viele Leute. Der Kellner führte sie an einen Tisch und brachte die Speisekarte. Der Vater sagte: „Bringen Sie, bitte, eine Suppe, Fleisch, Kartoffeln und Gemüse." Der Vater und die Mutter tranken ein Glas Bier, Karl und Anna tranken Mineralwasser. Nach dem Essen gingen sie wieder ins Hotel. Sie waren sehr müde und blieben einige Stunden in dem Hotel. Am Abend gingen sie in ein Kino und sahen einen interessanten Film. Dann gingen sie zu Bett.

IX. SUPPLEMENTARY VOCABULARY

der **Abend**, -s, -e   the evening
der **Arm**, -(e)s, -e   the arm
das **Badezimmer**, -s, -   the bathroom
das **Becken**, -s, -   the basin
das **Bett**, -(e)s, -en   the bed
das **Bier**, -(e)s, -e   the beer

das **Boot**, -(e)s, -e   the boat
brachte   brought (*past tense of* **bringen**   to bring)
die **Dame**, -, -n   the lady
endlich   finally
essen, aß   to eat
etwas   something, anything

der **Film**, -(e)s, -e   the film, moving picture

das **Fleisch**, -es   the meat

fließen, floß   to flow

führen   to lead, bring

das **Gemüse**, -s, -   the vegetable(s)

gerade   just

das **Glas**, -es, ⁻er   the glass

das **Hotel'**, -s, -s   the hotel

hungrig   hungry

interessant'   interesting

der **Kaffee**, -s, -s   the coffee

der **Kanal'**, -s, ⁻e   the canal

die **Kartof'fel**, -, -n   the potato

der **Kellner**, -s, -   the waiter

klein   little, small

das **Kino**, -s, -s   the moving picture house

lesen, las   to read

die **Leute** (*pl. only*)   the people

die **Limona'de**, -, -n   lemonade

mehrere   several

das **Mineral'wasser**, -s, -   the mineral water

der **Mittag**, -(e)s, -e   midday, noon

das **Mittagessen**, -s, -   the midday meal, dinner

müde   tired

neugierig   curious

plaudern   to chat

rein   clean

saßen   sat (*past tense of* **sitzen** to sit)

das **Schlafzimmer**, -s, -   the bedroom

der **See**, -s, -n   the lake

spät   late; **später**   later

die **Speisekarte**, -, -n   the bill of fare

standen   stood (*past tense of* **stehen** to stand)

die **Suppe**, -, -n   the soup

der **Tee**, -s, -s   the tea

um (+ *acc.*)   about, around, by, after, at, for

das **Wasserbecken**, -s, -   the basin of water

der **Wein**, -(e)s, -e   the wine

wurden   became (*past tense of* **werden** to become)

die **Zeitung**, -, -en   the newspaper

Aufgabe Neun

Plural of Weak, Mixed, and Irregular Nouns

I. READING SELECTION

Allerlei

In den Städten sind **Straßen**. Die **Straßen** sind groß und breit. Auf den **Straßen** fahren **Straßenbahnen**. Die Leute kaufen zuerst **Fahrkarten**, dann fahren sie in die Stadt oder aus der Stadt auf das Land. Die **Bauern** wohnen auf dem Lande. Dort sind keine **Straßenbahnen**. Die **Straßenbahnen** sind nur in den Städten. Also fahren die **Bauern** nicht oft mit der Straßenbahn. Nur in den Städten fahren die Leute mit den **Straßenbahnen**.

In den Städten sind auch viele **Schulen**. **Knaben** und Mädchen gehen in die Schulen. Die **Knaben** sind Schüler, die Mädchen sind **Schülerinnen**. Viele Schüler und **Schülerinnen** haben Brüder und **Schwestern**. Alle **Klassen** in den **Schulen** haben Lehrer oder **Lehrerinnen**. Die Lehrer sind Männer, die **Lehrerinnen** sind **Frauen**. An den Wänden der Schulzimmer sind **Tafeln**. Die Lehrer und **Lehrerinnen** schreiben die **Aufgaben** an die **Tafeln**. Sie schreiben mit der Kreide. Die Schüler und **Schülerinnen** schreiben die **Aufgaben** in die Hefte. Sie schreiben mit den Bleistiften oder den **Federn**. Dann lernen sie die **Aufgaben** auswendig. Die Lehrer und die **Lehrerinnen** stellen **Fragen** und die Schüler und **Schülerinnen** geben **Antworten**. Sie geben gern **Antworten**, denn sie haben die **Aufgaben** auswendig gelernt.

An den Wänden und in den Büchern sind **Karten** von Deutschland. Die **Farben** der **Karten** sind sehr schön. Die Farbe der **Türen** ist braun. Die **Farben** der Bücher sind rot

und schwarz. In den **Wohnungen** sind die **Türen** nicht oft rot oder schwarz.
Im Sommer machen viele **Familien Reisen** nach Europa.
Im Sommer haben die Schüler und die **Schülerinnen** Ferien, d.h. sie gehen nicht in die **Schulen.** Die Eltern, d.h. die Väter und die Mütter der Schüler und **Schülerinnen,** reisen dann auch nach Europa. Auf den Dampfern sind viele **Herren** und **Damen.** Viele Amerikaner und **Amerikanerinnen** reisen im Sommer und im Winter nach Europa. Die Reise nach Deutschland dauert nicht nur ein paar **Stunden,** sondern oft acht oder neun Tage. Die Amerikaner und **Amerikanerinnen** bleiben oft viele **Wochen** in Europa.

II. VOCABULARY

*Idioms { **auswendig lernen** to learn by heart, memorize
eine Frage stellen to ask a question
ein paar a few, several

*all (*pl.* **alle**) all
*also and so, therefore
*aus (+ *dat.*) out, of from
*auswendig by heart
*die Dame, -, -n the lady
*dauern, to last, take
*die Eltern (*pl. only*) the parents
*(das) Euro'pa, -s Europe
*die Ferien (*pl. only*) vacation
*die Frage, -, -n the question
*der Knabe, -n, -n the boy

*nach (+ *dat.*) toward, to, for, after, according to
*neun nine
*oft often
*das Paar, -(e)s, -e the pair, couple
*reisen (sein) to travel, take a trip
*schön beautiful
*stellen to place, put
*der Tag, -(e)s, -e the day
*der Winter, -s, - the winter

III. GRAMMAR

A. Weak Nouns

1. All four cases of the plural of weak nouns are formed by adding **-(e)n.** A list of the active weak nouns used up to and including this lesson follows.

die Amerikanerinnen	die Knaben
die Antworten	die Lehrerinnen
die Aufgaben	die Reisen
die Damen	die Schulen
die Fahrkarten	die Schülerinnen
die Familien	die Schwestern
die Farben	die Straßen
die Federn	die Straßenbahnen
die Fragen	die Stunden
die Frauen	die Tafeln
die Herren	die Türen
die Jungen	die Wochen
die Karten	die Wohnungen
die Klassen	

2. The vast majority of feminine nouns are weak. No neuter nouns and only a very few masculine nouns belong to this class. The only masculine nouns in the above list are **der Herr, der Junge, der Knabe.** Weak nouns never add Umlaut.

3. It will be recalled that feminine nouns never add any ending in the singular. Weak masculine nouns, however, also add **-(e)n** to form the genitive, dative, and accusative cases. **Der Herr** is slightly irregular in that it adds only **-n** in the singular, but **-en** in the plural.

4. Feminine nouns ending in **-in** regularly double the final **-n** before adding the ending **-en: die Lehrerinnen.** This doubling is necessary in order to keep the vowel short.

B. Mixed Nouns

A very few nouns are called mixed because they are declined like strong nouns in the singular and like weak nouns in the plural. Examples are **das Auge, des Auges, die Augen** *the eye;* **das Ohr, des Ohres, die Ohren** *the ear;* **der Doktor, des Doktors, die Doktoren; der Bauer** may be either weak or mixed: **der Bauer, -s** *or* **-n, -n.**

C. Irregular Nouns

Several nouns, such as **das Herz** *the heart* and **der Name** *the name*, resemble weak nouns except that they have the ending **-ens** in the genitive singular.   They really belong to the first class of strong nouns, having lost the -(**e**)**n** in the nominative singular.

D. *Examples of Declensions*

WEAK

Singular	der Herr	die Frau	die Lehrerin
	des Herrn	der Frau	der Lehrerin
	dem Herrn	der Frau	der Lehrerin
	den Herrn	die Frau	die Lehrerin
Plural	die Herren	die Frauen	die Lehrerinnen
	der Herren	der Frauen	der Lehrerinnen
	den Herren	den Frauen	den Lehrerinnen
	die Herren	die Frauen	die Lehrerinnen

MIXED   IRREGULAR

Singular	das Ohr	der Name
	des Ohres	des Namens
	dem Ohr(e)	dem Namen
	das Ohr	den Namen
Plural	die Ohren	die Namen
	der Ohren	der Namen
	den Ohren	den Namen
	die Ohren	die Namen

E. *Summary of General Rules*

1. The genitive singular of strong masculine and neuter nouns has the ending -(**e**)**s**.
2. Feminine nouns never have any endings in the singular.
3. The nominative, genitive, and accusative plural are always alike.
4. The dative plural always ends in -(**e**)**n**.
5. Always memorize the principal parts with each active noun.

IV. QUESTIONS

In your answers use plural forms of nouns whenever possible.

1. Wo sind Straßen? 2. Wie sind die Straßen? 3. Wo fahren die Straßenbahnen? 4. Was kaufen die Leute? 5. Wohin fahren sie dann? 6. Wo wohnen die Bauern? 7. Fahren die Bauern oft mit der Straßenbahn? 8. Wer geht in die Schulen? 9. Was sind die Knaben? 10. Was sind die Mädchen? 11. Was haben alle Klassen in den Schulen? 12. Was sind die Lehrer? 13. Was sind die Lehrerinnen? 14. Wo sind Tafeln? 15. Wer schreibt die Aufgaben an die Tafeln? 16. Wer schreibt die Aufgaben in die Hefte? 17. Wer lernt die Aufgaben auswendig? 18. Wer stellt Fragen? 19. Wo sind Karten von Deutschland? 20. Was machen viele Familien im Sommer? 21. Wann haben die Schüler und Schülerinnen Ferien?

V. GRAMMATICAL EXERCISES

(a) Change all nouns and verbs to the plural whenever possible:

1. Der Schüler schreibt mit dem Bleistift. 2. Die Schülerin schreibt mit der Feder. 3. Der Knabe hat einen Freund in der Schule. 4. An der Wand ist eine Tafel. 5. Die Tür in der Wohnung ist gelb. 6. Der Bauer hat ein Haus auf dem Lande. 7. Der Herr und die Dame reisen nach Europa. 8. Der Vater und die Mutter bleiben zu Hause. 9. Die Schwester hat die Aufgabe geschrieben. 10. Die Lehrerin hat eine Wohnung in der Stadt. 11. Die Straßenbahn ist auf der Straße gefahren. 12. In dem Buch ist eine Karte. 13. Wohin reisen der Amerikaner und die Amerikanerin? 14. Das Mädchen lernt die Aufgabe auswendig. 15. Die Lehrerin ist eine Frau.

(b) Change nouns and verbs to the singular:

1. Die Schülerinnen schreiben die Antworten in die Hefte. 2. In den Klassen sind Jungen und Mädchen. 3. In den Wohnungen sind Tische und Stühle. 4. Die Brüder und die Schwestern gehen in die Schulen. 5. Die Lehrerinnen machen gern Reisen. 6. Auf den Dampfern sind Herren und

Damen. 7. Die Straßenbahnen sind in den Städten. 8. Die Tafeln in den Schulzimmern sind schwarz. 9. Die Bauern kommen nicht oft in die Städte. 10. Die Amerikanerinnen sind zwei Wochen in Deutschland geblieben. 11. Die Schüler haben zuerst Fahrkarten gekauft. 12. Die Lehrer waren zwei Stunden in den Schulzimmern. 13. Die Farben der Karten sind schön. 14. Die Schülerinnen haben Bleistifte und Federn. 15. Sie schreiben die Aufgaben in die Hefte.

VI. TRANSLATION EXERCISES

1. The teachers (*fem.*) remained in school several hours (*note word order: time before place*). 2. Many ladies and gentlemen traveled to Europe. 3. The teachers (*masc.*) asked many questions. 4. The boys and girls had memorized their lessons. 5. The parents go to the country in summer (*note word order*). 6. The pupils (*fem.*) have vacation in summer. 7. Many people were on the steamers. 8. The families stayed only three weeks in Germany. 9. Many men and women rode in the street cars. 10. American men and women like to travel. 11. The pupils (*masc.*) wrote their lessons in their notebooks. 12. They wrote with pencils or pens. 13. On the walls are maps of Germany. 14. In the books are also maps. 15. The peasants came to the city and rode on the street car.

VII. VOCABULARY BUILDING

A German **d** frequently corresponds to an English *th*.

das Bad	the bath	**drei**	three
danken	to thank	**du**	thou
dein	thine	**dünn**	thin
denken	to think	**der Durst**	the thirst
dick	thick	**die Feder**	the feather; pen
der Dieb	the thief	**die Heide**	the heath
das Ding	the thing	**das Leder**	the leather
der Dorn	the thorn	**der Norden**	the north

VIII. SUPPLEMENTARY READING

Die Reise nach Berlin

Am nächsten Morgen hatte die Familie Braun ihr Frühstück im Hotel. Herr Braun sagte: „Hamburg ist die zweitgrößte Stadt in Deutschland und der drittgrößte Hafen der Welt. Wir haben nicht viel von Hamburg gesehen, aber wir bleiben nur ein paar Wochen in Deutschland, und in Deutschland sind viele interessante Städte. Wir fliegen heute nach Berlin. Berlin ist die größte Stadt in Deutschland und war die Hauptstadt des Deutschen Reiches. Berlin hatte damals mehr als vier Millionen Einwohner."

Nach dem Frühstück packten sie ihre Koffer, bezahlten die Rechnung und fuhren mit einem Auto zum Flugplatz. Es war ziemlich weit zum Flugplatz und die Fahrt kostete drei Mark 20 (zwanzig) Pfennig. Herr Braun gab dem Chauffeur 40 (vierzig) Pfennig Trinkgeld. Dann kauften sie Flugkarten nach Berlin und gingen zu dem Flugzeug. Es gehen auch Eisenbahnen nach Berlin, aber es ist besser zu fliegen. Die große Stadt ist von Amerikanern, Engländern, Franzosen und Russen besetzt. Rings um Berlin sind nur Russen. Sie inspizieren alle Eisenbahnzüge und sind mißtrauisch gegen Amerikaner. Im Jahr 1948 machten sie eine Blockade und ließen keine Züge aus dem Westen nach Berlin. Auch aus dem Osten kamen keine Züge nach dem amerikanischen Teil von Berlin. Nach kurzer Zeit hatten die Berliner nichts mehr zu essen und keine Kohle. Da begannen die Amerikaner, alle Lebensmittel und Rohmaterialien mit Flugzeugen nach Berlin zu fliegen. Jede Minute landete ein Flugzeug auf dem Flugplatz in Berlin. Die Berliner hatten nun zu essen und ihre Industrie arbeitete. Das war die sogenannte „Luftbrücke," die Amerikaner sagten „airlift." Erst nach einem Jahr beendeten die Russen diese Blockade. Von Hamburg nach Berlin ist es beinahe 300 (dreihundert) Kilometer, d.h. ungefähr 200 (zweihundert) amerikanische Meilen. Die Reise im Flugzeug dauerte etwas über eine Stunde.

Salzburg: Residenzplatz

Salzburg

Maria-Theresienplatz in Wien

Schloß Schönbrunn in Wien

Innsbruck: das goldene Dachl

Innsbruck: Relief von dem goldenen Dachl

IX. SUPPLEMENTARY VOCABULARY

arbeiten to work

beenden to terminate

der Berli'ner, -s, - the inhabitant (or native) of Berlin

besetzen to occupy, put, lay on

besser better

bezahlen to pay

die Blocka'de, -, -n the blockade

der Chauffeur', -s, -e the chauffeur

drittgrößt third largest

der Eisenbahnzug, -(e)s, "e the (railway) train

erst (*with expressions of time*) only, not until

essen, aß, hat gegessen to eat

die Fahrt, -, -en the journey, trip

fliegen, flog, ist geflogen to fly

die Flugkarte, -, -n the air ticket

der Flugplatz, -es, "e the airport

das Flugzeug, -(e)s, -e the airplane

der Franzo'se, -n, -n the Frenchman

das Frühstück, -(e)s, -e the breakfast

die Industrie', -, -en the industry

inspizie'ren to inspect

der Koffer, -s, - the trunk, suitcase

die Kohle, -, -n the coal

kurz short

lassen, ließ, hat gelassen to let

das Lebensmittel, -s, - the food, provisions

die Luftbrücke, -, -n the air bridge, airlift

die Minu'te, -, -n the minute

mißtrauisch distrustful

nächst next

nichts nothing

nun now

packen to pack

der Pfennig, -s, -e the pfennig (*100 pfennigs = 1 mark*)

die Rechnung, -, -en the bill

ringsum round about, all around

das Rohmaterial, -s, -ien the raw material

der Russe, -n, -n the Russian

sogenannt so-called

der Teil, -(e)s, -e the part

das Trinkgeld, -(e)s, -er the tip

über (+ *dat.* or *acc.*) over

die Welt, -, -en the world

die Zeit, -, -en the time

ziemlich rather, quite

der Zug, -(e)s, "e the train

Aufgabe Zehn

Der-*words and* **ein**-*words.*   *Present Tense of Strong Verbs*

I. READING SELECTION

Der Regenschirm

Heute ist Sonntag. An **diesem** Tage **fährt** Herr Schmidt mit der Straßenbahn in die Stadt. Er ist Lehrer und hat heute keine Schule. In der Stadt **trifft** Herr Schmidt einen Freund. Dieser Freund ist Arzt und heißt Doktor Krull. Mit **diesem** Freunde macht Herr Schmidt zuerst einen Spaziergang. Er **spricht** mit **seinem** Freunde über **dieses** und **jenes.** Um ein Uhr sagt Doktor Krull: ,,Ich gehe zum Mittagessen nach Hause, denn meine Frau wartet.'' Er **gibt** Herrn Schmidt die Hand und sagt: ,,Auf Wiedersehen.''
Herr Schmidt ist auch hungrig und geht in ein Restaurant. Der Kellner sagt ,,Guten Tag'' und **gibt** Herrn Schmidt die Speisekarte. Herr Schmidt **ißt** zuerst eine Suppe und dann Fleisch, Kartoffeln und Gemüse. Er trinkt auch ein Glas Bier. Dann **gibt** der Kellner Herrn Schmidt die Rechnung. Herr Schmidt bezahlt und **gibt** dem Kellner ein Trinkgeld. Der Kellner **nimmt** das Trinkgeld sehr gerne. Dann geht Herr Schmidt zu Fuß nach Hause.
Auf dem Wege nach Hause beginnt es zu regnen und Herr Schmidt hat keinen Regenschirm. Auf einmal **sieht** er einen Herrn mit einem Regenschirm. Dieser Herr geht eben in ein Restaurant und braucht also keinen Regenschirm. Herr Schmidt glaubt, es ist sein Freund Herr Müller. Er sagt zu dem Mann: ,,Bitte, geben Sie mir Ihren Regenschirm.'' Der Herr sagt nichts, sondern **gibt** Herrn Schmidt den Regen-

schirm und **läuft** schnell ins Restaurant. Jetzt ist Herr Schmidt sehr erstaunt, denn er hat den Herrn nie gesehen.

II. VOCABULARY

*Idioms { **um ein (zwei, drei) Uhr** at one (two, three) o'clock
zum Mittagessen for dinner
die Hand geben to shake hands

*bezahlen to pay
*das Bier, -(e)s, -e, (*pl. rare*) the beer
brauchen to need
*dieser, diese, dieses this; the latter
eben just
*essen, aß, hat gegessen, er ißt to eat
das Fleisch, -es (*no pl.*) the meat
das Gemüse, -s, - the vegetable
*das Glas, -es, ¨er the glass
glauben to believe
die Hand, -, ¨e the hand
*hungrig hungry
*jeder, jede, jedes each, every
*jener, jene, jenes that; the former
die Kartof'fel, -, -n the potato
der Kellner, -s, - the waiter
*mancher, manche, manches many a, much; *pl.* some
mir (*dat. of* ich) me
das Mittagessen, -s, - the midday meal, dinner
*nehmen, nahm, hat genommen, er nimmt to take

nichts nothing
nie never
die Rechnung, -, -en the bill
*der Regenschirm, -(e)s, -e the umbrella
*regnen to rain
*das Restaurant', -s, -s the restaurant
*solcher, solche, solches such
die Speisekarte, -, -n the bill of fare
*sprechen, sprach, hat gesprochen, er spricht to speak
die Suppe, -, -n the soup
*treffen, traf, hat getroffen, er trifft to meet
das Trinkgeld, -(e)s, -er the tip
über (+ *dat.* or *acc.*) over, at, above, concerning, about
*die Uhr, -, -en the clock, watch
*um (+ *acc.*) about, around, by, after, at, for; *with inf.*+
zu to, in order to
*welcher, welche, welches which, what, who
*zehn ten

NOTE: The third person singular of the present tense is added to the principal parts of strong verbs when a vowel change takes place.

III. GRAMMAR

A. Der-*words* and ein-*words*

der-words   ein-words

	dieser welcher			kein unser		
	jener mancher			mein euer		
	jeder solcher			dein ihr		
				sein Ihr		

		Masc.	Fem.	Neut.	Masc.	Fem.	Neut.
Sing.	Nom.	dieser	diese	dies(es)	kein	keine	kein
	Gen.	dieses	dieser	dieses	keines	keiner	keines
	Dat.	diesem	dieser	diesem	keinem	keiner	keinem
	Acc.	diesen	diese	dies(es)	keinen	keine	kein
Plural	Nom.	diese			keine		
	Gen.	dieser			keiner		
	Dat.	diesen			keinen		
	Acc.	diese			keine		

1. The declension of the **der**-words closely resembles that of the definite article.

2. The forms **dieses** in the nominative and accusative singular of the neuter are frequently shortened to **dies,** especially in colloquial speech. This does not apply to the other **der**-words.

3. The only difference between the **der**-words and the **ein**-words is in the nominative singular of the masculine and the nominative and accusative singular of the neuter. In these three cases the **ein**-words have no ending. This will be of considerable importance when the adjective endings are taken up.

4. The **er** of **unser** and **euer** is not an ending, but part of the stem. When an inflectional ending is added to **unser** and **euer** one of the last two **e**'s is usually dropped:

Sing.	Nom.	unser	euer
	Gen.	unsers or unsres	euers or eures
	Dat.	unserm or unsrem	euerm or eurem
	Acc.	unsern or unsren	euern or euren
Plural	Nom.	unsere or unsre	euere or eure
	Gen.	unserer or unsrer	euerer or eurer
	Dat.	unseren or unsren	eueren or euren
	Acc.	unsere or unsre	euere or eure

B. Present Tense of Strong Verbs

1. Many strong verbs change their stem vowels in the second person singular familiar and in the third person singular:

	a > ä	ē > ie
Sing.	1. ich fahre	1. ich sehe
	2. du fährst	2. du siehst
	3. er fährt	3. er sieht
	au > äu	ē > (sometimes) i
Sing.	1. ich laufe	1. ich gebe
	2. du läufst	2. du gibst
	3. er läuft	3. er gibt
	ĕ > i	
Sing.	1. ich spreche	1. ich nehme
	2. du sprichst	2. du nimmst
	3. er spricht	3. er nimmt

In the case of **nehmen** the **h** is inserted to indicate the length of the preceding vowel **e**. When this vowel is shortened in the second and third person singular to **i**, the **h** is dropped and the consonant **m** is doubled to indicate that the preceding vowel **i** is short.

2. The only other strong verbs hitherto used as active vocabulary that change the stem vowel in the present tense are **essen** and **treffen**.

1. ich esse	1. ich treffe
2. du ißt	2. du triffst
3. er ißt	3. er trifft

3. Hereafter such vowel changes will be indicated in the vocabulary by adding the third person singular of the present tense to the principal parts of strong verbs: **nehmen, nahm, hat genommen, er nimmt.**
4. Weak verbs NEVER change the stem vowel.

C. Nouns in Apposition

A noun directly following a noun of number, weight, or measure is used in apposition to, i.e., it has the same case as, the preceding noun.

Ein Glas Bier.

IV. QUESTIONS

1. Wie heißt die Aufgabe für heute? 2. Wohin fährt Herr Schmidt heute? 3. Was ist Herr Schmidt? 4. Hat Herr Schmidt an jedem Tage Schule? 5. An welchem Tage hat Herr Schmidt keine Schule? 6. Wo trifft Herr Schmidt einen Freund? 7. Was ist dieser Freund? 8. Wie heißt der Arzt? 9. Ist jeder Doktor Arzt? 10. Was macht Herr Schmidt mit jenem Freunde? 11. Wohin geht Doktor Krull zum Mittagessen? 12. Wann geht er nach Hause? 13. Wohin geht Herr Schmidt? 14. Was trinkt Herr Schmidt zum Mittagessen? 15. Wann regnet es? 16. Was hat Herr Schmidt nicht? 17. Wer gibt Herrn Schmidt einen Regenschirm? 18. Wohin läuft der Herr schnell?

V. GRAMMATICAL EXERCISES

(a) Supply the correct endings:

1. Manch— Leute reisen jed— Sommer (*acc.*) nach Europa. 2. In welch— Buche waren jen— Karten? 3. Die Farbe dies— Kreide ist weiß, die Farbe jen— Bleistifts ist gelb.

4. Dies— Mädchen geht zu sein— Großmutter. 5. Er gibt
jen— Manne sein— Hand. 6. Mit solch— Kreide schreibt
der Lehrer an die Tafel. 7. Sie spricht mit ihr— Lehrerin
über dies— und jen—. 8. An jed— Sonntag geht er mit
sein— Freunden in den Wald. 9. In dies— Wand ist eine
Tür, in jen— Wand ist ein Fenster. 10. Welch— Aufgabe
haben Sie gelernt? 11. Wir gehen mit unser— Vater in
jen— Haus. 12. Er schreibt sein— Freunde immer solch—
Briefe. 13. Manch— Mann hat solch— Lieder gesungen.
14. Ich schreibe mit mein— Bleistift, du schreibst mit dein—
Feder, er schreibt mit sein— Kreide. 15. In welch— Restaurant essen sie?

(b) Supply the correct forms in the present indicative of the
verbs in parentheses:

1. Er (laufen) schnell in das Haus. 2. Was (essen) du zum
Mittagessen? 3. Wo (kaufen) du die Fahrkarten? 4. Mit
welchem Manne (sprechen) er? 5. Karl (nehmen) die Feder
und schreibt in sein Heft. 6. Wo (treffen) Herr Schmidt
seinen Freund? 7. Dieser Herr (fahren) in einem Automobil.
8. Der Lehrer (stellen) eine Frage. 9. Das Mädchen (sehen)
eine Freundin. 10. Was (geben) der Lehrer dem Schüler?
11. Wohin (gehen) du zuerst? 12. Der Schüler (lernen) die
Aufgabe.

(c) Change all sentences in (b) to the past tense.
(d) Change all sentences in (b) to the perfect tense.

VI. TRANSLATION EXERCISES

1. Every pupil has a book. 2. The doctor eats in a restaurant. 3. In which restaurant does he eat? 4. He shakes
hands with his friend. 5. Some people have no umbrella.
6. That girl is going home at three o'clock (*note word order*).
7. He meets a friend on (auf) the steamer. 8. This pupil is
speaking to the teacher. 9. Where did that man go yesterday? 10. The teacher goes home for dinner (*note word order*).
11. Such songs are very beautiful. 12. He takes the umbrella

and runs into the restaurant. 13. He buys a ticket and rides home in the street car. 14. The boy writes with this pencil, but the girl writes with that pen. 15. Do you see that dog, Karl?

VII. VOCABULARY BUILDING

A German **ch** sometimes corresponds to a *k* in English.

der Becher	the beaker	die Milch	the milk
brechen	to break	der Mönch	the monk
das Buch	the book	der Rechen	the rake
das Joch	the yoke	der Storch	the stork
der Kuchen	the cake, cooky	wachen	to wake
machen	to make	die Woche	the week

VIII. SUPPLEMENTARY READING

In Berlin

Um elf Uhr kam die Familie Braun nach Berlin. Das Flugzeug landete und viele Leute warteten dort auf ihre Freunde. Aber niemand wartete auf Herrn Braun und seine Familie; denn er hatte niemand von seiner Ankunft in Berlin geschrieben. Ein Gepäckträger nahm ihr Gepäck und führte sie zu einem Auto. Dann fuhren sie in ein Hotel.

Es war gerade Zeit zum Mittagessen und darum speisten sie im Hotel. Herr Braun bestellte ein Mittagessen zu vier Mark pro Person, d.h. sie speisten Table d'hote und nicht nach der Karte. Aber sie tranken heute kein Bier, sondern Herr Braun bestellte eine Flasche Wein. Nach dem Mittagessen bezahlte Herr Braun die Rechnung, aber er gab dem Kellner kein Trinkgeld, denn das Trinkgeld, zehn Prozent, stand auf der Rechnung.

Sie waren alle neugierig, etwas von Berlin zu sehen, und darum machten sie gleich nach dem Mittagessen einen Spaziergang. Zuerst gingen sie zum Brandenburger Tor am westlichen Ende der Straße Unter den Linden. Hier beginnt der Tiergarten, früher ein großer, schöner Park in der Mitte Berlins. Nach dem Krieg haben die Berliner alle Bäume abgehauen, denn sie hatten keine Kohlen und brauchten das Holz. Die Straße Unter den Linden ist nur ungefähr ein Kilometer lang, aber sie ist ungefähr 60 (sechzig) Meter breit. Am östlichen Ende sind die Bibliothek, die Universität und das Opernhaus. Eine Brücke führt über einen Arm der Spree. Die Spree ist ein kleiner Fluß und fließt durch Berlin. Auf der anderen Seite der Brücke war rechts das Schloß. Hier wohnte in früheren Jahren der Deutsche Kaiser. Die Russen haben das Schloß vollkommen zerstört. An seiner Stelle ist jetzt ein großer Platz für die Paraden der Kommunisten. Die Familie Braun ging nicht in die Zone der Russen. Daher besuchten sie auch nicht die Stadt Potsdam. Sie war früher die zweite Residenz der Hohenzollern-Könige und verdankt ihre Bedeutung Friedrich dem Großen. Von König Friedrich erzählen zwei Anekdoten auf Seite 116 (hundertundsechzehn).

IX. SUPPLEMENTARY VOCABULARY

ab-hauen to cut down; **abgehauen** cut down (*past participle*)
ander other
die Ankunft, -, ̈e the arrival
der Baum, -(e)s, ̈e the tree
die Bedeutung, -, -en the significance, importance
bestellen to order
die Bibliothek', -, -en the library
das Brandenburger Tor the Brandenburg Gate
die Brücke, -, -en the bridge
daher therefore
darum therefore
elf eleven
das Ende, -s, -n the end
erzählen to relate, tell
die Flasche, -, -n the bottle

Friedrich der Große Frederick the Great
das Gepäck, -(e)s, -e the baggage
der Gepäckträger, -s, - the baggage carrier, porter
gleich immediately
die Hohenzollern the Hohenzollern(s)
das Holz, -es, ̈er the wood
hundert hundred
der Kommunist', -en, -en the Communist
der Krieg, -(e)s, -e the war
niemand no one, nobody
das Opernhaus, -es, ̈er the opera house
die Para'de, -, -n the parade
der Platz, -es, ̈e the place, room, seat; the square

(das) **Potsdam** Potsdam
pro per
das Prozent', -s, -e the percent
rechts to the right
die Residenz', -, -en the residence (royal)
das Schloß, -sses, ⁼sser the castle, palace
die Seite, -, -n the side; the page
speisen to dine
die Stelle, -, -n the place

Table d'hote table d'hôte
der Tiergarten, -s the Tiergarten
die Universität', -, -en the university
verdan'ken to owe to
vollkommen completely
warten (**auf** + *acc.*) to wait (for)
zerstören to destroy
die Zone, -, -n the zone

Aufgabe Elf

Conjugation of **werden.** *The Future Tenses.*
The Imperative

I. READING SELECTION

Der Wirt und der Student

Ein Professor ist Lehrer **an** einer Universität, ein Student
studiert **auf** der Universität. Jeder Professor war früher auch
Student. Mancher Student **wird** später auch Professor.
Viele Studenten sind arm, d.h. sie haben wenig Geld, aber
später **werden** sie oft reich.
Vor vielen Jahren lebte einmal ein Student in Deutschland.
Er war sehr arm und hatte seit ein paar Tagen nichts gegessen.
Nun **wurde** er sehr hungrig, aber er hatte kein Geld. Er ging
zu einem Freund, aber sein Freund hatte auch kein Geld.
Endlich machte er einen Spaziergang. Er ging in ein Wirts-
haus, d.h. in ein Restaurant, und bestellte zuerst eine Suppe,
dann Fleisch, Gemüse und Kartoffeln. Er trank auch eine
Flasche Wein. Dann rief er den Wirt und sagte: ,,Ich habe
kein Geld, um die Rechnung zu bezahlen. Aber ich **werde**
ein Lied **singen.** **Werden** Sie das Lied als Bezahlung für die
Rechnung **nehmen?**'' Der Wirt antwortete: ,,Nein, ich **werde**
das Lied nicht als Bezahlung **nehmen.** Ich verlange mein
Geld und kein Lied. **Bezahlen Sie,** bitte, die Rechnung!''
Aber der Student sagte: ,,Ich **werde** trotzdem ein Lied **singen.**
Wenn Sie sagen: ,Das Lied ist schön,' dann **werde** ich nicht
bezahlen. Sind Sie damit zufrieden?'' Der Wirt sagte: ,,Ja,
wenn ich sage: ,Das Lied ist schön,' dann brauchen Sie die
Rechnung nicht zu bezahlen.'' Nun begann der Student
viele Lieder zu singen, aber der Wirt sagte immer: ,,Nein, das
Lied ist nicht schön.'' Endlich steckte der Student die Hand
in die Tasche, nahm seinen Geldbeutel und begann zu singen:
,,Greif' in die Tasche, bezahle den Wirt'' usw. Der Wirt rief:

„Ja, das Lied ist schön." Der Student steckte den Geldbeutel schnell wieder in die Tasche und sagte: „Also brauche ich meine Rechnung nicht zu bezahlen."

II. VOCABULARY

*Idioms
- **an der Universität** at the university (referring to professors and non-students)
- **auf der Universität** at the university (referring to students)
- **usw. (und so weiter)** etc. (et cetera, and so forth)
- **vor fünf (zehn, vielen, usw.) Jahren** five (ten, many, etc.) years ago

als as
***arm** poor
bestellen to order
die Bezahlung, -, -en the payment
damit therewith, with that
***elf** eleven
endlich in the end, finally
die Flasche, -, -n the bottle
***das Fleisch, -es** the meat
***das Geld, -(e)s, -er** the money
der Geldbeutel, -s, - the money bag, purse
***das Gemüse, -s, -** the vegetable
greifen, griff, hat gegriffen to grip, grasp; reach
***die Hand, -, ̈e** the hand
***das Jahr, -(e)s, -e** the year
***die Kartof'fel, -, -n** the potato
***nichts** nothing
***nun** now; well
***der Profes'sor, -s, die Professo'ren** the professor
rufen, rief, hat gerufen to call, exclaim

***seit (+ dat.)** since, for
spät late; **später** later
stecken to stick, put
***der Student', -en, -en** the student
die Suppe, -, -n the soup
die Tasche, -, -n the pocket
trotzdem nevertheless, just the same
um (+ zu + inf.) to, in order to
***die Universität', -, -en** the university
verlangen to desire, demand
vor (+ dat. of a numerical time expression) ago
***der Wein, -(e)s, -e** the wine
***wenig** little
***wenn** if, when, whenever
***werden, wurde, ist geworden, er wird** to become
***wieder** again
***der Wirt, -(e)s, -e** the innkeeper
das Wirtshaus, -es, ̈er the inn
zufrieden satisfied

III. GRAMMAR

A. *Conjugation of* werden

	PRESENT	PRESENT PERFECT

Sing.	1. ich werde
	
	2. du wirst
	   Sie werden
	
	3. er ⎫
	   sie ⎬ wird
	   es ⎭
		1. ich bin ⎫
		
		2. du bist ⎪
		   Sie sind ⎬ geworden
		
		3. er ⎫ ⎪
		   sie ⎬ ist ⎪
		   es ⎭ ⎭

Plural	1. wir werden
	
	2. ihr werdet
	   Sie werden
	
	3. sie werden
		1. wir sind ⎫
		
		2. ihr seid ⎬ geworden
		   Sie sind ⎪
		
		3. sie sind ⎭

	PAST	PAST PERFECT

Sing.	1. ich wurde
	
	2. du wurdest
	   Sie wurden
	
	3. er ⎫
	   sie ⎬ wurde
	   es ⎭
		1. ich war ⎫
		
		2. du warst ⎪
		   Sie waren ⎬ geworden
		
		3. er ⎫ ⎪
		   sie ⎬ war ⎪
		   es ⎭ ⎭

Plural	1. wir wurden
	
	2. ihr wurdet
	   Sie wurden
	
	3. sie wurden
		1. wir waren ⎫
		
		2. ihr wart ⎬ geworden
		   Sie waren ⎪
		
		3. sie waren ⎭

1. **Werden,** like strong verbs, changes its stem vowel from **e** to **i** in the second person singular familiar and the third person singular. In addition these two forms are slightly irregular in that the second person drops the **d** of the stem, and the third person lacks the ending -(**e**)**t**.

2. The present perfect and past perfect tenses require **sein** as the auxiliary.

B. *The Future Tense*

Sing.	1. **ich werde** 2. **du wirst** **Sie werden** 3. **er** **sie** } **wird** **es**	**meinen Freund besuchen**
Plural	1. **wir werden** 2. **ihr werdet** **Sie werden** 3. **sie werden**	**meinen Freund besuchen**

1. The future tense is formed by conjugating **werden** with the infinitive of the given verb.

2. The infinitive follows all the modifiers, i.e., it comes at the end of a normal sentence.

3. In English the present tense is sometimes used in place of the future: *I am going down town today.* This practice is even more common in German, especially when the future is somehow expressed or understood.

Morgen machen wir einen Spaziergang.
Tomorrow we shall take a walk.

C. The Future Perfect Tense

I shall have learned the lesson, etc.

Sing.	1. ich werde 2. du wirst Sie werden 3. er sie } wird es	die Aufgabe gelernt haben
Plural	1. wir werden 2. ihr werdet Sie werden 3. sie werden	die Aufgabe gelernt haben

In German as in English the future perfect is used very infrequently. In the present book we shall have no further occasion to make use of it.

D. The Imperative

	sagen	fahren	sehen
2. Sing.	sag-e sag-en Sie	fahr-e fahr-en Sie	sieh seh-en Sie
2. Plural	sag-t sag-en Sie	fahr-t fahr-en Sie	seh-t seh-en Sie

	haben	sein	werden
2. Sing.	hab-e hab-en Sie	sei sei-en Sie	werd-e werd-en Sie
2. Plural	hab-t hab-en Sie	sei-d sei-en Sie	werd-et werd-en Sie

1. The imperative mood is limited to the second person singular and plural.
2. Except for special emphasis the familiar forms do not have the personal pronouns.
3. The imperative forms differ from the present indicative only in the second person singular familiar where the ending -st is replaced by -e. In the case of strong verbs changing the stem vowel from e to ie or i, this change is retained and the ending -e is dropped. The change from a to ä, however, is not retained. In colloquial speech the ending -e is frequently dropped, but in writing such an omission must be indicated by an apostrophe.
4. The polite forms have inverted order, making them identical with interrogative sentences. In conversation the difference is indicated by the tone of voice. In writing, the interrogative sentence is followed by a question mark, the imperative by an exclamation point.

E. Prepositions

The student has now encountered the following prepositions. Only those marked with an asterisk have so far been designated as active.

1. Prepositions governing the genitive:

| wegen | on account of |

2. Prepositions governing the dative:

*aus	out, of, from
*bei	by, at, near, with, at the house of
*mit	with, by, at
*nach	toward, to, for, after, according to
*seit	since
von	from, of, by
*zu	to, at, for, in, with,

3. Prepositions governing the accusative:

durch	through, by, by means of
gegen	against, towards, compared with, about
*um	about, around, by, after, at, for

4. Prepositions governing either the dative or accusative:[1]

*an	on, at, by, along, in, to, near
*auf	on, upon, at, in, to, for
*in	in, at, into, to, within
*über	over, at, above, concerning
*vor	before, in front of, from, for, ago
zwischen	between

IV. QUESTIONS

1. Welche Aufgabe haben wir heute? 2. Was ist ein Professor? 3. Wo studiert ein Student? 4. Was war jeder Professor früher auch? 5. Was werden manche Studenten später? 6. Wo lebte einmal ein Student? 7. Wann lebte er? 8. Wie war der Student? 9. Seit wann hatte er nichts gegessen? 10. Wie wurde er jetzt? 11. Was hatte er aber nicht? 12. Was machte er zuerst? 13. Wohin ging er dann? 14. Was aß er in dem Restaurant? 15. Trank er Wein oder Bier? 16. Was sagte er zu dem Wirt? 17. Was wird der Student singen? 18. Singen Sie gern?

V. GRAMMATICAL EXERCISES

(a) Change the following sentences to the past, future, and perfect tenses:

1. Herr Müller lebt in Amerika. 2. Er wird Arzt. 3. Der Student klopft an die Tür. 4. Wann kommt er nach Hause? 5. Der Schüler lernt seine Aufgabe. 6. Wir machen einen Spaziergang. 7. Ich kaufe ein Buch. 8. Er ißt Fleisch und Kartoffeln. 9. Er ist Professor an einer Universität. 10. Fährst du im Sommer nach Europa? 11. Die Schülerin fragt den Lehrer. 12. Der Mann gibt dem Kellner ein Trinkgeld. 13. Jener Herr geht auf das Land. 14. Die Eltern bleiben zu Hause. 15. Besucht ihr euren Großvater? 16. Der Student studiert auf der Universität. 17. Die Lehrerin stellt eine Frage. 18. Wir sprechen mit unserem Lehrer. 19. Der Stu-

[1] Concerning the use of the dative or accusative, cf. Lesson III.

dent trinkt eine Flasche Wein.   20. Er hat wenig Geld.   21.
Die Schüler singen Lieder.   22. Ich nehme die Kreide.   23.
Gehst du in die Schule?   24. Schreibst du einen Brief?   25.
Er trifft seinen Freund.

(b) Change the following sentences to all the forms of the
imperative:

1. Du nimmst das Buch.   2. Du gibst dem Wirt das Geld.
3. Du schreibst deine Aufgabe.   4. Du singst ein Lied.   5.
Du kommst morgen.

VI. TRANSLATION EXERCISES

1. He is going to be a doctor.   2. When did he live in
Germany?   3. The innkeeper said: That song is beautiful.
4. Many years ago he came to America.   5. He is now a professor at a university.   6. Formerly he studied at a university.   7. He has not eaten anything.   8. He will go into a
restaurant and eat meat, vegetables, and potatoes.   9. This
man drank beer, but that man drank wine.   10. Not every
man has much money.   11. Some students are poor.   12.
Please, give me your umbrella.   13. The student will sing a
song.   14. The boy became very hungry.   15. The innkeeper will take the money.

VII. VOCABULARY BUILDING

Sometimes a German **ch,** especially in the combination **cht,**
corresponds to an English *gh.*

acht   eight
dicht   tight, close
fechten   fight, fence
die Flucht   the flight
die Fracht   the freight
hoch   high

lachen   laugh
das Licht   the light
die Macht   the might
die Nacht   the night
recht   right
die Sicht   the sight

VIII. SUPPLEMENTARY READING

Die Reise von Berlin nach München

Am folgenden Morgen sagte Herr Braun: „Die Berliner sind fleißig und arbeiten viel. Sie werden ihre Stadt vielleicht schon bald wieder aufgebaut haben. Aber jetzt ist sie voll von Ruinen. Wir werden daher heute nach München fahren." „Werden wir fliegen?" riefen Karl und Anna. „Nur bis Hannover," antwortete der Vater, „dort werden wir den Zug nehmen." Nach ein paar Stunden waren sie auf dem Bahnhof in Hannover.

Die deutschen Eisenbahnen haben erste, zweite und dritte Klasse. Die erste Klasse ist sehr teuer und nur Amerikaner und Millionäre reisen erster Klasse. Die zweite Klasse ist auch ziemlich teuer und nur ungefähr fünf Prozent aller Reisenden fahren zweiter Klasse. Die meisten Leute fahren dritter Klasse, denn sie ist viel billiger. Herr Braun war kein Millionär, aber er war reich, und so reisten sie zweiter Klasse und zwar Schlafwagen.

Nach ein paar Minuten kam der Zug in den Bahnhof. Er war sehr lang und hatte 10 (zehn) Wagen. Ein paar Wagen hatten Abteile erster und zweiter Klasse, aber die meisten hatten Abteile dritter Klasse. In den Abteilen erster und zweiter Klasse sind die Sitze gepolstert, in den Abteilen dritter Klasse sind die Sitze aus Holz. Ein Abteil erster Klasse ist für vier Personen, ein Abteil zweiter Klasse ist für sechs Personen und ein Abteil dritter Klasse ist für acht Personen. In einem Schlafwagenabteil zweiter Klasse sind zwei Betten, eins unten und eins oben, und ein Waschtisch. In einem Schlafwagenabteil erster Klasse ist nur ein Bett und ein Waschtisch. Frau Braun und Anna schliefen in dem einen Abteil, Herr Braun und Karl in einem anderen.

Von Hannover nach München ist es ungefähr 700 (siebenhundert) Kilometer, d.h. über 500 (fünfhundert) amerikanische Meilen. Die Reise dauerte beinahe zehn Stunden.

IX. SUPPLEMENTARY VOCABULARY

das (*or* **der**) **Abteil, -(e)s, -e** the compartment

auf-bauen to erect, build up; rebuild; **aufgebaut** built up

der Bahnhof, -(e)s, ⁼e the railway station

bis (+ *acc.*) to, as far as, until

fleißig diligent, industrious

folgend following, next, subsequent

gepolstert upholstered

(das) Hannover, -s (city of) Hanover

der Millionär', -s, -e the millionaire

oben above

die Person', -, -en the person

der Reisende, -n, -n the traveler

die Rui'ne, -, -n the ruin

schlafen, schlief, hat geschlafen, er schläft to sleep

der Schlafwagen, -s, - the sleeping car

das (*or* **der**) **Schlafwagenabteil, -(e)s, -e** the sleeping car compartment

schon already

der Sitz, -es, -e the seat

unten below

vielleicht perhaps

voll full

der Wagen, -s, - the wagon, carriage

der Waschtisch, -es, -e the washing stand

zwar indeed, to be sure

Aufgabe Zwölf

Word Order. Conjunctions. Time Expressions

I. READING SELECTION

Der Professor und die Medizin

Eines Abends besuchte ein Professor seinen Freund. Er ging zu Fuß, obgleich es ziemlich weit zu der Wohnung seines Freundes **war**. Wenn das Wetter schön **war**, ging der Professor immer gern zu Fuß. Die Freunde sprachen über dieses und jenes. Als es Zeit **war**, nach Hause zu gehen, sah der Professor, daß es stark **regnete**. Da weder er noch sein Freund einen Regenschirm **hatte**, sagte sein Freund: ,,Wenn Sie in diesem Regen nach Hause **gehen**, werden Sie gewiß krank. Bleiben Sie diese Nacht hier!'' Aber der Professor antwortete: ,,Nein, das geht nicht. Jeden Abend, ehe ich zu Bett **gehe**, nehme ich Medizin. Wenn ich die Medizin nicht **nehme**, werde ich nicht schlafen. Aber die Medizin ist in meinem Schlafzimmer zu Hause.'' Sein Freund sagte: ,,Das macht nichts. Ich werde mein Dienstmädchen nach Ihrem Hause schicken, um die Medizin zu holen.'' Als der Professor damit zufrieden **war**, führte sein Freund ihn in ein Schlafzimmer.

Als der Herr des Hauses später wieder in das Wohnzimmer **kam**, sah er den Professor vor dem Feuer sitzen, aber er sah auch, daß seine Kleider ganz naß waren. Er war sehr erstaunt und fragte: ,,Aber Herr Professor, was ist geschehen? Wo waren Sie denn?'' Der Professor antwortete: ,,Nun, sehen Sie, nachdem Sie aus dem Zimmer gegangen **waren**, dachte ich: meine Frau ist vielleicht schon zu Bett gegangen und schläft. Das Dienstmädchen wird sie gewiß stören. Außerdem wird meine Frau die Medizin vielleicht gar nicht finden. Also bin ich selbst nach Hause gegangen und habe sie geholt."

II. VOCABULARY

*Idioms
{
das geht nicht   that won't do, that's impossible
das macht nichts   that doesn't matter
gar nicht (nichts)   not (nothing) at all
gar kein Geld   no money at all
}

*der Abend, -s, -e the evening
*als (*conj.*) when; as
außerdem besides
*das Bett, -es, -en the bed
*da there, here; (*conj.*) as, since, because
*daß (*conj.*) that
denken, dachte, hat gedacht to think
*ehe (*conj.*) before
*finden, fand, hat gefunden to find
führen to lead
ganz whole, entire(ly), very
*geschehen, geschah, ist geschehen, es geschieht to happen
gewiß certain(ly), sure(ly)
*hier here
*holen to fetch, go and get, call for
ihn (*acc.* of **er**) him
das Kleid, -es, -er dress; *pl.* clothes
*krank sick

*nachdem (*conj.*) after
*die Nacht, -, ⁼e the night
naß wet
*obgleich (*conj.*) although
der Regen, -s the rain
schicken to send
*schlafen, schlief, hat geschlafen, er schläft to sleep
das Schlafzimmer, -s, - the bedroom
*schon already
*selbst *or* **selber** self; **ich selbst** I myself, etc.
*sitzen, saß, hat gesessen to sit
stark strong; hard
stören to disturb
*vielleicht perhaps
weder . . . noch neither . . . nor
das Wetter, -s the weather
die Zeit, -, -en the time
ziemlich rather, quite, fairly
*zwölf twelve

III. GRAMMAR

A. *Normal and Inverted Word Order*

1. In simple declarative sentences the finite verb (i.e., the inflected form of the verb) is the second element in the sen-

tence. This is true of both the so-called normal and inverted word order (cf. Lesson V).

> Der Professor **nimmt** jeden Abend Medizin, ehe er zu Bett geht.
> Jeden Abend **nimmt** der Professor Medizin, ehe er zu Bett geht.
> Ehe er zu Bett geht, **nimmt** der Professor jeden Abend Medizin.
> Medizin **nimmt** der Professor jeden Abend, ehe er zu Bett geht.
> Jeden Abend, ehe er zu Bett geht, **nimmt** der Professor Medizin.
> Wer **nimmt** jeden Abend Medizin?
> Was **nimmt** der Professor jeden Abend?

2. In questions, however, without an interrogative pronoun or adverb, the word order is the same as in English, i.e., the question begins with the verb.

Ist er zu Hause?

Such German questions are usually rendered in English by the progressive or emphatic forms.

Schreibt er den Brief?
Is he writing the letter?
Does he write the letter?

3. Imperative sentences likewise begin with the verb.

Bleiben Sie diese Nacht hier!

B. Dependent Word Order

1. In dependent word order the finite verb comes at the end of the dependent clause.

A dependent (or subordinate) clause is any statement containing a subject and verb that does not form an independent sentence, but depends for its meaning on the main clause of the sentence.

> Independent sentence: Er **nimmt** die Medizin nicht.
> Dependent clause: Wenn er die Medizin nicht **nimmt.**

The latter clause is dependent on some independent statement, such as: Er wird nicht schlafen, (wenn er die Medizin nicht nimmt).

2. Such dependent clauses may be introduced by a subordinating conjunction, such as **als, da, daß, ehe, nachdem, obgleich, wenn,** etc.

3. All relative clauses are dependent clauses.

Der Mann, der gestern hier war, heißt Herr Müller.
The man who was here yesterday is called Mr. Müller.

4. All clauses introduced by an indefinite relative pronoun are dependent.

Wer die Aufgabe geschrieben hat, darf nach Hause gehen.
He who (Whoever) has written the lesson may go home.

5. All indirect questions are dependent clauses.

Direct: **Wer hat das Buch gelesen?**
Indirect: **(Er fragt), wer das Buch gelesen hat.**

6. All dependent clauses are set off by commas.

C. Coördinating Conjunctions

Coördinating conjunctions connect words, clauses, or sentences and do not affect the word order. The most common are: **aber, denn, oder, sondern, und.**

D. Word Order: Infinitive

In all infinitive clauses the verb comes at the end.

Ich werde mein Dienstmädchen schicken, um die Medizin zu **holen.**

E. Time Expressions

1. Indefinite time and also the time of customary action may be expressed adverbially by the genitive case.

Indefinite time: **eines Abends**
                     eines Tages
                     eines Morgens

Customary action: **abends** (*in the evening*)
morgens
vormittags
nachmittags

The latter, being treated as adverbs, are not capitalized.
2. Definite time or extent of time is expressed by the accusative case.

Definite time: **jeden Tag**
jeden Abend
jeden Morgen

Extent of time: **den ganzen Tag** (*the entire day*)

F. Denn, nun, selbst (selber)

1. **Denn,** ordinarily a coördinating conjunction, is frequently added to questions to make them less abrupt, more natural. Occasionally it implies surprise or impatience. It is rendered in English more by the tone of voice than by any specific translation.
2. **Nun** and **jetzt** both mean *now*. **Jetzt** is used in a more absolute sense, whereas **nun** has more direct reference to what has preceded, often implying *and now* (*as a consequence*).

Wir haben die Aufgabe gelesen, nun werden wir sie schreiben.

When followed by a comma, however, **nun** means well.

Nun, haben Sie das Buch gelesen?

3. **Selbst** (**selber**) is indeclinable and the same form is used with all genders, cases, and numbers.

Der Vater hat es selbst gesagt.
Father said so himself.

Die Mutter hat den Brief selbst geschrieben.
Mother wrote the letter herself.

Selbst (not **selber**) may precede a word and then it means *even*.

Selbst der Vater hat es gesagt.
Even father said so.

G. Als, wann, wenn

1. **Als** is used as the conjunction when referring to a definite event in the past.

   Als ich nach Hause kam, war mein Bruder schon da.

2. **Wann** is used only in questions, both direct and indirect.

   Wann kam er nach Hause?

   Ich weiß nicht, wann er nach Hause kam.
   I don't know when he came home.

3. In all other cases **wenn** is used, i.e., in the present and future tenses and in the past tense for *whenever* (repeated action).

   Wenn es morgen regnet, bleiben wir zu Hause.

IV. QUESTIONS

1. Wann besuchte ein Professor seinen Freund? 2. Fuhr er mit der Straßenbahn? 3. Wann ging der Professor immer zu Fuß? 4. Wann regnete es? 5. Was hatte der Professor nicht? 6. Wer hatte auch keinen Regenschirm? 7. Was sagte der Freund zu dem Professor? 8. Wie wird der Professor, wenn er nach Hause geht? 9. Was nimmt der Professor jeden Abend, ehe er zu Bett geht? 10. Was geschieht, wenn der Professor die Medizin nicht nimmt? 11. Wo war die Medizin? 12. Wer wird die Medizin holen? 13. Wohin kam der Herr des Hauses wieder? 14. Wer saß vor dem Feuer? 15. Wie war der Freund, als er den Professor sah? 16. Was fragte er den Professor? 17. Wer schlief vielleicht schon? 18. Wer wird die Medizin vielleicht nicht finden? 19. Wohin ist der Professor selbst gegangen? 20. Was hat er geholt?

V. GRAMMATICAL EXERCISES

Connect the following sentences by using the subordinating conjunctions given in parentheses.

(a) Make the second sentence subordinate to the first:

1. Der Professor wird gewiß krank. Er geht in dem Regen nach Hause. (wenn) 2. Der Schüler ging zu Bett. Er hatte die Aufgabe gelernt. (nachdem) 3. Er wurde ganz naß. Er hatte keinen Regenschirm. (da) 4. Er war damit zufrieden. Das Dienstmädchen holte die Medizin. (daß) 5. Er schrieb seinem Freund. Er besuchte ihn. (ehe) 6. Wir machten heute keinen Spaziergang. Das Wetter war sehr schön. (obgleich)

(b) Make the first sentence subordinate to the second. The main clause following the dependent clause requires inverted word order:

1. Es war nicht sehr weit zu der Wohnung seines Freundes. Er ging zu Fuß. (da) 2. Der Student hatte das Lied gesungen. Der Wirt sagte: „Das Lied ist schön." (nachdem) 3. Er nimmt die Medizin. Er wird gut schlafen. (wenn) 4. Der Mann ist früher sehr arm gewesen. Er wurde später sehr reich. (obgleich) 5. Herr Braun ging aus dem Restaurant. Er gab dem Kellner ein Trinkgeld. (ehe) 6. Der Student ging in das Restaurant. Er hatte kein Geld. (als)

(c) Make either sentence subordinate to the other, depending on the meaning.

1. Ich habe wenig Zeit. Ich werde in die Stadt gehen. (obgleich) 2. Morgen machen wir einen Spaziergang. Das Wetter ist schön. (wenn) 3. Der Schüler wohnte auf dem Lande. Er ging nicht in die Schule. (als) 4. Der Student hatte kein Automobil. Er fuhr mit der Straßenbahn. (da) 5. Der Bauer war sehr hungrig. Er aß das Fleisch und die Kartoffeln. (ehe) 6. Er schrieb seinem Freunde wieder einen Brief. Er hatte ein paar Tage gewartet. (nachdem)

VI. TRANSLATION EXERCISES

1. When I visited my friend one evening, he sat in the living room. 2. Since I had not seen the man for a few days, I first wrote him (ihm) a letter. 3. He sleeps very well (gut) every night, although he takes no medicine. 4. Before I went

home, I saw that it was raining. 5. The professor went home, although he had no umbrella. 6. If he remains here this night, he will not get sick. 7. When his friend saw the professor before the fire, he was greatly astonished. 8. After the student had sung a song, the innkeeper said: No, that is not beautiful. 9. Many years ago a student went into a restaurant, although he had no money. 10. Although they are now poor, many students later become rich. 11. The professor said: I shall go home to get the medicine. 12. His friend answered: No, I shall send my maid. 13. The student became very hungry, for he had not eaten anything (*not anything* = *nothing*) for several days. 14. He ate meat, potatoes, and vegetables. 15. He spoke with a friend about this and that.

VII. VOCABULARY BUILDING

German **pf** frequently corresponds to English *p* or *pp*.

der Apfel	the apple	das Pflaster	the plaster, pavement
das Kupfer	the copper	die Pflaume	the plum
der Pfad	the path	pflücken	to pluck
die Pfanne	the pan	der Pfosten	the post
der Pfennig	the penny	das Pfund	the pound
die Pflanze	the plant	stampfen	to stamp

VIII. SUPPLEMENTARY READING

München

München ist die größte Stadt in Süddeutschland und liegt zum größten Teil auf dem linken Ufer eines kleinen Flusses, der Isar. München ist berühmt durch sein Bier und seine Kunst, aber es ist auch eine wichtige Industriestadt. Vor 150 (hundertfünfzig) Jahren war es noch ein kleiner und unbedeutender Ort. König Ludwig I. von Bayern (1825–1848) war nicht damit zufrieden, so rief er bedeutende Maler, Bildhauer und Architekten nach München und baute einen neuen Stadtteil im klassischen Stil. Als sein **Sohn Otto 1830 König** von Griechenland geworden war, fanden viele alte Kunstwerke aus Griechenland ihren Weg nach München. Für sie baute Ludwig ein Museum, das erste in Deutschland. Später folgten Galerien für alte und für neuere Malerei. Da diese Neubauten viele Künstler und Handwerker nach München zogen, entstanden Kunstschulen, und immer mehr junge Künstler kamen zu der Stadt an der Isar. Auch Musik und Theater blühten. Dichter und Schriftsteller lebten in München, weil sie die künstlerische Atmosphäre der Stadt liebten. So kam es, daß München eine Kunst-[1] und Musikstadt wurde. Ein großer Vorteil für München ist die Nähe der Alpen. An manchen Tagen, besonders vor Eintritt von schlechtem Wetter und nach Gewitterregen sieht man das Gebirge von München aus ganz deutlich. In den Bergen treibt man viel Wintersport.

Eine Anekdote von Richard Wagner

Als Richard Wagner in München wohnte, kamen viele fremde Leute zu ihm, nur um den berühmten Meister zu sehen. Dies war ihm sehr unangenehm. Eines Tages trat ein Herr auf der Straße zu ihm, zog den Hut und sagte: „Verzeihen Sie, mein Name ist Meier . . . " Ehe er weiter sprechen konnte, antwortete ihm Richard Wagner: „Ich verzeihe es Ihnen!" und ging schnell weiter.

IX. SUPPLEMENTARY VOCABULARY

alt old
der Architekt', -s, -en the architect
die Atmosphä're, -, -n the atmosphere
bauen to build
bedeutend significant, important

berühmt famous
besonders especially
der Bildhauer, -s, - the sculptor
blühen to bloom, flourish
deutlich clear, distinct
der Dichter, -s, - the poet
der Eintritt, -(e)s, -e the entrance; beginning

[1] A hyphen after a word indicates that it is to be joined up with the last part of the next compound word: Kunststadt.

folgen (sein) (+ *dat.*)   to follow
fremd   strange
die Galerie', -, -n   the gallery
der Gewitterregen, -s, -   the thunder shower
das Griechenland, -(e)s   Greece
der Handwerker, -s, -   the artisan
die Isar,-   the Isar (*river flowing through Munich*)
jung   young
klassisch   classical
können, konnte, hat gekonnt, er kann   can, to be able, may
die Kunst, -, ⁻e   the art
der Künstler, -s, -   the artist
künstlerisch   artistic
die Kunstschule, -, -n   the art school
die Kunststadt, -, ⁻e   the art city
das Kunstwerk, -(e)s, -e   the work of art
lieben   to love
link   left
der Maler, -s, -   the painter
die Malerei, -, -en   the painting
der Meister, -s, -   the master
das Muse'um, -s, die Muse'en   the museum
die Musik', -   the music
die Musik'stadt, -, ⁻e   the city of music
die Nähe, -, -n   the proximity
der Name, -ns, -n   the name

der Neubau, -es, -e *or* -ten   the building in course of erection; **die Neubauten** (*m. pl.*)   the new buildings
der Ort, -(e)s, -e *or* ⁻er   the place, locality
schlecht   bad, poor
der Schriftsteller, -s, -   the author, writer
der Sohn, -(e)s, ⁻e   the son
der Stadtteil, -(e)s, -e   the quarter, section (of a city)
der Stil, -(e)s, -e   the style
(das) Süddeutschland, -s   Southern Germany
das Thea'ter, -s, -   the theatre
treiben, trieb, hat getrieben   to drive; pursue; **Wintersport treiben**   to engage in winter sports
treten, trat, ist getreten, er tritt   to step, walk
das Ufer, -s, -   the bank, shore
un'angenehm   disagreeable
un'bedeutend   insignificant, unimportant
verzeihen, verzieh, hat verziehen   to forgive, pardon
der Vorteil, -(e)s, -e   the advantage
weil   because
wichtig   important
der Wintersport, -s, -e   winter sports
ziehen, zog, hat gezogen   to draw, pull

Aufgabe Dreizehn

Separable and Inseparable Prefixes

I. READING SELECTION

Der Bauer und das Streichholz

Eines Tages machte Herr Müller eine Reise, um seinen Freund auf dem Lande zu besuchen. Das tat er sehr oft. Er **stand** um sechs Uhr **auf,** obgleich das sehr früh war, denn er wünschte, mit dem Zuge um acht Uhr **abzufahren.** Nachdem er sein Frühstück gegessen hatte, bestellte er ein Auto und **kam** zehn Minuten vor Abfahrt des Zuges auf dem Bahnhof **an.** Der Zug stand schon da und Herr Müller **stieg ein.** Er nahm Platz in einem Abteil für Raucher. Noch ein paar Leute, zwei Herren, eine Dame und ein Bauer, kamen in das Abteil. Da es sehr warm war, **nahm** Herr Müller den Hut **ab** und **machte** das Fenster **auf.** Pünktlich um acht Uhr **fuhr** der Zug **ab.** Herr Müller nahm ein Buch aus seiner Reisetasche und **fing** zu lesen **an.** Nun wünschte er eine Zigarette zu rauchen, aber er fand, daß er kein Streichholz hatte. Da er sah, daß der Bauer eine Pfeife rauchte, bat er ihn um ein Streichholz. Der Bauer nahm eine Schachtel Streichhölzer aus der Tasche, aber er gab Herrn Müller nicht die Schachtel, sondern nur ein Streichholz. Um seine Dankbarkeit zu zeigen, reichte Herr Müller dem Bauern eine Handvoll Zigarren. Aber dieser nahm nicht eine, sondern die ganze Handvoll. Als er sah, daß Herr Müller sehr erstaunt war, **dachte** er einen Augenblick **nach,** und nachdem er die Zigarren in die Tasche gesteckt hatte, sagte er: „Bitte, nehmen Sie noch ein paar Streichhölzer!"

II. VOCABULARY

*Idioms {
bitten um (+ *acc.*)   to ask for, request
noch ein paar   a few more
Platz nehmen   to take a seat, sit down
}

*ab-fahren, fuhr ab, ist abge-
fahren, er fährt ab to
depart, leave
die Abfahrt, -, -en   the departure
*ab-nehmen, nahm ab, hat
abgenommen, er nimmt ab
to take off
das (*or* der) Abteil, -s, -e   the
compartment
*an-fangen, fing an, hat ange-
fangen, er fängt an to
begin
*an-kommen, kam an, ist ange-
kommen   to arrive
*auf-machen, machte auf, hat
aufgemacht   to open
*auf-stehen, stand auf, ist auf-
gestanden   to get up
der Augenblick, -s, -e   the
moment
*der Bahnhof, -s, ͏̈e   the rail-
road station
*bestellen   to order
*bitten, bat, hat gebeten to
request, ask
die Dankbarkeit, -   the gratitude
dreizehn   thirteen
ein-steigen, stieg ein, ist eingestiegen   to get in
*das Frühstück, -s   the break-
fast

die Handvoll, -   the handfull
*der Hut, -(e)s, ͏̈e   the hat
lesen, las, hat gelesen, er liest
to read
*die Minu'te, -, -n   the minute
nach-denken, dachte nach,
hat nachgedacht   to think
over, meditate, reflect
die Pfeife, -, -n   the pipe
der Platz, -es, ͏̈e   the place
pünktlich   punctual(ly),
prompt(ly)
*rauchen   to smoke
der Raucher, -s, -   the
smoker
reichen   to reach, hand
die Reisetasche, -, -n   the
traveling bag
die Schachtel, -, -n   the
(small) box
*stehen, stand, hat gestanden
to stand
*das Streichholz, -es, ͏̈er   the
match
*tun, tat, hat getan   to do
*warm   warm
*warum   why
*wünschen   to wish
zeigen   to show
die Zigar're, -, -n   the cigar
die Zigaret'te, -, -n   the cigarette
*der Zug, -(e)s, ͏̈e   the train

Die Bergstadt Schwaz in Tirol

Courtesy of the German Tourist Information Office

Heuernte bei Oberammergau

Festspielhaus in Oberammergau

Courtesy of the German Tourist Information Office

Der Dom in Eichstätt (Bayern)

Die Inselstadt Lindau im Bodensee

III. GRAMMAR

A. *Compound Verbs with Inseparable and Separable Prefixes*

1. The German language contains a large number of compound verbs, i.e., simple verbs with a prefix. Some of these prefixes (**be-, emp-, ent-, er-, ge-, ver-, zer-**) are never separated from the verb proper. Such inseparable verbs are treated in all respects like simple verbs except that the prefix never has the accent and that the past participle does not add the additional prefix **ge-**. The meaning of compound verbs with inseparable prefixes, however, is frequently radically different from that of simple verbs.

suchen	*to seek*	**stellen**	*to place*
besuchen	*to visit*	**bestellen**	*to order*
fallen	*to fall*	**hören**	*to hear*
gefallen	*to please*	**gehören**	*to belong*

2. Separable prefixes are usually adverbs or prepositions. In English there is a similar phenomenon, but it is not as widely used.

He got **up.**
He sat **down.**
He took the book **back.**
He picked the paper **up.**

Such separable prefixes in German are separated from the verb only in the simple tenses, i.e., in the present and past tenses, and in the imperative. Such prefixes always have the accent and they usually come at the end of the clause.

Infinitive: **aufmachen**
Pres. Tense: **Ich mache das Fenster auf.**
Past Tense: **Er machte das Fenster auf.**
Imperative: **Machen Sie das Fenster auf!**

Infinitive: **abfahren**
Pres. Tense: **Ich fahre um drei Uhr ab.**
Past Tense: **Der Zug fuhr um drei Uhr ab.**
Imperative: **Fahren Sie um drei Uhr ab!**

3. Even in the simple tenses the prefix is not separated when the verb is used in a dependent clause.

Als er das Fenster aufmachte, sah er einen Mann.

4. In the past participle the regular prefix **ge-** is placed between the separable prefix and the verb.

Ich habe das Fenster aufgemacht.
Der Zug ist um drei Uhr abgefahren.

5. Where **zu** is required with the infinitive, it is likewise placed between the prefix and the verb.

Ich fing an, das Fenster aufzumachen.

6. Hereafter the principal parts of separable verbs will be indicated in the vocabulary as follows:

ab-fahren, fuhr ab, ist abgefahren, er fährt ab.

B. Articles instead of Possessive Adjectives

When referring to parts of the body, clothing, etc., or whenever there is no ambiguity, it is common in German to use the definite article instead of the possessive adjective.

Er steckte die Hand in die Tasche.
Der Vater und die Mutter fahren auch nach Europa.

IV. QUESTIONS

1. Wer machte eines Tages eine Reise? 2. Warum machte er eine Reise? 3. Wo wohnte sein Freund? 4. Wann stand Herr Müller auf? 5. Warum stand er so früh auf? 6. Was bestellte er, nachdem er sein Frühstück gegessen hatte? 7. Wohin fuhr er? 8. Wann kam er dort an? 9. Was stand schon da? 10. Was nahm Herr Müller ab? 11. Warum nahm Herr Müller den Hut ab? 12. Was machte er auf? 13. Wann fuhr der Zug ab? 14. Wer war auch in dem Zug? 15. Was wünschte Herr Müller zu tun? 16. Was hatte er aber nicht? 17. Wer rauchte auch? 18. Um was bat er den Bauern? 19. Was gab der Bauer Herrn Müller?

V. GRAMMATICAL EXERCISES

(a) Change the following sentences to the past, future, present perfect, and past perfect tenses:

1. Er steht um sechs Uhr auf.
2. Ich fahre um acht Uhr ab.
3. Er kommt zehn Minuten vor acht an.
4. Wir nehmen den Hut ab.
5. Sie machen das Fenster auf.

(b) Change the above sentences to infinitive phrases, by making them dependent on er wünscht.

(c) In the following groups make one of the two sentences dependent upon the other by using the subordinating conjunctions in parentheses:
1. Ich fahre um acht Uhr ab. Ich werde früh aufstehen. (da)
2. Er sah einen Mann auf der Straße. Er machte das Fenster auf. (als)
3. Er kam sehr früh am Bahnhof an. Der Zug stand schon da. (obgleich)
4. Mein Freund sagt. Der Zug fährt um acht Uhr ab. (daß)
5. Er nimmt den Hut ab. Er wird krank. (wenn)

(d) Change the following sentences to all the forms of the imperative:

1. Du machst das Buch auf.
2. Du nimmst den Hut ab.
3. Du stehst früh auf.

VI. TRANSLATION EXERCISES

1. Mr. Müller often visited a friend in the country. 2. He left on the eight o'clock train. 3. Since he got up at six o'clock, he ate his breakfast very early. 4. After he had ordered a car, he drove to the station. 5. After ten minutes

he arrived at the station.   6. Since the train was already there, he took a seat.   7. After he had taken his hat off, he opened the window.   8. A few more people came into the train.   9. The peasant began to smoke.   10. Mr. Müller also wished to smoke, but he had no match.   11. When he saw that the peasant was smoking, he asked him for a match.   12. The peasant said: Please take a few more matches.

VII. VOCABULARY BUILDING

A g in German sometimes corresponds to a y in English.

das Garn	the yarn	legen	to lay
gelb	yellow	sagen	to say
gestern	yesterday	der Tag	the day
der Honig	the honey	der Weg	the way

Occasionally a j in German corresponds to a y in English.

ja	yea	das Joch	the yoke
die Jacht	the yacht	jodeln	to yodle
das Jahr	the year	jung	young

VIII. SUPPLEMENTARY READING

Zwei Anekdoten von Friedrich dem Großen

Einmal kam ein Student, ein Kandidat der Theologie, zu Friedrich dem Großen und bat ihn um eine Stellung. Der König fragte ihn: „Wo sind Sie geboren?"—„In Berlin," war die Antwort.—„Wenn Sie in Berlin geboren sind," sagte der König, „dann bekommen Sie die Stellung nicht, denn alle Berliner sind nichts wert."—„Das ist sehr richtig, Majestät," antwortete der Kandidat, „aber es gibt zwei Ausnahmen."— „So," sagte der König, „welches sind die?"—„Eure Majestät und ich," war die Antwort des Kandidaten. Der König war mit dieser Antwort so zufrieden, daß er dem Studenten die Stellung gab.

Ein Franzose war einmal Soldat in dem Heere Friedrichs des Großen, aber er verstand wenig Deutsch. Eines Tages rief ihn ein Offizier und sagte: ,,Der König wird heute kommen und drei Fragen stellen. Zuerst wird er fragen: Wie alt bist du? Dann antwortest du: 21 (einundzwanzig) Jahre. Zweitens wird er fragen: Wie lange bist du schon in meinem Heere? Deine Antwort wird sein: Zwei Jahre. Die letzte Frage des Königs ist: Bist du immer mit dem Essen und deinem Lohn zufrieden gewesen? Dann antwortest du: Beides." Später am Tage kam der König wirklich. Als er den Franzosen sah, fragte er ihn zuerst: ,,Wie lange bist du schon in meinem Heere?" Er war sehr erstaunt, als er die Antwort bekam: ,,Einundzwanzig Jahre." Deshalb fragte er ihn weiter: ,,Wie alt bist du denn?" Als der Soldat antwortete: ,,Zwei Jahre," wurde der König ungeduldig und sagte: ,,Entweder bist du ein Esel oder ich." ,,Beides richtig," war die Antwort.

IX. SUPPLEMENTARY VOCABULARY

die Ausnahme, -, -n the exception
bekommen, bekam, hat bekommen to get, receive
deshalb therefore
entwe'der either
der Esel, -s, - the donkey, ass, fool
das Essen, -s the food
geben; es gibt there is, there are
geboren born
das Heer, -(e)s, -e the army
der Kandidat', -en, -en the candidate
letzt last
der Lohn, -(e)s, ⁼e pay, wages
die Majestät', -, -en majesty

der Offizier', -s, -e the officer
richtig right, correct, true
der Soldat', -en, -en the soldier
die Stellung, -, -en the position
die Theologie', - theology
ungeduldig impatient
verstehen, verstand, hat verstanden to understand
weiter-fragen to continue to ask, ask further
wert worth; nichts wert no good
wirklich real(ly)
zweitens secondly, in the second place

Aufgabe Vierzehn

Personal Pronouns

I. READING SELECTION

Die Frau und der Schneider

Eines Tages im Frühling, als das Wetter wieder schön wurde, ging Frau Müller zu einem Schneider. Eine Freundin von **ihr** hatte **ihr** aus Europa fünf Meter Stoff geschickt. Sie ging also **damit** zu dem Schneider, zeigte **ihm** den Stoff und sagte zu **ihm**: „Bitte, machen Sie **mir** ein Kleid **daraus**! Wieviel kostet es?" Aber der Schneider antwortete: „Es tut **mir** leid, aber fünf Meter Stoff sind nicht genug für ein Kleid. Sie brauchen noch ein Meter." Frau Müller glaubte das nicht. Da aber in diesem Hause noch ein Schneider wohnte, ging sie zu **ihm** und fragte **ihn**: „Glauben Sie, daß fünf Meter Stoff genug sind für ein Kleid für **mich**?" Dieser Schneider sagte: „Ja, fünf Meter sind mehr als genug," und er versprach, das Kleid für sie zu machen.

Nach einer Woche kam Frau Müller wieder, um ihr Kleid zu holen. Es paßte **ihr** sehr gut und sie war sehr **damit** zufrieden. Nun fragte sie den Schneider: „Wieviel schulde ich **Ihnen**?" Er antwortete: „Gewöhnlich bekomme ich 30 (dreißig) Mark **dafür**." Frau Müller war auch **damit** zufrieden, nahm Geld aus der Tasche und bezahlte die Rechnung. In diesem Augenblick kam die Tochter des Schneiders in das Zimmer. Sie hatte auch ein Kleid aus ihrem Stoff. Frau Müller war sehr erstaunt und fragte den Schneider: „Wie ist das möglich? Vor kurzem war ich bei Ihrem Nachbar, Schneider Wolf. Dieser sagte, daß fünf Meter Stoff nicht genug sind für ein Kleid, und Sie haben zwei Kleider **daraus** gemacht." „Sie haben recht," antwortete er, „aber die Antwort ist sehr einfach. Meine Tochter ist nicht so groß wie die Tochter jenes Schneiders."

II. VOCABULARY

*Idioms { **noch ein (Meter, usw.)**   another (meter, etc.)
recht haben   to be right
vor kurzem   a short time ago, recently

*der Augenblick, -s, -e**   the
moment, instant
*bekommen, bekam, hat be-
kommen**   to get, receive
besonders   especially
*brauchen**   to need; use
einfach   simple
die Freundin, -, -nen   the
friend (*fem.*)
*der Frühling, -s, -e**   the
spring
*genug**   enough
*gewöhnlich**   usual(ly)
*glauben**   to believe, think
*gut**   good; *adv.* well
*das Kleid, -(e)s, -er**   the
dress; *bl.* clothes
*kosten**   to cost
kurz   short
mehr   more
*das (or der) Meter, -s, -**   the
meter (*about 39 inches*)

möglich   possible
der Nachbar, -s, -n   the
neighbor
passen (+ *dat.*)   to fit
*die Rechnung, -, -en**   the bill
*recht**   right
*schicken**   to send
der Schneider, -s, -   the tailor
schulden   to owe
der Stoff, -(e)s, -e   cloth,
material
*die Tasche, -, -n**   the pocket;
handbag
*die Tochter, -, -̈**   the daughter
*versprechen, versprach, hat
versprochen, er verspricht**
(+ *dat.*)   to promise
vierzehn   fourteen
*das Wetter, -s**   the weather
*wieviel**   how much
zeigen   to show
*zufrieden**   satisfied

III. GRAMMAR

A. Personal Pronouns

		1ST PERSON		2ND PERSON		3RD PERSON		
Sing.	Nom.	ich	*I*	du	Sie	er	sie	es
	Gen.	(meiner	*of me*)	(deiner)	(Ihrer)	(seiner)	(ihrer)	(seiner)
	Dat.	mir	*to me*	dir	Ihnen	ihm	ihr	ihm
	Acc.	mich	*me*	dich	Sie	ihn	sie	es
Plural	Nom.	wir	*we*	ihr	Sie		sie	
	Gen.	(unser	*of us*)	(euer)	(Ihrer)		(ihrer)	
	Dat.	uns	*to us*	euch	Ihnen		ihnen	
	Acc.	uns	*us*	euch	Sie		sie	

1. The genitive forms of the personal pronouns may still occasionally be found in older German or in elevated discourse, but are exceedingly rare in colloquial German. Instead either the direct object or a prepositional phrase is used, as in English.

FORMER USAGE	PRESENT USAGE
Er gedenkt meiner.	**Er denkt an mich.**
He thinks of me.	
Vergiß meiner nicht.	**Vergiß mich nicht.**
Forget me not.	

2. The dative is used as the indirect object or after certain prepositions. Note the following:

> **Er ist ein Freund von mir, von dir, von ihm, usw.**
> *He is a friend of mine, of yours, of his, etc.*

3. The accusative is used as the direct object or after certain prepositions.

4. The personal pronoun in the third person must agree in gender and number with the noun to which it refers.

Gestern kam mein **Freund** und ich ging mit **ihm** in die Stadt.
Annas **Freundin** kam auch und sie machte mit **ihr** einen Spaziergang.

5. The personal pronoun in the third person, when referring to a lifeless object, is not used after a preposition. Instead a compound formed of **da** + a preposition is used (**dar** before prepositions beginning with a vowel).

> **damit** *therewith, with it* (instead of **mit ihm**)
> **darin** *therein, in it*
> **davon** *thereof, of it*
> **dadurch** *through it*

B. Prepositional Contractions

Prepositions plus the dative and accusative of the definite article are commonly contracted, especially in colloquial German.

an dem = am	an das = ans
in dem = im	auf das = aufs
zu dem = zum	in das = ins
zu der = zur	vor das = vors

IV. QUESTIONS

1. Wie wird das Wetter im Frühling? 2. Wer ging im Frühling zu dem Schneider? 3. Wer hatte Frau Müller Stoff geschickt? 4. Was sagte Frau Müller zu dem Schneider? 5. Hatte sie genug Stoff für ein Kleid? 6. Wieviel Meter brauchte sie noch? 7. Wo wohnte noch ein Schneider? 8. Was fragte Frau Müller diesen Schneider? 9. Was versprach dieser Schneider zu machen? 10. Wann kam Frau Müller wieder? 11. Wie war sie mit dem Kleid zufrieden? 12. Wieviel bekam der Schneider gewöhnlich dafür? 13. Was nahm Frau Müller aus der Tasche? 14. Warum nahm sie Geld aus der Tasche? 15. Wer kam in diesem Augenblick in das Zimmer? 16. Wie war Frau Müller, als sie die Tochter sah? 17. Wie viele Kleider hatte der Schneider gemacht?

V. GRAMMATICAL EXERCISES

(a) Supply the correct form of the personal pronoun given in parentheses:

1. Hast du (sie) das Buch gegeben? 2. Es tut (ich) leid, daß er krank ist. 3. Es tut (er) leid, daß wir nicht hier bleiben. 4. Es tut (wir) leid, daß er kein Geld hat. 5. Er wird die Rechnung für (ich) bezahlen. 6. Ein Freund von (er) hat (wir) besucht. 7. Er hat (du) nicht gesehen. 8. Wird er mit (Sie) nach Deutschland reisen? 9. Am Mittwoch werden wir bei (ihr) sein. 10. Warum schreiben Sie (ich) nicht? 11. Wer hat (du) gefragt? 12. Unsre Eltern gingen am Freitag auf das Land, aber wir sind nicht mit (sie) gegangen.

(b) Substitute personal pronouns or compounds with **da** for the words in parentheses:

1. Frau Müller hat (die Rechnung) heute bekommen. 2. (Der Student) hat gestern eine Feder gekauft. Jetzt schreibt er (mit der Feder). 3. (Der Schneider) hat zwei Kleider (aus dem Stoff) gemacht. 4. Morgen werde ich (meine Großmutter) besuchen. 5. (Die Lehrerin) war (mit der Antwort) zufrieden. 6. (Das Dienstmädchen) hat (die Medizin) nicht geholt. 7. (Der Bauer) hat viel Geld für (den Hund) bekommen. 8. (Der Student) hat nichts (für das Essen) bezahlt. 9. (Das Kleid) hat (die Frau) vierzig Mark gekostet. 10. Sagen Sie (Ihrem Bruder), daß ich (das Buch) bald brauche. 11. (Der Lehrer) schreibt (mit der Kreide). 12. Die Schülerin) hat (die Aufgabe) gelernt. 13. (Die Frau) nahm Geld (aus der Tasche).

VI. TRANSLATION EXERCISES

1. A lady ordered a dress and Mr. Schneider promised to make it for her. 2. A friend (*fem.*) of hers also went to him. 3. She asked him: Are five meters enough for a dress for me? 4. After a few days she called for it (holen + *acc.*). 5. She asked him: How much does it cost? 6. Mr. Schneider sent her a bill and she paid it. 7. When she saw the dress, she was satisfied with it. 8. She had a handbag and she took money out of it. 9. The student had a pocket, but there was no money in it. 10. In spring the weather is usually beautiful. 11. My medicine is at home. 12. If I do not take it, I shall not sleep. 13. I am sorry, but I did not see him. 14. He is right as usual. 15. She needed another meter for the dress.

VII. VOCABULARY BUILDING

A German **v** sometimes corresponds to an English *f*.

bevor	before	**vier**	four
der Vater	the father	**das Volk**	the folk
vergessen	to forget	**voll**	full

Sometimes **tz** in German corresponds to a *t* in English.

die Katze	the cat	**setzen**	to set
das Netz	the net	**sitzen**	to sit
schwitzen	to sweat	**der Witz**	the wit

VIII. SUPPLEMENTARY READING

Salzburg

In München mietete die Familie Braun ein Auto und fuhr damit auf der Autobahn nach Salzburg. Diese alte Stadt hat eine wundervolle Lage. Sie liegt auf beiden Ufern der Salzach zwischen steilen Hügeln mit alten Festungswerken und Türmen. Im Hintergrund sieht man die mächtigen Ketten der Alpen. Salzburg war früher die Hauptstadt eines Erzbistums. Damals regierten Bischöfe ihre Länder genau so wie andere Prinzen; sie hatten Polizei und Militär, sie machten Krieg und schloßen Frieden. Die meisten Bischöfe kamen aus aristokratischen Familien und waren reich. Im Lauf der Jahrhunderte bauten sie viele schöne Kirchen und Paläste mit breiten Plätzen und schönen Gärten. Auf den Plätzen waren die Paraden der kleinen Armee, in den Gärten spazierten die Herren und Damen des Hofes, in den Palästen fanden Feste und Konzerte statt. Besonders schön waren die Ställe und die Reitschule. Hier ritten die Kavaliere des Bischofs die edlen spanischen Pferde. Heute ist die Reitschule ein Theater. Jeden Sommer finden darin Konzerte und Opern statt. Zu ihnen kommen viele berühmte Musiker von Europa. Die meisten Kirchen und Paläste sind im Barockstil. Die Familie Braun hatte noch nie so viele Gebäude in diesem Stil gesehen. „Mir gefällt dieser Stil nicht," sagte Karl. „Wir haben so etwas nicht in Amerika." „Du hast recht," antwortete sein Vater, „aber wir reisen ja nicht, um alles so zu finden, wie es zu Hause ist. Wenn wir mehr davon gesehen haben, wird das Barock uns vielleicht besser gefallen und auch seine letzte Phase. Man nennt diese Phase Rokoko. Heute Abend werden wir eine Oper im

Rokokostil hören: ‚Figaros Hochzeit.' Sie ist von Mozart,
und Mozart ist hier in Salzburg geboren. Wir werden uns
jetzt sein Geburtshaus ansehen."

IX. SUPPLEMENTARY VOCABULARY

an-sehen, sah an, hat angesehen, er sieht an   to look at
aristokra'tisch   aristocratic
die Armee', -, -n   the army
die Autobahn, -, -en   the super
highway
das Barock', -s   the baroque
(style)
der Barockstil, -(e)s   the baroque style (architecture of the
17th century, coming between
Renaissance and Rococo)
besser   better
der Bischof, -s, ⁼e   the bishop
darin   therein, in it
davon   of that, therefrom
edel   noble
das Erzbistum, -s, ⁼er   the
archbishopric
das Fest, -es, -e   the festival,
fete
das Festungswerk, -(e)s, -e   the
fortification
Frieden schließen   to make
peace
der Garten, -s, ⁼   the garden
das Gebäude, -s, -   the building
das Geburtshaus, -es, ⁼er   the
house where a person was
born
gefallen, gefiel, hat gefallen,
er (es) gefällt   to please; like;
es gefällt mir   I like
genau   exactly

der Hintergrund, -es, ⁼e   the
background
die Hochzeit, -, -en   the wed-
ding, marriage, festivity
der Hof, -es, ⁼e   the court,
court-yard
hören   to hear
der Hügel, -s, -   the hill
ja   yes, indeed (emphatic)
der Kavalier', -s, -e   the cavalier, courtier
die Kette, -, -n   the chain,
range
die Kirche, -, -n   the church
das Konzert', -(e)s, -e   the
concert
die Lage, -, -n   the situation,
site
der Lauf, -(e)s, ⁼e   the course,
career
mächtig   mighty, huge
mieten   to hire, rent
das Militär', -s   the military,
soldiers
der Musiker, -s, -   the musician
nennen, nannte, hat genannt
to name, call
noch nie   never yet
die Oper, -, -n   the opera
der Palast', -es, ⁼e   the palace
das Pferd, -(e)s, -e   the horse
die Pha'se, -, -n   the phase
die Polizei', -, -en   the police
der Prinz, -en, -en   the prince

regieren to govern, rule, manage

die Reitschule, -, -n the riding school

das Roko′ko, -s the rococo (*style*)

der Rokokostil, -(e)s the rococo style

die Salzach, - the Salzach (*river flowing through Salzburg*)

(das) Salzburg, -s (city of) Salzburg

schließen, schloß, hat geschlossen, er schließt to shut, close, conclude

spanisch Spanish

spazie′ren to promenade

der Stall, -es, ¨e the stall

statt-finden, fand statt, hat stattgefunden to take place

steil steep

der Turm, -(e)s, ¨e the tower

wundervoll wonderful

Aufgabe Fünfzehn

Declension of Adjectives

I. READING SELECTION

Zwei Anekdoten

Es gibt in Deutschland viele Anekdoten über Dichter und Professoren. Heute werden wir zwei solche Geschichten lesen. Die erste Geschichte handelt von einem bekannten Dichter. Dieser bekannte Dichter heißt Ludwig Uhland und lebte in der ersten Hälfte des letzten Jahrhunderts. Er schrieb schöne Lieder und lange Gedichte, aber meistens nur sehr kurze Briefe. Einmal besuchte der alte Dichter mit seiner lieben Frau einen alten Freund. Während des Gesprächs sagte Uhland: „Jedes Ding hat zwei Seiten." Seine Frau lächelte und sagte: „Nein, ein Ding hat nicht zwei Seiten." Neugierig fragte Uhland: „Was ist das?" Schnell antwortete seine Frau: „Deine Briefe haben immer nur eine Seite." Nun lachten auch der Dichter und sein alter Freund.

Die zweite Geschichte handelt von einem bekannten Professor, und Professoren sind oft zerstreut. Dieser zerstreute Professor hatte zwei Paar Schuhe, ein gelbes Paar und ein schwarzes Paar. Eines Tages zog er einen schwarzen Schuh auf seinen linken Fuß und einen gelben Schuh auf seinen rechten Fuß an. Auf der Straße blieben viele Leute stehen, sahen seine Füße an und lächelten. Endlich merkte der zerstreute Professor, warum die Leute stehenblieben und lächelten. Dann blieb er auch stehen und sagte zu ihnen: „Sie sind

erstaunt, nicht wahr? Aber glauben Sie mir, zu Hause habe
ich noch ein Paar wie dieses."

II. VOCABULARY

*Idioms
es gibt (+ acc.)   there is; there are
handeln von (+ dat.)   to treat of, to deal with
stehenbleiben   to stop; er bleibt stehen   he stops
was für ein   what kind of; what a

*alt old
an-sehen, sah an, hat angesehen, er sieht an   to look at
*an-ziehen, zog an, hat ange-
zogen   to put on, to dress
*bekannt   known, well-known
*der Dichter, -s, -   the poet
*das Ding, -(e)s, -e   the thing
*endlich   at last, finally
*erst   first
fünfzehn   fifteen
der Fuß, -es, ⁝e   the foot
*das Gedicht, -(e)s, -e   the
poem
*die Geschichte, -, -n   the
story; history
das Gespräch, -(e)s, -e   the
conversation
die Hälfte, -, -n   half
*handeln   to act; to deal
das Jahrhundert, -s, -e   the
century

*kurz   short
*lächeln   to smile
*lachen   to laugh
*lang   long
*lesen, las, hat gelesen, er liest
to read
letzt   last
lieb   dear
*link   left
meistens   mostly
merken   to notice
neugierig   curious
*der Schuh, -(e)s, -e   the shoe
*die Seite, -, -n   the page; side
*über (+ dat. or acc.)   over,
at, above, concerning
*von (+ dat.)   from, of, by
während (+ gen.)   during
zerstreut   absent-minded
zweit   second

III. GRAMMAR

A. Declension of Adjectives

1. Adjective endings are commonly classified as strong and
weak. The strong endings are those of the der-words:

	MAS.		FEM.		NEUT.	
Sing.	dies	er	dies	e	dies	es
	dies	es	dies	er	dies	es
	dies	em	dies	er	dies	em
	dies	en	dies	e	dies	es

Plural	dies	e
	dies	er
	dies	en
	dies	e

The weak endings are **-en** with the exception of five cases, viz. the three forms of the nominative singular and consequently also the accusative of the feminine and neuter, since these two accusative cases are always identical with the nominative case.

	MAS.	FEM.	NEUT.
Sing.	e	e	e
	en	en	en
	en	en	en
	en	e	e

Plural	en
	en
	en
	en

2. We differentiate between pronominal (or limiting) adjectives and descriptive adjectives.

The pronominal adjectives (all the **der**-words and **ein**-words) always take the endings which you have already learned (cf. Lesson X).

Descriptive adjectives may be used either predicatively or attributively.

Predicate adjectives never take endings.

Das Haus ist groß.

Attributive adjectives, i.e., adjectives preceding a noun, **must** take an ending, and if they are descriptive adjectives

the ending will have to be strong or weak according to circumstances.
3. The original function of the strong endings was to indicate gender, number, and case. To be sure, at the present time some of these endings are identical so that they no longer fully perform this function, but in practice one may follow the general principle:
The strong endings must appear, either in the pronominal adjective, or failing that, in the descriptive adjective.
4. Descriptive adjectives with strong endings.

	MASCULINE	FEMININE	NEUTER
Sing.	alt-er Mann	groß-e Tür	klein-es Fenster
	alt-en Mannes	groß-er Tür	klein-en Fensters
	alt-em Mann	groß-er Tür	klein-em Fenster
	alt-en Mann	groß-e Tür	klein-es Fenster
Plural	alt-e Männer	groß-e Türen	klein-e Fenster
	alt-er Männer	groß-er Türen	klein-er Fenster
	alt-en Männern	groß-en Türen	klein-en Fenstern
	alt-e Männer	groß-e Türen	klein-e Fenster

Note that in the genitive singular, masculine and neuter, the weak ending **-en** is now generally used instead of the strong ending **-es**.
5. When the strong endings appear in the pronominal adjective, the descriptive adjective following has weak endings.

	MASCULINE		FEMININE	
Sing.	dies-er alt-e	Mann	dies-e groß-e	Tür
	dies-es alt-en	Mannes	dies-er groß-en	Tür
	dies-em alt-en	Mann	dies-er groß-en	Tür
	dies-en alt-en	Mann	dies-e groß-e	Tür
Plural	dies-e alt-en	Männer	dies-e groß-en	Türen
	dies-er alt-en	Männer	dies-er groß-en	Türen
	dies-en alt-en	Männern	dies-en groß-en	Türen
	dies-e alt-en	Männer	dies-e groß-en	Türen

NEUTER

	dies-es	klein-e	Fenster
Sing.	dies-es	klein-en	Fensters
	dies-em	klein-en	Fenster
	dies-es	klein-e	Fenster

	dies-e	klein-en	Fenster
Plural	dies-er	klein-en	Fenster
	dies-en	klein-en	Fenstern
	dies-e	klein-en	Fenster

6. You will recall that all the **ein**-words lack endings in the nominative singular of the masculine and the nominative and accusative singular of the neuter. Following our general rule, the descriptive adjective in these three cases must take the strong endings. In all other cases the descriptive adjective has weak endings, since all the other forms of the **ein**-words have the full strong endings. These endings are sometimes called mixed endings.

MASCULINE   FEMININE

	ein	alt-er	Mann	ein-e	groß-e	Tür
Sing.	ein-es	alt-en	Mannes	ein-er	groß-en	Tür
	ein-em	alt-en	Mann	ein-er	groß-en	Tür
	ein-en	alt-en	Mann	ein-e	groß-e	Tür

	alt-e	Männer	kein-e	groß-en	Türen
Plural	alt-er	Männer	kein-er	groß-en	Türen
	alt-en	Männern	kein-en	groß-en	Türen
	alt-e	Männer	kein-e	groß-en	Türen

NEUTER

	ein	klein-es	Fenster
Sing.	ein-es	klein-en	Fensters
	ein-em	klein-en	Fenster
	ein	klein-es	Fenster

	uns(e)r-e	klein-en	Fenster
Plural	uns(e)r-er	klein-en	Fenster
	unser-(e)n	klein-en	Fenstern
	uns(e)r-e	klein-en	Fenster

B. Was für ein

The **was für** in this idiomatic phrase is indeclinable in all cases, singular and plural. The **ein** is regularly declined in the singular, but omitted entirely in the plural.

> **Was für ein Buch ist es?**
> **Mit was für einem Bleistift schreiben Sie?**
> **Was für einen Hut hat er?**
> **Was für Bücher lesen Sie?**

C. Es ist, es sind; es gibt

Es gibt is followed by the accusative case and the same singular form of the verb is used with both the singular and plural of nouns. It is sometimes difficult to tell precisely whether to use **es gibt** or **es ist** (**es sind**). In general **es gibt** stresses existence only.

> **Es gibt einen Gott.**
> *There is a God.*

> **Es gibt viele gute Bücher.**
> *There are many good books.*

Es ist and **es sind** express existence in a definite place of limited extent.

> **Es ist ein Buch auf dem Tisch.**
> **Es sind viele Leute auf dem Dampfer.**

IV. QUESTIONS

1. Wo gibt es viele Geschichten über Dichter und Professoren? 2. Was für Geschichten haben wir heute gelesen? 3. Welche Geschichte handelt von einem bekannten Dichter? 4. Wie heißt dieser Dichter? 5. Was für Gedichte schrieb Uhland? 6. Wie waren seine Briefe oft? 7. Wen (*whom*) besuchte der alte Dichter einmal? 8. Was sagte Uhland zu seinem alten Freund? 9. Was tat seine Frau, als er dies sagte? 10. Was sagte sie? 11. Was hatte immer nur eine

Seite? 12. Wieviel Paar Schuhe hatte ein bekannter Professor? 13. Was war die Farbe der zwei Paar Schuhe? 14. Was zog der Professor eines Tages an? 15. Was taten viele Leute auf der Straße? 16. Wer blieb auch stehen? 17. Was sagte der Professor zu den Leuten?

V. GRAMMATICAL EXERCISES

Supply the missing endings:
1. In dem Schulzimmer sind ein groß— Fenster, eine breit— Tür, ein braun— Tisch und zwei braun— Stühle. 2. An der gelb— Wand ist eine groß— Karte von Deutschland. 3. Der klein— Schüler schreibt mit einem gelb— Bleistift, die groß— Schülerin schreibt mit einer schwarz— Feder, der Lehrer schreibt mit weiß— Kreide. 4. In unserem rot— und schwarz— Buche sind viel— Geschichten. 5. Ein schnell— Zug ist ein Schnellzug (*express*). 6. Der hungrig— Student ging mit seinem arm— Freunde in ein klein— Restaurant. 7. Der krank— Mann ging zu einem bekannt— Arzt. 8. Mit was für ein— Bleistift schreiben Sie? 9. Ein bekannt— Professor hatte einen gelb— Schuh an seinem recht— Fuß und einen schwarz— Schuh an seinem link— Fuß. 10. Im Sommer haben wir oft warm— Wetter. 11. Mein groß— Bruder hat seinen alt— Lehrer seit viel— Jahren nicht gesehen. 12. Die klein— Tochter des Schneiders hatte ein rot— Kleid. 13. Was für ein— Hut hat die schön— Dame? 14. Es ist ein weit— Weg von Berlin nach Wien. 15. Die zufrieden— Dame bezahlte die groß— Rechnung gern. 16. Unser deutsch— Lehrer fährt auf einem deutsch— Dampfer nach Deutschland.

VI. TRANSLATION EXERCISES

1. A well-known poet wrote only short letters. 2. Yesterday we read a long story in our German book. 3. Our German teacher will visit his old friend in Germany. 4. The old poet and his good friend smiled. 5. A beautiful story is not always true. 6. Tomorrow we shall have warm weather

again. 7. The astonished woman paid the big bill. 8. Many people stopped on the street and smiled. 9. His sick friend did not have a good doctor. 10. The little girl sang a beautiful song. 11. A hungry student once had no money. 12. Her poor father was very sick. 13. The windows in their old house are small. 14. There are rich and poor students. 15. What kind of book do you wish?

VII. VOCABULARY BUILDING

There are numerous cognates in German and English having the same vowel changes. In some cases the consonants remain the same, in others they are likewise changed. German **a** may correspond to English *ea*.

der Bart the beard; **ja** yea; **das Jahr** the year; **klar** clear

German **a** may correspond to English *o*.

alt old; **der Kamm** the comb; **lang** long; **die Nase** the nosr

German **au** may correspond to English *ou*.

aus out; **das Haus** the house; **die Maus** the mouse; **sauer** sour

VIII. SUPPLEMENTARY READING

Eine Anekdote von Mozart

Wolfgang Amadeus Mozart war ein Wunderkind. Eɪ war erst vier Jahre alt, als sein Vater, halb im Scherz, ihn lehrte, Klavier zu spielen. Im nächsten Jahr erhielt er eine kleine Violine, aber er hatte noch keinen Unterricht. Eines Tages spielte der Vater Mozart mit seinen Freunden Schachtner und Wentzl einige Trios. „Bitte, Vater," sagte der kleine Junge, „laß mich die zweite Violine spielen, bitte, bitte!" „Nein," antwortete der Vater, „du hast ja noch nie Unterricht gehabt, geh zur Mutter." Das Kind begann bitterlich zu weinen, und Herr Schachtner sagte mitleidig: „Spiele nur mit mir

zusammen, Wolferl, aber spiele so leise, daß dich niemand
hört. Verstehst du?" Die Mutter wischte dem Kind die
Tränen ab und setzte es auf einen Stuhl. Das erste Trio
begann. Schachtner spielte und sah mit einem Auge auf
Wolfgang. Nach einigen Minuten war es klar, daß er überflüssig war. Der fünfjährige Junge spielte die zweite Violine
vollkommen richtig. Schachtner legte still seine Violine
nieder und sah heimlich auf die anderen Spieler. Aus den
Augen des Vaters liefen Tränen, während er weiter spielte.
Niemand sagte etwas, bis sie alle sechs Trios gespielt hatten.
Dann erst begann der Jubel. Die drei Männer lobten und
küssten das Kind. Die Mutter weinte vor Freude. Und der
kleine Fünfjährige wurde so aufgeregt, daß er rief: ,,Jetzt spiele
ich auch die erste Violine!" Und das tat er, wenn auch nicht
ganz so gut.

Um dieselbe Zeit begann Mozart Menuette zu kompo-
nieren. Der Vater schrieb sie alle in ein Heft. Und bald
machte er mit dem Knaben und seiner auch sehr musikali-
schen Schwester eine Konzertreise nach München und ein
Jahr später nach Wien. Dort spielten die Kinder vor der
Kaiserin Maria Theresia. Das war eine große Ehre. Aber
der kleine Mozart war gar nicht schüchtern, sondern kletterte
auf den Schoß der Kaiserin, einer freundlichen und mütter-
lichen Dame, und gab ihr einen Kuß.

IX. SUPPLEMENTARY VOCABULARY

ab-wischen to wipe off, wipe
  away
aufgeregt excited
**auf-sehen, sah auf, hat auf-
  gesehen, er sieht auf** to look
  upon, observe
auf-setzen to set on, put up
das Auge, -s, -n the eye
bitterlich bitterly
derselbe, dieselbe, dasselbe
  the same
die Ehre, -, -n the honor

**erhalten, erhielt, hat erhalten,
  er erhält** to preserve, keep;
  receive
die Freude, -, -n the joy
freundlich friendly
halb half
heimlich secretly
-jährig years old
der Jubel, -s the jubilation,
  rejoicing
die Kaiserin, -, -nen the
  empress

das Kind, -(e)s, -er the child
das Klavier', -s, -e the piano
klettern to climb
komponie'ren to compose
die Konzertreise, -, -n the concert tour
der Kuß, Kusses, Küsse the kiss
küssen to kiss
leise softly
loben to praise
Maria Theresia, -s Maria Theresa
das Menuett', -s, -e the minuet
mitleidig compassionate(ly), sympathetic(ally)
musika'lisch musical
mütterlich motherly
nieder-legen to lay down

der Scherz, -es, -e the jest, joke
der Schoß, -es, ̈-e the lap
schüchtern shy
spielen to play
still still, silent(ly)
die Träne, -, -n the tear
das Trio, -s, -s the trio
überflüssig superfluous
der Unterricht, -es the instruction, lessons
die Violi'ne, -, -n the violin
weinen to cry
weiter-spielen to continue to play
das Wunderkind, -(e)s, -er the child prodigy
zusammen together, jointly
zusammen-spielen to play together

Aufgabe Sechzehn

Declensional Details

I. READING SELECTION

Zwei Anekdoten

Es gibt nicht nur viele deutsche Anekdoten über Dichter und Professoren, sondern man findet auch in anderen Ländern ähnliche Geschichten. Vielleicht können Sie selber einige interessante Geschichten erzählen. Aber tun Sie es auf deutsch! Heute werden wir wieder zwei deutsche Anekdoten lesen. Die erste Geschichte handelt wieder von einem bekannten deutschen Dichter. Der Name dieses deutschen Dichters ist Gotthold Ephraim Lessing (1729–1781). Einmal kam ein Bekannter zu ihm und sie sprachen über ein neues Buch. Der Bekannte fragte Lessing: ,,Glauben Sie nicht, daß es viel Wahres und Neues in dem Buche gibt?'' Lessing überlegte eine Weile, dann antwortete er: ,,Sie haben recht. Es gibt viel Neues und Wahres in dem Buch, aber das Neue darin ist nicht wahr und das Wahre darin ist nicht neu.''

Die zweite Geschichte handelt nicht von einem Professor an einer Universität, sondern von dem Lehrer einer Volksschule. Am Ende jedes Schuljahres prüfte er die Schüler. Zu dieser Prüfung kamen auch die Eltern der Schüler und einige andere Lehrer. Jedesmal, wenn der Lehrer eine Frage stellte, hob jeder Schüler die Hand auf und der Lehrer bekam nie eine falsche Antwort. Jeder Schüler gab laut und deutlich die richtige Antwort, ob die Frage schwer oder leicht war. Niemand gab eine falsche Antwort. Alle Leute, auch die anderen Lehrer, waren sehr erstaunt. Endlich war die Prüfung zu Ende. Ein anderer Lehrer war neugierig. Er ging zu dem Lehrer der Volksschule und fragte ihn leise: ,,Wie

kommt es, daß Sie nie eine falsche Antwort bekommen?"
„Das ist sehr einfach," antwortete der Lehrer, „wenn ein
Schüler die richtige Antwort weiß, hebt er die rechte Hand
auf, und wenn er sie nicht weiß, hebt er die linke Hand auf."

II. VOCABULARY

*Idioms
- **auf deutsch, englisch, usw.**   in German, English, etc.
- **am Ende**   at the end
- **zu Ende**   at an end, over

ähnlich   similar, like
*ander   other
*auf-heben, hob auf, hat aufgehoben   to raise, to pick up
deutlich   distinct(ly)
*einige   several, a few
*das Ende, -s, -n   the end
*erzäh'len   to tell, relate
*falsch   false, wrong
*interessant'   interesting
jedesmal   everytime
können, konnte, hat gekonnt, er kann   can, to be able
*laut   loud(ly)
*leicht   light, easy
*leise   low, soft, in a low voice
*man   one
*der Name, -ns, -n   the name
*neu   new

*nie   never
*niemand   nobody
*ob   whether, if
prüfen   to examine
die Prüfung, -, -en   the examination
*richtig   right, correct
das Schuljahr, -(e)s, -e   the school year
*schwer   heavy, difficult
*sechzehn   sixteen
überle'gen   to reflect, think a thing over
die Volksschule, -, -n   elementary public school
*die Weile, -   space of time, while
wissen, wußte, hat gewußt, er weiß   to know

III. GRAMMAR

A. Declensional Details

1. Two or more descriptive adjectives take the same endings.

> armer kranker Mann
> dieser arme kranke Mann

2. Adjectives used as nouns take the same endings as descriptive adjectives, but are capitalized. Only the masculine and feminine form plurals.

der Bekannte (Mann)	**die Bekannte (Frau)**
the acquaintance	*the acquaintance*
ein Bekannter (Mann)	**eine Bekannte (Frau)**
an acquaintance	*an acquaintance*

das Bekannte
that which is familiar
Bekanntes
familiar things

3. After **viele, wenige, andere, einige, manche** (*some*), **mehrere** (*several*), the nominative and accusative plural of the descriptive adjective take the ending **-e** instead of **-en**.

viele deutsche Geschichten
einige interessante Anekdoten

After **alle** the regular weak ending **-en** is used.

alle guten Leute

4. An adjective used as a noun after **nichts, viel, wenig,** **etwas** (*something*) is capitalized and takes the strong endings.

viel Neues und Wahres

After **alles,** which has the strong endings, the adjective takes weak endings.

alles Neue und Wahre

5. The present participle of verbs is formed by adding **-d** to the infinitive.

schlafen	**schlafend**
to sleep	*sleeping*

Both present and past participles are used as adjectives.

der schlafende Junge
der geschriebene Brief

6. The uninflected form of the adjective is used as the adverb.

Er antwortete laut und deutlich.

Note that in German the predicate adjective and the adverb are identical.

Das Wetter ist gut. *The weather is good.*
Er schläft gut. *He sleeps well.*

Remember that adverbs cannot stand between the subject and verb in declarative statements.

B. Man

The forms **einem** und **einen** serve as the dative and accusative singular, respectively, of the impersonal **man.**

Es tut einem leid. *One feels sorry.*

The impersonal **man** is frequently used in German in place of the passive.

Man erzählt viele Geschichten. *Many stories are told.*

IV. QUESTIONS

1. Wo findet man auch Geschichten über Dichter und Professoren? 2. Was haben wir heute wieder gelesen? 3. Wie heißt ein bekannter deutscher Dichter? 4. Wer kam einmal zu Lessing? 5. Über was sprachen sie? 6. Was fragte der Bekannte den Dichter Lessing? 7. Was antwortete Lessing? 8. Wie war das Neue in dem Buch? 9. Wie war das Wahre darin? 10. Welche Geschichte handelt von einem Lehrer? 11. Wer kam auch zu der Prüfung am Ende des Jahres? 12. Was tat jeder Schüler, wenn der Lehrer eine Frage stellte? 13. Was für eine Antwort bekam der Lehrer nie? 14. Was für eine Antwort bekam der Lehrer, wenn die Frage schwer war? 15. Wie waren alle Leute? 16. Wer ging nach der Prüfung zu dem Lehrer? 17. Was fragte er ihn? 18.

Welche Hand hob ein Schüler auf, wenn er die richtige Antwort wußte?

V. GRAMMATICAL EXERCISES

(a) Supply the missing endings:

1. Ich ging gestern mit einem alt— Bekannt— in die Stadt. 2. Ein arm— hungrig— Mann hatte kein Geld. 3. Die Frau hatte gestern viel Neu— zu erzählen. 4. Nicht alles Neu— ist wahr. 5. Ein alt— Bekannt— von mir besuchte mich vor einigen Tagen. 6. Viele reich— Leute reisen im Sommer nach Europa. 7. Alle arm— Leute bleiben zu Hause. 8. Geben Sie mir etwas Leicht— zu lesen! 9. Es gibt auch andere schön— Geschichten. 10. Die Groß— sind oft nicht so schnell wie die Klein—. 11. Man hat wenig Gut— über ihn gesagt. 12. Haben Sie viele Bekannt—?

(b) Substitute German words for the English words in parentheses and supply the missing endings:

1. In Deutschland sieht man viele schön—, alt— Häuser. 2. Erzählen Sie (us) etwas Interessant—! 3. Dieser Mann ist (a) Deutsch—, jener ist Amerikaner. 4. Bei (my) alt— Freunde traf ich (several) schön— Mädchen. 5. Der Schüler gab (few) falsch— Antworten. 6. Er hat (little) Neu— in dem Briefe geschrieben. 7. Welch— arm— Mann hat er das Geld gegeben? 8. (All) Schön— ist gut.

VI. TRANSLATION EXERCISES

1. An old poet told us much that was interesting. 2. The new teacher asked many difficult questions. 3. The pupil answered in German. 4. The little boy quickly ran to his mother. 5. An acquaintance of mine will visit me tomorrow. 6. Is there much that is new in this book? 7. Yesterday we read two German stories. 8. At the end of the year the parents also came. 9. Several pupils raised their right hands (*sing.*) and others their left hands. 10. The teacher always

received a correct answer. 11. My good friend bought this old, beautiful house. 12. That which is new is not always true. 13. She sang this little song very beautifully. 14. Not all good books are interesting. 15. He went to Europe with an old acquaintance.

VII. VOCABULARY BUILDING

An **e** in German may correspond to an *i* in English.

geben to give; **leben** to live; **recht** right; **die Schwester** sister.

German **ei** may correspond to English *i*.

beißen to bite; **die Meile** mile; **treiben** to drive; **der Wein** the wine.

German **ei** may correspond to English *ea*.

die Heide the heath; **heilen** to heal; **reichen** to reach; **der Schweiß** the sweat.

VIII. SUPPLEMENTARY READING

Ein Brief

Wien, den 1. (ersten) August 195–

Lieber Onkel und liebe Tante!

Vor einigen Wochen sind wir glücklich in Deutschland angekommen. Wir hatten herrliches Wetter während der ganzen Fahrt und alles war neu und interessant für uns. Es tat uns beinahe leid, daß die Fahrt schon zu Ende war. Wir landeten in Cuxhaven und fuhren dann mit der Eisenbahn nach Hamburg. Von dort flogen wir nach Berlin, blieben aber nur einen Tag, denn mein Vater wünschte, sobald wie möglich nach Süddeutschland zu kommen, wo er früher gelebt hat. So sind wir zuerst nach München gereist und von da nach Salzburg. Diese wunderschöne Stadt liegt schon in Österreich. Von dort reisten wir nach Wien, der Hauptstadt

dieses Landes. Hier wohnen wir in einem Hotel am „Ring."
Diese Straße hat man an der Stelle der früheren Festungswerke
um die alte Stadt gebaut. Auch hier hat der Krieg viele
Gebäude zerstört oder beschädigt. Besonders hat der berühmte Stephansdom gelitten, die größte und schönste Kirche
von Wien. Man hat ihn aber wieder aufgebaut. Wir hörten
in ihm ein Konzert des Knabenchors von St. Stephan. Den
hohen Turm des Domes sieht man von allen Punkten der
Umgebung. Das ist das Schönste an Wien: die Stadt ist an
drei Seiten von ziemlich hohen Bergen umgeben. Sie sind
bedeckt mit Wäldern. An einigen Punkten sind hübsche
Restaurants. Vorgestern aßen wir in einem von ihnen zu
Abend. Es heißt Cobenzl und war früher ein Schlößchen.
Von dort hatten wir eine herrliche Aussicht über die ganze
Stadt mit ihren vielen Lichtern. Während des Essens spielte
eine Kapelle Wiener Walzer von Johann Strauss. Es gibt in
Wien wie in den anderen großen deutschen Städten sehr gute
Theater. Sehr berühmt ist das Burgtheater. Leider ist es
während des Sommers geschlossen. Morgen werden wir in
ein anderes Theater gehen. Ich hoffe, daß ich alles verstehen
werde. Übermorgen reisen wir weiter nach Tirol.
Mit vielen herzlichen Grüßen

Euer Neffe
Karl

IX. SUPPLEMENTARY VOCABULARY

die Aussicht, -, -en the view
bedeckt covered
beschädigen to damage, injure
das Burgtheater, -s the Burg
(castle) Theater
der Dom, -(e)s, -e the cathedral
glücklich happy, safe(ly)
der Gruß, -es, ⁼e the greeting
herrlich fine, splendid, glorious

herzlich hearty, sincere
hoch (*when followed by* e *of the
inflected cases* ch *becomes* h, *as*
hoher, hohe, hohes) high
hoffen to hope
hübsch pretty
die Kapelle, -, -n the band
der Knabenchor, -(e)s, ⁼e the
boys' choir
leiden, litt, hat gelitten to
suffer
leider unfortunately

das Licht, -(e)s, -er   the light
der Neffe, -n, -n   the nephew
der Onkel, -s, -   the uncle
der Punkt, -(e)s, -e   the point
das Schlößchen, -s, -   the small
    castle
das Schönste   the most beauti-
    ful
sobald   as soon
der Stephansdom, -(e)s   the
    Cathedral of St. Stephen
die Tante, -, -n   the aunt
(das) Tirol, -s   the Tyrol
übermorgen   the day after to-
    morrow

umgeben   surrounded
die Umge'bung, -, -en   the
    surroundings
vorgestern   the day before
    yesterday
der Walzer, -s, -   the waltz
weiter-reisen, reiste weiter, ist
    weitergereist   to continue a
    journey
Wiener   Viennese
wunderschön   wondrously
    beautiful
zu Abend   in the evening

Aufgabe Siebzehn

Interrogative and Relative Pronouns

I. READING SELECTION

Drei Anekdoten

Heute werden wir noch ein paar Geschichten lesen, **die** von Professoren und Lehrern handeln. Ein Professor, **der** oft zerstreut war, machte eines Tages einen Spaziergang, **was** er sehr gerne tat. Auf der Straße begegnete er einem lieben Bekannten, **den** er seit langer Zeit nicht gesehen hatte und **dessen** Vater vor einigen Monaten gestorben war. Beide Männer blieben stehen. Der Professor fragte: „Wie geht es Ihnen, Herr Beyer?" Herr Beyer dankte ihm und antwortete: „Danke, es geht mir ganz gut." Der Professor, **der** sehr höflich war, sagte: „Ich hoffe, es geht Ihrem lieben Vater auch gut?" Herr Beyer, in **dessen** Hause der Professor oft als Gast gewesen war, war erstaunt, diese Frage zu hören, und sagte: „Haben Sie denn vergessen, daß mein Vater vor einigen Monaten gestorben ist?" „Ach, verzeihen Sie," antwortete der Professor, „ich wollte nur fragen, ob Ihr Vater noch immer tot ist."

Ein anderer Professor, **der** auch zerstreut war, ging einmal von der Universität zu Fuß nach Hause, **was** er sehr oft tat. Auf der Straße begegnete er einem Dienstmädchen, **das** mit zwei kleinen Kindern einen Spaziergang machte. Der Professor blieb stehen und sagte zu dem Mädchen: „Was für schöne Kinder! **Wem** gehören sie denn?" Das Dienstmädchen antwortete: „Beide gehören Ihnen, Herr Professor."

Ein Lehrer, **dessen** Schüler nicht sehr fleißig waren, hatte einen Schüler, **der** besonders faul war. Einmal sagte der Lehrer zu diesem Schüler: „Als Alexander der Große so alt war wie Sie, war er Herr über beinahe die ganze Welt." Der Schüler, **der** nicht dumm war, antwortete schnell: „Ja, aber

144

Courtesy of the German Tourist Information Office

Schloß Meersburg am Bodensee

Mädchen im Schwarzwald

Courtesy of the German Tourist Information Office

Ein Schwarzwaldhaus

Das Höllental im Schwarzwald

Kloster Hirsau im Schwarzwald

Rothenburg ob der Tauber: vor dem Burgtor

Rothenburg ob der Tauber

das war nicht sehr schwer für ihn, denn Aristoteles war sein Lehrer."

II. VOCABULARY

*Idioms
{
danke (schön) thanks, thank you (very much)
es geht mir (dir, ihm, usw.) gut I (you, he, etc.) am well; wie geht es Ihnen? how are you?
immer noch (noch immer) still
}

*ach ah, oh, alas
Aristo'teles Aristotle
*begegnen, begegnete, ist begegnet (+ dat.) to meet (by chance)
*beide both
*beinah(e) almost
besonders especially
*danken (+ dat.) to thank
*dumm stupid
*faul lazy; rotten
*fleißig diligent
*ganz whole, entire; adv. quite, very
*der Gast, -es, ̈e the guest
*gehören (+ dat.) to belong
*hoffen to hope
höflich courteous, polite

*hören to hear
*das Kind, -(e)s, -er the child
*lieb dear
*der Monat, -(e)s, -e the month
siebzehn seventeen
*sterben, starb, ist gestorben er stirbt to die
tot dead
*vergessen, vergaß, hat vergessen, er vergißt to forget
verzeihen, verzieh, hat verziehen to forgive, pardon
*die Welt, -, -en the world
wollen, wollte, hat gewollt, er will to wish, want
*die Zeit, -, -en the time

III. GRAMMAR

A. Interrogative Pronouns: wer, was

Nom.	wer who	was what
Gen.	wessen whose	wessen of what
Dat.	wem whom, to whom	————
Acc.	wen whom	was what

1. There are no plural forms of **wer** and **was**. **Wer** is used with both masculine and feminine nouns and may be the subject of a plural form of **sein**.

Wer ist der Mann?
Wer ist die Frau?
Wer sind die Leute?

2. In place of the missing dative of **was** a compound form of **wo** + the preposition (**wor** before prepositions beginning with a vowel) is used. (Cf. similar compounds of **da** + the preposition, Lesson XIV.)

Womit schreiben Sie?
With what (wherewith) are you writing?

3. A compound of **wo** + the preposition is also generally used in place of the preposition + the accusative of **was.**

Wofür wünschen Sie es?
What do you want it for?

B. *Relative Pronouns:* **der, welcher**

		MASCULINE	FEMININE	NEUTER
Sing.	Nom.	der *who*	die	das
	Gen.	dessen *whose*	deren	dessen
	Dat.	dem *whom, to whom*	der	dem
	Acc.	den *whom*	die	das
Plural	Nom.	die		
	Gen.	deren		
	Dat.	denen		
	Acc.	die		
Sing.	Nom.	welcher	welche	welches
	Gen.	(dessen)	(deren)	(dessen)
	Dat.	welchem	welcher	welchem
	Acc.	welchen	welche	welches
Plural	Nom.	welche		
	Gen.	(deren)		
	Dat.	welchen		
	Acc.	welche		

1. The relative pronoun **der** is declined like the definite article except in the genitive singular and plural and in the dative plural. These five forms add **-en,** and the **s** of the masculine and neuter is doubled.

2. The relative pronoun **welcher** is declined like the **der**-words except that in place of the missing genitive the corresponding forms of the relative **der** are used.

3. There is no difference in meaning between **der** and **welcher** as relative pronouns. Generally the **der** forms, being shorter, are preferred.

4. The relative pronoun must agree in gender and number with its antecedent, i.e., with the noun to which it refers. Its case, however, is determined by its use in the clause.

> Der Mann, **der** (**welcher**) gestern hier war.
> Der Schüler, **dessen** Bruder krank ist.
> Der Student, **dem** (**welchem**) ich das Buch gab.
> Der Freund, **den** (**welchen**) wir besucht haben.

5. The relative pronoun may not be omitted in German as is possible in English.

> Das Buch, **das** ich lese.
> *The book (that, which) I am reading.*

6. Compounds of **wo** + a preposition (**wor** before prepositions beginning with a vowel) *may* be used in place of a relative when referring to lifeless objects.

> Das Haus, **worin** (in dem) er wohnt.
> Der Bleistift, **womit** (mit dem) ich schreibe.

7. All relative clauses are dependent clauses. They must have dependent word order and be set off by commas (cf. Lesson XII).

C. Indefinite Relative Pronouns: **wer, was**

1. **Wer** and **was** as indefinite relative pronouns are declined like the interrogative pronouns **wer** and **was.**

2. **Wer** never has a definite antecedent.

Wer faul ist, lernt nicht viel.
He who (Whoever) is lazy does not learn much.

3. **Was** may also be used without an antecedent.

Was neu ist, ist nicht immer wahr.
What (That which) is new is not always true.

4. **Was** is also used when the antecedent is an indefinite neuter pronoun like **alles, nichts, etwas** (*something*).

Alles, **was** er hatte, gab er dem Manne.
All that he had he gave the man.

Nichts, **was** er sagt, ist richtig.
Nothing that he says is correct.

5. **Was** is used when the antecedent is a neuter adjective used as a noun, especially in the superlative.

Es war das Beste, **was** er gehört hatte.

6. Finally, **was** is used when the antecedent is an entire clause.

Er machte einen Spaziergang, **was** er sehr gerne tat.

IV. QUESTIONS

1. Was für Geschichten werden wir heute lesen? 2. Was tat ein Professor sehr gerne? 3. Wem begegnete er auf der Straße? 4. Wen hatte er seit langer Zeit nicht gesehen? 5. Wessen Vater war vor einigen Monaten gestorben? 6. Was fragte der Professor den Bekannten? 7. Was antwortete Herr Beyer? 8. In wessen Hause war der Professor oft als Gast gewesen? 9. Was hatte der Professor vergessen? 10. Wohin ging ein anderer Professor einmal? 11. Wem begegnete er auf der Straße? 12. Mit wem machte das Mädchen einen Spaziergang? 13. Was fragte der Professor das Mädchen? 14. Was antwortete das Mädchen? 15. Was für einen Schüler

hatte ein Lehrer? 16. Was sagte der Lehrer einmal zu dem Schüler? 17. Wie war der Schüler nicht? 18. Wer war der Lehrer Alexanders des Großen?

V. GRAMMATICAL EXERCISES

(a) Supply the correct forms of the relative pronoun **der**:

1. Die Dame, von ——— Sie sprechen, ist Amerikanerin. 2. Das Bett, in ——— ich schlafe, ist braun. 3. Der Zug, mit ——— ich fahre, ist ein Schnellzug. 4. Der Doktor, ——— Tochter Gedichte schreibt, ist ein Bekannter von uns. 5. Der Wein, ——— er trinkt, ist weiß. 6. Der Bauer, ——— ich ein Streichholz gab, ist nicht dumm. 7. Der Stuhl, auf ——— ich sitze, ist schwarz. 8. Das Buch, ——— er mir geschickt hat, ist sehr interessant. 9. Ein Brief, ——— nicht zwei Seiten hat, ist kurz. 10. Eltern, ——— Kinder fleißig sind, sind zufrieden.

(b) In the above sentences supply the correct forms of **welcher.**

(c) In the above sentences use compounds with **wo** whenever possible.

(d) In the sentences below supply the correct forms of **wer** or **was:**

1. ——— immer seine Aufgabe lernt, ist fleißig. 2. Nicht alles, ——— man hört, ist wahr. 3. Er stand früh auf, ——— er immer tat. 4. Nichts, ——— ich in dem Buche gelesen habe, war interessant. 5. ——— kein Geld hat, ist arm. 6. Es war das Beste, ——— er gesehen hatte.

(e) Change the second sentence in each group below to a relative clause:

EXAMPLE:
{Der Professor blieb stehen. Die Kinder gehörten ihm.
Der Professor, dem (welchem) die Kinder gehörten, blieb stehen.

1. Er begegnete einem Freund. Sein Vater war gestorben.
2. Das Feuer war ausgegangen. Das Dienstmädchen hatte es
gemacht. 3. Der Zug fährt um neun Uhr ab. Wir fahren
damit. 4. Die Dame brauchte noch ein Meter. Sie bestellte
ein Kleid. 5. Der Student war hungrig. Ich gab ihm das
Geld. 6. Die Leute lächelten. Wir begegneten ihnen.

VI. TRANSLATION EXERCISES

1. The man who lives in this house is in the country.
2. The acquaintance whose father had died was astonished.
3. The student (to) whom I sent a letter did not answer.
4. The peasant whom we saw today was smoking. 5. The
pencil with which I write is yellow. 6. My friend (*fem.*)
whose mother was sick went to a doctor. 7. The friend whom
the professor met said: How are you? 8. Whoever believes
that is stupid. 9. I gave the poor man all that I had. 10.
The lady to whom this book belongs is in Europe. 11. Whose
pen is this? 12. The child whose mother was in the country
was lazy. 13. The pupil to whom this pencil belongs
remained at home. 14. The answer which the teacher
received was wrong. 15. He had forgotten almost everything
that he had learned.

VII. VOCABULARY BUILDING

German **ei** may correspond to English *o*.

beide both; **das Heim** the home; **meist** most; **der Stein**
the stone.

German **ie** may correspond to English *ee*.

das Bier the beer; **fliehen** to flee; **der Kiel** the keel; **das
Knie** the knee.

German **o** may correspond to English *ea*.

die Bohne the bean; **das Ohr** the ear; **ost** east; **der Strom**
the stream.

VIII. SUPPLEMENTARY READING

In Tirol

Am frühen Morgen packte die Familie Braun ihre Koffer. Dann klingelten sie nach dem Hausdiener, der nach einigen Minuten kam, um die Koffer hinunterzutragen. Unten im Hotel bezahlte Herr Braun die Rechnung. Dann fuhren sie nach dem Bahnhof. Dort riefen sie einen Gepäckträger, der ihre Koffer nahm und sie in den Bahnhof trug. Spät am Nachmittag kamen sie in Innsbruck an, der schönen Hauptstadt von Tirol. Sie liegt an einer Stelle, an der eine Brücke über den Fluß Inn führt; daher hat man sie Innsbruck genannt. Als die Familie Braun die breite Maria-Theresienstraße entlang ging, glaubten sie ein dunkles Gewitter über den Häusern der Stadt zu sehen. Was sie sahen, waren aber die dunklen Wälder auf den Bergen, die direkt hinter der Stadt steil aufsteigen bis zu einer Höhe von ungefähr 2500 (zweitausendfünfhundert) Metern d.h. 7500 (siebentausend-fünfhundert) Fuß. Von Innsbruck führt eine Straße nach Süden zu dem Brenner-Paß, welcher der niedrigste Paß über die Alpen ist. Schon die alten Römer haben diese Straße benutzt. Auf dem Brenner ist die italienische Grenze, aber noch 80 (achtzig) Meilen weiter sprechen die meisten Leute deutsch. Bis zu dem ersten Weltkrieg gehörte dieses Gebiet zu Österreich. Besonders malerisch ist die alte Stadt Bozen, welche die Italiener Bolzano nennen. In ihrer Nachbar-schaft ist der größte deutsche Dichter des Mittelalters, Walther von der Vogelweide, geboren. Die Landschaft hat einen süd-lichen Charakter. Weinberge und Obstbäume sind überall; die Bauernhöfe und die vielen Schlösser um Bozen sind umgeben von Walnuß- und Kastanienbäumen. Aber oben auf den Bergen stehen die Tannen, die für den Norden charak-teristisch sind. Von Bozen aus sieht man die Felsen der Dolomiten, die bei Sonnenuntergang ganz rot werden. Man nennt sie Rosengarten. Nach einer alten Legende hatte Laurin, der König der Zwerge, in diesen Felsen einen Rosen-garten, den nur ganz wenige Menschen gesehen haben. An schönen Tagen reflektieren die Felsen, so sagt die Legende, die rote Farbe der Rosen.

IX. SUPPLEMENTARY VOCABULARY

auf-steigen, stieg auf, ist auf-gestiegen, er steigt auf to ascend, rise

der Bauernhof, -es, ⁻e the farm

benutzen to use

(das) Bozen, -s (city of) Bolzano

der Brenner-Paß, -Passes the Brenner Pass

der Charak′ter, -s, -e the character

charakteris′tisch characteristic

die Dolomiten (*pl.*) the Dolomites (*Alps of the Southern Tyrol*)

entlang along

der Felsen, -s, - the cliff

das Gebiet, -(e)s, -e the district

das Gewitter, -s, - the thunderstorm

der Hausdiener, -s, - the house servant, porter

hinter (+ *dat.* or *acc.*) behind

hinunter-tragen, trug hinunter, hat hinunter-getragen, er trägt hinunter to carry down

die Höhe, -, -n the height

der Inn, -s the Inn (*river flowing through Innsbruck*)

(das) Innsbruck, -s (city of) Innsbruck

der Italie′ner, -s, - the Italian

italie′nisch Italian

der Kasta′nienbaum, -(e)s, ⁻e the chestnut tree

klingeln nach (+ *dat.*) to ring for

die Landschaft, -, -en the landscape

die Legen′de, -, -n the legend

malerisch picturesque

die Maria-Theresienstraße, - Maria Theresa Street

der Mensch, -en, -en the man, human being; *pl.* people

das Mittelalter, -s the Middle Ages

die Nachbarschaft, -, -en the neighborhood, vicinity

der Nachmittag, -(e)s, -e the afternoon

niedrig low; **niedrigste** lowest

der Obstbaum, -(e)s, ⁻e the fruit-tree

der Paß, Passes, Pässe the pass

reflecktie′ren to reflect

der Römer, -s, - the Roman

die Ro′se, -, -n the rose

der Rosengarten, -s, ⁻ the rose garden

der Sonnenuntergang, -(e)s, ⁻e the sunset

südlich southern

die Tanne, -, -n the fir

tragen, trug, hat getragen, er trägt to carry; wear

überall everywhere

der Walnußbaum, -(e)s, ⁻e the walnut tree

der Weinberg, -(e)s, -e the vineyard

der Zwerg, -(e)s, -e the dwarf

Aufgabe Achtzehn

Reflexive Pronouns and Verbs

I. READING SELECTION

Eine schwere Frage

Die Geschichte, die wir heute lesen, handelt von einer „jungen Dame," die sechs Jahre alt war und die wir Gretchen nennen werden. Gretchen hatte Angst vor allem. Wenn sie allein in einem Zimmer war, fürchtete sie **sich**, besonders wenn es dunkel war. Sie fürchtete **sich** auch, wenn es donnerte und blitzte. Außerdem hatte sie Angst vor allen Tieren, z.B. vor dem Hund, der Katze, dem Pferd und der Kuh. Eines Tages wurde ihr Vater böse und sagte zu ihr: „Schäme **dich**, immer solche Angst zu haben!" „Vater," fragte Gretchen, „hast du keine Angst, wenn du eine Kuh siehst?" „Nein, gewiß nicht," antwortete der Vater. „Hast du auch keine Angst vor dem Pferd?" fragte sie weiter. Wieder antwortete der Vater: „Natürlich nicht." „Aber, Vater," sagte sie, „gewiß fürchtest du **dich**, wenn es donnert und blitzt?" „Gar nicht, du dummes Mädchen," war die Antwort. Jetzt wunderte **sich** die Tochter und schwieg eine Weile. Dann fragte sie plötzlich: „Vater, fürchtest du **dich** vor gar nichts in der ganzen Welt außer vor der Mutter?"

II. VOCABULARY

*Idioms {
Angst haben vor (+ *dat.*)   to be afraid of
sich fürchten vor (+ *dat.*)   to be afraid of
z.B. (**zum Beispiel**)   for example
}

achtzehn eighteen
*allein′ alone
*die Angst, -, ⸚e the fear
*außer (+ *dat.*) besides, except

*das Beispiel, -(e)s, -e the example
*blitzen to lighten, to emit lightning
*böse bad; angry

*donnern to thunder
*dunkel dark
*fürchten to fear; sich
    fürchten to be afraid
*gewiß certain(ly)
(das) Gretchen (*diminutive
    of* Margarete) Margery,
    Maggy, Peggy
*jung young
*die Katze, -, -n the cat
*die Kuh, -, ⸚e the cow
*natür'lich natural(ly); of
    course
nennen, nannte, hat genannt
    to name, call
*das Pferd, -(e)s, -e the horse

*plötzlich sudden(ly)
*sich schämen to be (feel)
    ashamed
schweigen, schwieg, hat
    geschwiegen to be silent
*sich himself, herself, itself,
    themselves, yourself, oneself
*das Tier, -(e)s, -e the animal
weiter farther, further; con-
    tinue
weiter-fragen, fragte weiter,
    hat weitergefragt to con-
    tinue to ask
*sich wundern to wonder, to
    be surprised

III. GRAMMAR

A. *Reflexive Pronouns*

1. Reflexive pronouns are pronoun objects which refer back to the subject of the sentence or clause, i.e., the person or thing represented by the pronoun object is identical with the person or thing of the subject.

> **Er sieht mich.** *He sees me.*
> **Ich sehe mich.** *I see myself.*

In the first of the above sentences **mich** is a personal pronoun, for the person represented by **mich** is different from the subject. In the second sentence **mich** is a reflexive pronoun (although identical in form with the personal pronoun), for the object pronoun **mich** stands for the same person as the subject **ich.**

2. Since the reflexive pronouns are pronoun *objects*, there are no nominative forms, and the genitive is exceedingly rare. In the first and second persons, the forms of the reflexive pronouns are identical with those of the personal pronouns.

All you need remember is that there is only one distinctive form of the reflexive pronoun which is **sich** *for the third person, dative and accusative, all genders, singular and plural.*

Naturally then the reflexive pronoun for the conventional form of address is also **sich**. Note that this is *not* capitalized.

Fürchten Sie sich nicht?

B. *Reflexive Verbs*

1. There are many transitive verbs, in English as well as in German, which may or may not be used with a reflexive pronoun object, but such verbs are more common in German.

> **Die Mutter zieht das Kind an.**
> *The mother dresses the child.*
>
> **Der Junge zieht sich an.**
> *The boy dresses himself (gets dressed).*

In German, however, certain verbs always require the reflexive pronoun to render the specific meaning of the verbal phrase.

> **Ich schäme mich.**
> **Ich fürchte mich.**
> **Ich wundere mich.**

2. Conjugation of Reflexive Verbs.

	DATIVE	ACCUSATIVE
Sing.	1. ich hole **mir** ein Buch	1. ich fürchte **mich**
	2. du holst **dir** ein Buch Sie holen **sich** ein Buch	2. du fürchtest **dich** Sie fürchten **sich**
	er ⎱ 3. sie ⎬ holt **sich** ein Buch es ⎰	er ⎱ 3. sie ⎬ fürchtet **sich** es ⎰
Plural	1. wir holen **uns** ein Buch	1. wir fürchten **uns**
	2. ihr holt **euch** ein Buch Sie holen **sich** ein Buch	2. ihr fürchtet **euch** Sie fürchten **sich**
	3. sie holen **sich** ein Buch	3. sie fürchten **sich**

C. Impersonal Verbs

1. In German and in English certain verbs are used impersonally, but this construction again is more common in German.

Es regnet. Es donnert. Es blitzt.

2. Some reflexive verbs may also be used impersonally, in which case they are no longer reflexive.

Es wundert mich.
Es wundert ihn.

3. Certain idioms in German have the impersonal construction. When such a construction has a pronoun object, either dative or accusative, it is conjugated by changing the pronoun to the different persons. Such pronouns, however, are never reflexive, but always personal.

	DATIVE	ACCUSATIVE
Sing.	1. es tut **mir** leid	1. es wundert **mich**
	2. es tut **dir** leid es tut **Ihnen** leid	2. es wundert **dich** es wundert **Sie**
	3. es tut {**ihm** / **ihr** / **ihm**} leid	3. es wundert {**ihn** / **sie** / **es**}
Plural	1. es tut **uns** leid	1. es wundert **uns**
	2. es tut **euch** leid es tut **Ihnen** leid	2. es wundert **euch** es wundert **Sie**
	3. es tut **ihnen** leid	3. es wundert **sie**

D. Note the following constructions:

1. **Ich bin es.** *It is I.*
2. **Du bist es.** *It is you.*
   Sie sind es. *It is you.*
3. **Er ist es.** *It is he.*
   Sie ist es. *It is she.*
   Es ist es. *It is it.*
1. **Wir sind es.** *It is we.*
2. **Ihr seid es.** *It is you.*
   Sie sind es. *It is you.*
3. **Sie sind es.** *It is they.*

IV. QUESTIONS

1. Von wem handelt die Geschichte, die wir heute gelesen haben? 2. Wie alt war die „junge Dame"? 3. Wie hieß das Mädchen? 4. Wovor hatte Gretchen immer Angst? 5. Was tat sie, wenn sie allein in einem Zimmer war? 6. Wann fürchtete sie sich auch? 7. Wovor hatte sie auch Angst? 8. Geben Sie ein paar Beispiele! 9. Wie wurde ihr Vater eines Tages? 10. Was sagte er zu ihr? 11. Was fragte sie ihren Vater? 12. Was antwortete der Vater? 13. Was fragte sie ihn weiter? 14. Was antwortete der Vater wieder? 15. Was sagte Gretchen jetzt zu ihrem Vater? 16. Welche Antwort bekam sie? 17. Was tat die Tochter jetzt? 18. Was fragte sie?

V. GRAMMATICAL EXERCISES

(a) Conjugate in the present, past, and present perfect tenses:

1. Ich nehme mir Zeit.
2. Ich schäme mich.
3. Es geht mir gut.

(b) Supply the correct forms of the reflexive pronoun:

1. Wir ziehen ——— an. 2. Die Schülerin zieht ———
an. 3. Die Kinder ziehen ——— an. 4. Ihr zieht ———
an. 5. Das junge Mädchen zieht ——— an. 6. Gretchen
schämt ——— nicht. 7. Wunderst du ———? 8. Ich
fürchte ——— nicht. 9. Die Dame bestellt ——— ein Kleid.
10. Die Eltern fürchten ——— nicht. 11. Schämen Sie
——— nicht? 12. Der Kellner wundert ——— nicht.

VI. TRANSLATION EXERCISES

1. The name of the "young lady" who was six years old was
Gretchen. 2. We read a story about her today. 3. She was
afraid to be alone in a room. 4. She was also afraid when
there was thunder and lightning (*use impersonal construction*).
5. Was the little girl afraid of the dog and the cat? 6. What
did she do, when she saw a horse or a cow? 7. Her father
said to her one day: It is stupid to have such fear. 8. The
father was not afraid when he saw a horse. 9. He had no
fear of the dog or the cat either. 10. Are you afraid when
there is thunder and lightning? 11. Her father was afraid of
nothing but mother. 12. Not all animals sleep when it is
dark. 13. Of course we were surprised. 14. The man will
certainly feel ashamed. 15. Please do not be angry.

VII. VOCABULARY BUILDING

German **o** may correspond to English *u*.

> **der Donner** the thunder; **der Onkel** the uncle; **der Som-
> mer** the summer; **die Sonne** the sun.

German **u** may correspond to English *oo*.

> **das Buch** the book; **der Fuß** the foot; **die Schule** the
> school; **der Stuhl** the stool (chair).

German **u** may correspond to English *ou*.

> **jung** young; **rund** round; **die Suppe** the soup; **die
> Wunde** the wound.

VIII. SUPPLEMENTARY READING

Oberammergau

Von Tirol begab sich die Familie Braun wieder nach Bayern, um das berühmte Passionsspiel von Oberammergau zu sehen. Vor mehr als dreihundert Jahren war die Pest in Oberammergau und viele Menschen starben. Damals gelobten die frommen Bauern, ein großes Passionsspiel zu Ehren des Herrn aufzuführen. Seitdem haben sie das regelmäßig alle zehn Jahre getan. Früher führten sie das Spiel auf dem offenen Marktplatz auf, heute findet es in einem besonderen Gebäude statt.

Als die Familie Braun am Vormittag in dem Dorf spazieren ging, sahen sie überall ältere und jüngere Bauern und Handwerker mit langen Bärten. „Sie spielen alle im Passionsspiel," erklärte ihnen ein Herr, den sie fragten. Am Nachmittag begaben sie sich in das Theater, das 6000 (sechstausend) Sitze hat. Der Zuschauerraum und ein Teil der Bühne haben ein Dach, denn es regnet sehr oft in den bayrischen Alpen. Die Aufführung dauerte sieben bis acht Stunden, fünfhundert Personen spielten mit. Obgleich das Passionsspiel heute etwas kommerzialisiert ist, fanden sich die meisten Zuschauer doch ergriffen von dem Ernst und der Aufrichtigkeit, mit der die bäuerlichen Schauspieler ihre Aufgabe lösten.

Es war die letzte Aufführung des Jahres. Als am anderen Morgen die Familie Braun die Dorfstraße entlang ging, hörten sie aus allen Häusern das Klappern von Scheren. „Jetzt schneiden sie die Bärte ab," lächelte Herr Braun, „erst in neun Jahren werden sie sie wieder wachsen lassen."

IX. SUPPLEMENTARY VOCABULARY

ab-schneiden, schnitt ab, hat abgeschnitten to cut off
ältere older
auf-führen to perform
die Aufführung, -, -en the performance, production

die Aufrichtigkeit, -, -en the uprightness, sincerity
der Bart, -es, ⸚e the beard
bäuerlich peasant (*adj.*); country, rural
sich begeben, begab sich, hat

sich begeben, er begibt sich
to betake (oneself), go, set out
besonder special
die Bühne, -, -n the stage
das Dach, -(e)s, ̈er the roof
doch nevertheless, yet
das Dorf, -(e)s, ̈er the village
die Dorfstraße, -, -n the village
street
ergriffen deeply stirred
erklären to explain
der Ernst, -es the earnestness,
seriousness
**sich finden, fand sich, hat sich
gefunden** to find oneself
fromm pious
geloben to vow
der Herr, -n, -en the gentleman; the Lord God
jüngere younger
das Klappern, -s, - the clatter,
click
kommerzialisiert commercialized
lösen loosen, untie; eine
Aufgabe lösen to accomplish a task

der Marktplatz, -es, ̈e the
market place
mit-spielen to join in the play
with
(das) Oberammergau, -s
(village of) Oberammergau
offen open
das Passions'spiel, -(e)s, -e
the Passion play
die Pest, -, -en the plague
regelmäßig regularly, always
der Schauspieler, -s, - the
actor
die Schere, -, -n the scissors
seitdem since that time
**spazieren-gehen, ging spa-
zieren, ist spazierengegangen**
to go for a walk
das Spiel, -(e)s, -e the play
**wachsen, wuchs, ist gewachsen,
er wächst** to grow
der Zuschauer, -s, - the spectator
der Zuschauerraum, -(e)s, ̈e
the house (*opposite to the stage*),
auditorium

Aufgabe Neunzehn

Comparison of Adjectives and Adverbs

I. READING SELECTION

Eine Anekdote von Beethoven

Zwei der **bekanntesten** deutschen Komponisten sind Ludwig van Beethoven (1770–1827) und Richard Wagner (1813–1883). Beethoven lebte **früher** als Wagner, aber Wagner wurde **älter** als Beethoven. Alle beide arbeiteten sehr fleißig und schufen viele **höchst** interessante Werke. Von Beethovens Werken sind seine Sinfonien **am bekanntesten.** Seine **größte** und **berühmteste** Sinfonie ist die Neunte. Wagner ist **am bekanntesten** durch seine Musikdramen oder Opern. Während seiner Jugend lebte Beethoven in Deutschland. Im Jahre 1792 (siebzehnhundertzweiundneunzig) ging er nach Wien und blieb dort bis zu seinem Tode. Man erzählt die folgende Geschichte von ihm. Jeden Tag ging Beethoven in ein gewisses Restaurant in Wien, um dort sein Mittagessen zu essen. Eines Mittags setzte er sich an seinen gewöhnlichen Platz, ohne einen von den Gästen am Tische zu grüßen. Der Kellner, der ihn oft gesehen hatte, stellte Brot und Butter und eine Flasche Wein auf den Tisch und brachte ihm die Speisekarte. Beethoven nahm ein kleines Heft aus der Tasche, stützte den Kopf auf den rechten Arm, und von Zeit zu Zeit schrieb er etwas in das Heft. Der Kellner kam immer wieder, aber Beethoven merkte es nicht. Es wurde immer später, aber Beethoven blieb bis sechs Uhr abends sitzen. Plötzlich rief er den Kellner und sagte: „Kellner, die Rechnung bitte!" „Aber Sie haben heute noch nichts gegessen," antwortete der Kellner. „So? Auch gut!" sagte Beethoven, nahm seinen Hut und ging.

II. VOCABULARY

*Idioms
{
alle beide   both of them
noch nicht(s)   not yet (anything); noch nie   never yet
immer später (länger, usw.)   later and later (longer and longer, etc.)
immer wieder   again and again
}

*arbeiten   to work
*der Arm, -(e)s, -e,   the arm
berühmt   famous
*bis (+ *acc.*)   to, as far as, until; *conj.* until, before
*bringen, brachte, hat gebracht   to bring
*das Brot, -(e)s, -e   the bread
*die Butter, -   the butter
*durch (+ *acc.*)   through, by, by means of
*etwas   something
*folgen (sein) (+ *dat.*)   to follow
grüßen   to greet
*hoch, höher, höchst   high, higher, highest
die Jugend, -   youth, adolescence
*der Kellner, -s, -   the waiter
der Komponist', -en, -en   the composer
*der Kopf, -(e)s, -̈e   the head
*der Mittag, -(e)s, -e   midday, noon

*das Mittagessen, -s, -   the midday meal, dinner
das Musik'drama, -s, -dramen   the music drama, opera
neunt   ninth
neunzehn   nineteen
*ohne (+ *acc.* or *inf. with* **zu**)   without
die Oper, -, -n   the opera
*der Platz, -es, -̈e   the place; plaza
schaffen, schuf, hat geschaffen   to create
*setzen   to set; **sich setzen**   to sit down
die Sinfonie', -, -n   the symphony
*spät   late
stützen   to support
der Tod, -(e)s, -e   the death
*während (+ *gen.*)   during; *conj.* while
*das Werk, -(e)s, -e   the work

III. GRAMMAR

Comparison of Adjectives and Adverbs

1. The comparative is formed by adding **-er**, the superlative by adding **-st (-est)** to the adjective stem. Adjectives

ending in a t or s sound add -est to form the superlative.
Constructions corresponding to the English *more* and *most* are
not used.

POSITIVE	COMPARATIVE	SUPERLATIVE	
breit	breiter	der, die, das breiteste	am breitesten
faul	fauler	der, die, das faulste	am faulsten
interessant	interessanter	der, die, das interessanteste	am interessantesten
klein	kleiner	der, die, das kleinste	am kleinsten
weit	weiter	der, die, das weiteste	am weitesten

2. Certain adjectives in addition take Umlaut in the comparative and superlative. There is no way of telling whether or not an adjective requires Umlaut. Such forms must be memorized. Of the adjectives so far employed as active words the following take Umlaut.

POSITIVE	COMPARATIVE	SUPERLATIVE	
alt	älter	der, die, das älteste	am ältesten
arm	ärmer	der, die, das ärmste	am ärmsten
dumm	dümmer	der, die, das dümmste	am dümmsten
jung	jünger	der, die, das jüngste	am jüngsten
krank	kränker	der, die, das kränkste	am kränksten
kurz	kürzer	der, die, das kürzeste	am kürzesten
lang	länger	der, die, das längste	am längsten
schwarz	schwärzer	der, die, das schwärzeste	am schwärzesten
warm	wärmer	der, die, das wärmste	am wärmsten

3. A small number of adjectives have irregular forms. Of the adjectives so far employed as active words the following are irregular.

POSITIVE	COMPARATIVE	SUPERLATIVE	
groß	größer	der, die, das größte	am größten
gut	besser	der, die, das beste	am besten
hoch	höher	der, die, das höchste	am höchsten
viel	mehr	der, die, das meiste	am meisten

4. The comparative and superlative forms are declined like any other adjective.

> **der ältere Bruder**
> **mein älterer Bruder**

5. The superlative forms **der, die, das (faulste)** may be used in the predicate when a noun is distinctly understood.

> **Von allen Schülern ist Fritz der faulste (Schüler).**
> *Of all the pupils Fred is the laziest (one).*

When the superlative is used as a genuine predicate adjective, or as an adverb, the am-forms are used. These are in reality dative singular forms **(an dem längsten).**

> **Im Sommer sind die Tage am längsten.**
> *In summer the days are longest.*
>
> **Dieses Kind sang das Lied am besten.**
> *This child sang the song best.*

6. The adverb **gern** is compared irregularly.

> **Anna geht gern in die Schule.**
> *Anna likes to go to school.*
>
> **Karl geht lieber auf das Land.**
> *Karl prefers to go to the country.*
>
> **Der Vater fährt am liebsten nach Europa.**
> *Father likes most of all to go to Europe.*

7. Both the comparative and the superlative are sometimes used in an absolute manner with no actual comparison implied.

Eine ältere Dame.
An elderly lady.

Eine höchst interessante Geschichte.
A highly (most) interesting story.

8. The double comparative is rendered by **immer** + the comparative.

Es wird immer wärmer.
It is getting warmer and warmer.

9. **Wie** is used after the positive, **als** after the comparative.

Karl ist nicht so dumm **wie** Fritz.
Karl is not so stupid as Fred.

Im Sommer ist es wärmer **als** im Winter.
In summer it is warmer than in winter.

IV. QUESTIONS

1. Wer sind zwei der bekanntesten deutschen Komponisten?
2. Wer lebte früher, Beethoven oder Wagner? 3. Wer wurde am ältesten? 4. Wie arbeiteten alle beide? 5. Wo lebte Beethoven während seiner Jugend? 6. Wohin ging er später? 7. Wo starb er? 8. Wohin ging Beethoven jeden Tag? 9. Warum ging er in das Restaurant? 10. Wohin setzte er sich eines Mittags? 11. Wen grüßte er nicht? 12. Was stellte der Kellner auf den Tisch? 13. Was nahm Beethoven aus der Tasche? 14. Was tat er von Zeit zu Zeit? 15. Wie lange blieb er dort sitzen? 16. Wen rief er plötzlich? 17. Was sagte er zu dem Kellner? 18. Was antwortete der Kellner? 19. Was tat Beethoven?

V. GRAMMATICAL EXERCISES

(a) Supply the comparative and the superlative:

1. Karl ist (jung) als Fritz. Anna ist ———. 2. Im Herbst sind die Tage (kurz) als im Sommer. Im Winter sind

sie ———. 3. Der Bleistift ist (lang) als das Streichholz.
Das Bett ist ———. 4. Was tun Sie (gern), lesen oder
schreiben? Was tun Sie ———? 5. Die Mutter ist (alt)
als die Tochter. Die Großmutter ist ———. 6. Der Sonntag ist (schön) als der Montag. Die Ferien sind ———. 7.
Der Schüler spricht (laut) als die Schülerin. Der Lehrer
spricht ———. 8. Der Abend ist (warm) als der Morgen.
Der Mittag ist ———. 9. Der Junge schläft (viel) als seine
Eltern. Das Kind schläft ———. 10. Das Pferd läuft
(schnell) als die Kuh. Der Hund läuft ———. 11. Der
Wein ist (weiß) als das Bier. Die Kreide ist ———. 12.
Der Tisch ist (groß) als der Stuhl. Das Haus ist ———.
13. Die Tochter ist (klein) als die Mutter. Das Kind ist
———. 14. Die Tür ist (hoch) als der Tisch. Das Fenster
ist ———. 15. Der Bauer hat (wenig) Geld als der Wirt.
Der Student hat ———.

(b) Supply the missing endings:

1. Fritz ist der faulst— und der dümmst— Schüler in der
Klasse. 2. Ich habe nie einen fauler— und dümmer—
gesehen. 3. Wer hat sich am schnellst— angezogen? 4. Ich
habe um ein kleiner— Glas Wein gebeten. 5. Dies ist ein
kürzer— Gedicht als jenes. 6. Diese Seite war am schwerst—.

VI. TRANSLATION EXERCISES

1. Who is the laziest pupil in the class? 2. What do you
prefer to eat, meat or potatoes? 3. Karl likes to eat bread
and butter most of all. 4. The waiter put the wine on the
table. 5. The days are getting shorter and shorter. 6. He
always ate his dinner in a certain restaurant. 7. The train
has not yet arrived. 8. This is the most interesting story I
have read. 9. During the winter I work more diligently than
during the summer. 10. Again and again he wrote something in his notebook. 11. The dog followed me home. 12.
In which month are the days shortest? 13. I sat down at my
usual place. 14. The table is higher than the bed, but the
door is highest. 15. Without the medicine he will not sleep.

VII. VOCABULARY BUILDING

While the recognition of cognates will aid you in remembering many words, there are also certain pitfalls. A number of words, while originally related, have developed entirely different meanings. The following is only a partial list.

GERMAN	ENGLISH	COGNATE
die Allee′	the avenue	alley
also	therefore	also
der Artist′	the acrobat	artist
blank	polished, bright	blank
denn	for	then
famos′	excellent	famous
fatal′	disagreeable, annoying	fatal
der Feind	the enemy	fiend
handeln	to act	handle
der Knabe	the boy	knave
die Mappe	the portfolio	map
namentlich	especially	namely
weil	because	while
die Zeit	the time	tide
das Zimmer	the room	timber

VIII. SUPPLEMENTARY READING

Bodensee und Schwarzwald

Von Oberammergau fuhr die Familie Braun an den Bodensee. Das ist der größte See im Gebiet der deutschen Sprache. Deutschland, Österreich und die Schweiz grenzen an ihn. Das südliche Schweizer Ufer ist hügeliger und waldiger als das Nordufer, aber von diesem hat man eine schönere Aussicht. An klaren Tagen sieht man die ganze Kette der Schweizer Schneeberge. An dem Ostteil des Sees liegt auf einer Insel die Stadt Lindau. Dort ging die Familie Braun auf einen Dampfer und fuhr nach Westen, vorüber an Friedrichshafen, wo einst Graf Zeppelin seine Luftschiffe baute, und an dem malerischen Städtchen Meersburg. Dort wohnte in ihren

letzten Lebensjahren die Dichterin Annette von Droste-
Hülshoff, die in der deutschen Literatur so bekannt ist wie
Emily Dickinson in der amerikanischen.   In Konstanz verließ
die Familie Braun das Schiff und fuhr in den Schwarzwald.
„Jetzt werden wir einmal reisen, wie ich das in meiner Jugend
getan habe," sagte Herr Braun, „nämlich zu Fuß. Wir
kaufen uns Rucksäcke, in die wir die nötigsten Dinge packen.
Die Koffer schicken wir voraus nach Baden-Baden.   Ein gut
markierter Weg führt von Basel aus nach Norden, wir folgen
ihm einfach und kommen sicher zu den schönsten Punkten."
So geschah es auch, und die Familie wanderte tagelang über
weite Höhen, durch dunkle Tannenwälder und grüne Wiesen-
täler, in denen die malerischen Bauernhäuser mit weit über-
hängenden mächtigen Dächern standen.   Über Nacht blieben sie in einfachen kleinen Gasthäusern, die sehr billig waren.
Am Sonntag sahen sie die bunten Kostüme, die die Schwarzwälder Bäuerinnen tragen, wenn sie in die Kirche gehen.
Manchmal fuhren sie auch in einem Autobus, wenn sie müde
waren.   Der Schwarzwald gefiel ihnen sehr gut, aber sie
freuten sich doch, als sie schließlich in Baden-Baden ankamen.
Das ist der bekannteste und eleganteste Kurort in Deutschland, den Menschen aus allen Ländern gern besuchen.   Hier
blieb die Familie Braun einige Zeit und machte Ausflüge in
die weitere Umgebung.

IX. SUPPLEMENTARY VOCABULARY

**an-grenzen, grenzte an, ist
angegrenzt** to border upon
der Ausflug, -(e)s, ⁀e the outing, picnic; **einen Ausflug
machen** to take a trip (for
pleasure)
der Autobus, -ses, -se the
motor-bus
(das) Baden-Baden, -s (city
of) Baden-Baden
(das) Basel, -s (city of) Basle

die Bäuerin, -, -nen the peasant woman
das Bauernhaus, -es, ⁀er the
peasant's house
der Bodensee, -s the Lake of
Constance
bunt gay-colored
die Dichterin, -, -nen the
poetess
elegant′ elegant
sich freuen to be pleased

(das) Friedrichshafen, -s (town of) Friedrichshafen

das Gasthaus, -es, ⁼er the inn

hügelig hilly

die Insel, -, -n the island

(das) Konstanz (town of) Constance

das Kostüm, -s, -e the costume

der Kurort, -(e)s, -e *or* ⁼er the watering-place, spa

das Lebensjahr, -(e)s, -e the year of one's life

(das) Lindau, -s (city of) Lindau

die Literatur', - the literature

das Luftschiff, -(e)s, -e the airship

manchmal sometimes

markiert' marked

(das) Meersburg, -s (town of) Meersburg

nämlich namely, that is to say

das Nordufer, -s, - the north shore

nötig necessary

der Ostteil, -(e)s, -e the eastern part

der Rucksack, -s, ⁼e the knapsack

das Schiff, -(e)s, -e the ship, boat

schließlich finally, at last

der Schneeberg, -(e)s, -e the snow-capped mountain

Schwarzwälder Black Forest (*adj.*)

Schweizer Swiss (*adj.*)

sicher certain(ly), sure(ly)

die Sprache, -, -n the language, speech

das Städtchen, -s, - the small town

tagelang day after day

der Tannenwald, -(e)s, ⁼er the fir-wood

überhängend overhanging

verlas'sen, verließ, hat verlassen, er verläßt to leave, desert

voraus in front, on ahead

vorüber along by, past

waldig wooded

wandern (sein) to travel (on foot), wander

das Wiesental, -(e)s, ⁼er the fertile valley

Aufgabe Zwanzig

Numerals. Time Expressions. Prepositions

I. READING SELECTION

Das Zählen

Die Zahlen von eins bis neunzehn haben Sie schon gelernt und heute haben wir Aufgabe zwanzig. Die übrigen Zahlen sind nicht sehr schwer. Man zählt weiter: einundzwanzig, zweiundzwanzig, dreiundzwanzig, usw. Aber die Zahl für 30 ist nicht dreizig, sondern dreißig. Man sagt auch nicht sechszig für 60, sondern sechzig, und für 70 gewöhnlich nicht siebenzig, sondern siebzig. Wenn Sie jetzt noch die Zahlen hundert und tausend lernen, dann können Sie leicht bis zu einer Million zählen.

Die vier Jahreszeiten haben Sie auch schon gelernt: der Frühling, der Sommer, der Herbst, der Winter. Ein Jahr hat zwölf Monate. Die Monate heißen: der Januar, der Februar, der März, der April, der Mai, der Juni, der Juli, der August, der September, der Oktober, der November, der Dezember. Ein Jahr hat dreihundertfünfundsechzig Tage und zweiundfünfzig Wochen. Eine Woche hat sieben Tage. Die Tage der Woche heißen: der Sonntag, der Montag, der Dienstag, der Mittwoch, der Donnerstag, der Freitag, der Sonnabend (oder Samstag).

Wenn heute Mittwoch ist, dann war gestern Dienstag und vorgestern Montag. Heute über acht Tage ist es dann auch Mittwoch. Morgen über acht Tage ist es Donnerstag. Wenn heute Donnerstag ist, dann ist es morgen Freitag und übermorgen Sonnabend. Heute vor acht Tagen war es auch Donnerstag. Gestern vor acht Tagen war es Mittwoch.

Ein Tag hat vierundzwanzig Stunden. Eine Stunde hat

sechzig Minuten. Eine Minute hat sechzig Sekunden. Die Tageszeiten sind der Morgen, der Vormittag, der Mittag, der Nachmittag, der Abend, die Nacht, die Mitternacht. Der Mittag ist zwischen dem Vormittag und dem Nachmittag. Der Abend ist zwischen dem Nachmittag und der Nacht. Gegen Abend wird es dunkel, gegen Morgen wird es wieder hell. Dienstag ist der **dritte** Tag der Woche. August ist der **achte** Monat des Jahres. Wenn heute der **vierte** Dezember ist, dann war gestern der **dritte** und vorgestern der **zweite** Dezember. Heute über acht Tage ist dann der **elfte** Dezember, in vierzehn Tagen der **achtzehnte** Dezember. Weihnachten ist immer am **fünfundzwanzigsten** Dezember, der Tag vor Weihnachten oder Weihnachtsabend ist der **vierundzwanzigste** Dezember, und der Tag nach Weihnachten ist der **sechsundzwanzigste** Dezember. Der letzte Tag des Jahres ist der **einunddreißigste** Dezember. Am **ersten** Januar ist Neujahr.

> Dreißig Tage hat November,
> April, Juni und September.
> Februar hat viermal sieben.
> Alle, die noch übrig blieben,
> Haben einunddreißig.

Die Zeit

sieben Uhr

(ein) Viertel nach sieben
(ein) Viertel acht
(ein) Viertel auf acht
sieben Uhr fünfzehn

halb acht
sieben Uhr dreißig

(ein) Viertel vor acht	zehn Minuten vor	zwanzig Minuten
drei Viertel acht	acht	nach acht
drei Viertel auf acht	sieben Uhr fünfzig	acht Uhr zwanzig
sieben Uhr fünfund-vierzig		

Karl steht morgens um sieben Uhr auf. Dann nimmt er ein Bad. Um viertel acht (viertel auf acht, viertel nach sieben) ist er damit fertig. Dann zieht er sich an. Um halb acht ißt er sein Frühstück. Um dreiviertel acht (dreiviertel auf acht, viertel vor acht) ist er auch damit fertig. Um zehn Minuten vor acht fängt er an, seine Aufgaben zu lernen. Später fragt er seine Mutter: „Wieviel Uhr ist es?" Sie antwortet: „Zwanzig Minuten nach acht." Dann geht Karl zur Schule, denn die Schule fängt um halb neun an.

II. VOCABULARY

*Idioms
- heute (gestern) vor acht Tagen   a week ago today (yesterday)
- heute (morgen) über acht Tage   a week from today (tomorrow)
- wieviel Uhr ist es?   what time is it?

der April', - or -s, -e April
der August', - or -es, -e August
das Bad, -(e)s, ̈er the bath
der Dezem'ber, - or -s, - December
*der Donnerstag, -(e)s, -e Thursday
*dreißig thirty

*dritt third
der Februar, - or -s, -e February
fertig finished, ready
*gegen (+ acc.) against, towards, about, compared with
halb half
hell light, bright, clear

*hundert hundred; **das Hundert, -s, -e** the hundred

die Jahreszeit, -, -en the time of year, season

der Januar, - *or* **-s, -e** January

der Ju′li, - *or* **-s, -s** July

der Ju′ni, - *or* **-s, -s** June

*letzt last

der Mai, - *or* **-(e)s, -e** May

der März, -en *or* **-** *or* **-es, -e** March

*die Million′, -, -en the million

die Mitternacht, -, ̈e the midnight

morgens in the morning

*der Nachmittag, -s, -e the afternoon

das Neujahr, -(e)s, -e the New Year

der Novem′ber, - *or* **-s, -** November

der Okto′ber, - *or* **-s, -** October

der Samstag, -(e)s, -e Saturday

*sechzig sixty

*die Sekun′de, -, -n the second

der Septem′ber, - *or* **-s, -** September

*der Sonnabend, -s, -e Saturday

die Tageszeit, -, -en the time of day

*tausend thousand; **das Tausend, -s, -e** the thousand

*übermorgen day after tomorrow

übrig remaining left

viermal four times

*das Viertel, -s, - the quarter

*vorgestern day before yesterday

*der Vormittag, -s, -e the forenoon

*die Weihnacht, -, *or* **die Weihnachten, -, -** Christmas

der Weihnachtsabend, -s, -e Christmas eve

weiter-zählen to continue to count

die Zahl, -, -en the number

*zählen to count

*zwanzig twenty

*zwischen (+ *dat.* or *acc.*) between

III. GRAMMAR

A. Numerals

	CARDINALS	ORDINALS
1	eins	der, die, das **erste**
2	zwei	zweite
3	drei	**dritte**
4	vier	vierte
5	fünf	fünfte
6	sechs	sechste

CARDINALS		ORDINALS
7	sieben	sieb(en)te
8	acht	**achte**
9	neun	neunte
10	zehn	zehnte
11	elf	elfte
12	zwölf	zwölfte
13	dreizehn	dreizehnte
14	vierzehn	vierzehnte
15	fünfzehn	fünfzehnte
16	**sechzehn**	sechzehnte
17	**siebzehn**	siebzehnte
18	achtzehn	achtzehnte
19	neunzehn	neunzehnte
20	**zwanzig**	**zwanzigste**
21	einundzwanzig	einundzwanzigste
22	zweiundzwanzig	zweiundzwanzigste
23	dreiundzwanzig	dreiundzwanzigste
30	**dreißig**	dreißigste
40	vierzig	vierzigste
50	fünfzig	fünfzigste
60	**sechzig**	sechzigste
70	**siebzig**	siebzigste
80	achtzig	achtzigste
90	neunzig	neunzigste
100	hundert	hundertste
101	hundertundeins	hundertunderste
102	hundertundzwei	hundertundzweite
200	zweihundert	zweihundertste
1000	tausend	tausendste
1 000 000	eine Million	millionste

1. Cardinals.

(a) The form **eins** is used in counting, **eins, zwei, drei, vier, fünf,** etc., and with expressions of time when the noun **Uhr** is omitted.

> **Es ist eins.**
> *It is one (o'clock).*

> **Es ist halb eins.**
> *It is half past twelve.*

(b) Note the irregular forms **sechzehn, siebzehn, zwanzig, dreißig, sechzig, siebzig.**

(c) All numbers are written as one word.

Ein Jahr hat dreihundert(und)fünfundsechzig Tage.

2. Ordinals.

(a) Ordinals are formed by adding the ending **-te** to the cardinals from 2–19, and **-ste** from 20 on.

(b) Note the irregular forms **erste, dritte, (siebte), achte.**

(c) Ordinals are declined like attributive adjectives.

(d) A period after an Arabic or Roman figure indicates that it is an ordinal and the reader must supply the correct form.

der 5. (fünfte) Dezember
Wilhelm I. (der Erste)

(e) Dates of letters, indicating definite time, are in the accusative.

Berlin, den 9. (neunten) November 1955

Note that there is no comma between the month and the year.

B. Time Expressions

In ordinary German usage the half-hour is always indicated by looking forward to the next hour.

Es ist halb acht (7:30).

This is also the usual practice when indicating the quarter-hours.

(ein) Viertel (auf) acht (7:15)
drei Viertel (auf) acht (7:45)

In referring to railroad schedules German resembles English usage except that the twenty-four hour system is used, beginning at midnight.

Neunzehn Uhr fünfundzwanzig (7:25 P.M.)

C. Prepositions

1. While there are numerous prepositions governing the genitive case, the only one so far designated as an active word is **während** *during*. Two other fairly common prepositions requiring the genitive are **anstatt** (**statt**) *instead of* and **wegen** *on account of*

2. The following prepositions governing the dative have all been employed and designated as active words.

> **aus**   *out, of, from*
> **außer**   *besides, except*
> **bei**   *by, at, near, with, at the house of*
> **mit**   *with, by, at*
> **nach**   *toward, to, for, after, according to*
> **seit**   *since*
> **von**   *from, of, by*
> **zu**   *to, at, for, in, with*

3. The following prepositions governing the accusative have all been used and designated as active.

> **bis**   *to, as far as, until*
> **durch**   *through, by, by means of*
> **für**   *for*
> **gegen**   *against, towards, compared with, about*
> **ohne**   *without*
> **um**   *about, around, by, after, at, for*

4. The following governing either the dative or the accusative have been designated as active. Concerning the use of the dative or accusative, cf. Lesson III.

> **an**   *on, at, by, along, in, to, near*
> **auf**   *on, upon, at, in, to, for*
> **in**   *in, at, into, to, within*
> **über**   *over, at, above, concerning*
> **vor**   *before, in front of, from, for, ago*
> **zwischen**   *between*

To this group belong also the following three, not yet designated as active words.

Rothenburg ob der Tauber: das Hegereiterhaus im Spitalhof

Heidelberg am Neckar

Heidelberg: Blick von dem Philosophenweg auf die Stadt

Der Römer in Frankfurt a.M.

hinter *behind*
neben *next to, near, beside*
unter *under, below, among*

IV. QUESTIONS

1. Welche Aufgabe haben wir heute? 2. Welche Zahlen haben Sie schon gelernt? 3. Wie zählt man von zwanzig weiter? 4. Welches sind die vier Jahreszeiten? 5. Wie viele Monate hat ein Jahr? 6. Wie viele Tage hat ein Jahr? 7. Wie viele Wochen hat ein Jahr? 8. Wie viele Tage hat eine Woche? 9. Wie heißen die Tage der Woche? 10. Was war vorgestern, wenn heute Sonnabend ist? 11. Was ist übermorgen, wenn heute Freitag ist? 12. Was war gestern vor acht Tagen? 13. Was ist morgen über acht Tage? 14. Wie viele Stunden hat ein Tag? 15. Wie viele Minuten hat eine Stunde? 16. Wie viele Sekunden hat eine Minute? 17. Welche Tageszeit ist zwischen dem Vormittag und dem Nachmittag? 18. Welches ist der fünfte Tag der Woche? 19. Welcher Tag ist Weihnachten? 20. Wann ist Neujahr? 21. Wieviel Uhr ist es jetzt? 22. Wann fängt diese Stunde an? 23. Wann stehen Sie gewöhnlich auf? 24. Wann gehen Sie zur Schule? 25. Wann gehen Sie gewöhnlich zu Bett?

V. GRAMMATICAL EXERCISES

(a) Read (or write out) the following sentences:

1. In unserer Schule sind 687 Schüler. 2. Die Schule fing am 25. September an. 3. Heute vor acht Tagen war der 3. Januar. 4. 30 und 30 macht 60. 5. Kolumbus kam im Jahre 1492 nach Amerika. 6. 26 weniger 9 ist 17. 7. Der 22. Februar 1732 ist George Washingtons Geburtstag (*birthday*). 8. Goethes Geburtstag ist der 28. August 1749. 9. George Washington war also 17 Jahre älter als Goethe. 10. Ein Jahr hat 365 Tage. 10. Der letzte Tag des Jahres ist der 31. Dezember. 12. Karl steht jeden Morgen um 7.15 auf. 13. Der Zug nach Berlin fährt um 9.45 ab. 14. 12 mal (*times*) 12 ist 144. 15. Morgen über acht Tage ist der 18.

Januar. 16. Friedrich II. lebte von 1712 bis 1786. 17. Der Zug kam um 12.30 in Hamburg an.

(b) Supply the correct endings:

1. D— Amerikanerin wohnte bei ein— lieb— Freundin. 2. D— Gast bat den Wirt um ein— gut— Wein. 3. D— klein— Kind fürchtete sich vor d— schwarz— Katze. 4. Während d— schön— Herbstes blieb d— Familie auf d— Lande. 5. D— Wirt stellte d— Glas Bier auf d— Tisch. 6. D— Kind saß zwischen d— Großvater und d— Großmutter. 7. Anna hat heute ein— Brief von ihr— alt— Freundin bekommen. 8. Auf d— Wege zu— Schule gingen die Schüler durch ein— groß— Park. 9. D— Eltern gingen mit d— Kindern in d— Stadt. 10. Seit jen— Augenblick habe ich ihn nicht gesehen. 11. D— arm— Mann hat zwei Mark für d— Brot und d— Butter bezahlt. 12. Man trinkt aus ein— Glas.

VI. TRANSLATION EXERCISES

In the following sentences write out all the numerals:
1. An hour has 60 minutes or 3600 seconds. 2. The train arrived at 4:30, but I was at the station at 4:20. 3. At what time did you get up? 4. Goethe was 83 years old when he died in the year 1832. 5. Schiller was 46 years old when he died in the year 1805. 6. A week ago today it was the 23rd. 7. A week from today it will be the 30th. 8. Seven months have 31 days, four have 30 days, and one month usually has 28 days. 9. Saturday is the seventh day of the week. 10. It is almost 300 kilometers from Berlin to Hamburg. 11. About four million people live in Berlin. 12. We ate our breakfast at 7:45. 13. The vacation lasted 13 weeks. 14. Day before yesterday was the last day of the month. 15. This is the third book which I bought this week.

VII. VOCABULARY BUILDING

Compound words, i.e., words composed of two or more independent elements, are far more common in German than in

English. The last element in such compounds is the basic one and determines the gender of the noun. When you meet such words, try to resolve them into their component parts.
1. The most frequent combination is that of two or more nouns.

der Abendsonnenschein the evening sunshine
die Hafenstadt the harbor city, port
der Herbstnachmittag the autumn afternoon
das Vaterland the fatherland, native country

2. Compounds may consist of an adjective and a noun.

das Freigepäck the free baggage
die Großstadt the cosmopolitan city
der Schnellzug the express train
der Schwarzwald the Black Forest

3. Compounds may be formed from a verb and a noun.

das Schreibpapier the writing paper, stationery
der Spazierstock the walking stick, cane
die Studierlampe the study lamp
der Zeigefinger the pointing finger, index finger

4. Compounds may be formed from a preposition (or adverb) and a noun.

der Hintergrund the background
der Oberkellner the head waiter
der Übermensch the superman
die Unterwelt the underworld

5. Compounds may be formed from two adjectives.

altmodisch old-fashioned
dunkelblau dark blue
hellfarbig light-colored
weitbekannt widely known

VIII. SUPPLEMENTARY READING

Rothenburg ob der Tauber

In früheren Zeiten besuchten die meisten Amerikaner die Stadt Nürnberg, weil sie ein so klares Bild von dem Charakter der alten deutschen Städte, von ihrem Reichtum und ihrem Interesse für Kunst gab. Aber die Bomben des zweiten Weltkrieges haben sie fast vollständig zerstört. Die Familie Braun fuhr daher in eine kleinere aber ebenso malerische Stadt, Rothenburg ob der Tauber. Sie liegt auf der Höhe am Rande eines Tales, durch das die Tauber, ein kleines Flüßchen, fließt. Aus dem Tal steigt man zu der Stadt hinauf und passiert verschiedene alte Tore, bevor man in das Innere der Stadt kommt. Sie ist ganz von Mauern und Türmen umgeben; vor den Mauern sind breite Gräben, die früher mit Wasser gefüllt waren. Die Familie Braun ging auf den Mauern beinahe um die ganze Stadt herum und schaute auf die braunen und roten Dächer der alten Häuser hinab. Eine große gotische Kirche, die St. Jakobskirche, beherrscht das Stadtbild und ist von überall her zu sehen. Sie stammt aus dem 14. Jahrhundert. In ihr befindet sich ein geschnitzter Altar von Tilmann Riemenschneider (1460–1531), einem berühmten Bildhauer. Er lebte in derselben Zeit wie der große Nürnberger Maler Albrecht Dürer (1473–1528), dessen Werke in den Museen der ganzen Welt zu sehen sind. Riemenschneider arbeitete in der gotischen Tradition, während Dürer dem Renaissancestil nahe kam.

In der alten Zeit war Rothenburg eine freie Reichsstadt wie Hamburg und Bremen, d.h. es gehorchte nur dem Kaiser, aber keinem anderen Fürsten. Im 16. Jahrhundert war es reich, aber in dem 30 jährigen Krieg (1618–1648) verlor es seinen Reichtum und verarmte. Da es keine Industrie hatte und von der Eisenbahn entfernt lag, blieb es auch im 19. Jahrhundert genau so, wie es früher gewesen war. Selten kam ein Reisender nach Rothenburg, das Leben war sehr still, Gras wuchs auf den Straßen. Lange Zeit war es vergessen, bis um 1860 Maler und Dichter seine Schönheit wiederentdeckten und der Welt davon erzählten.

IX. SUPPLEMENTARY VOCABULARY

der Altar', -s, ⸚e   the altar
sich befinden, befand sich, hat
  sich befunden   to be, feel; to
  be found
beherrschen   to command
bevor   before
das Bild, -es, -er   the picture
die Bombe, -, -n   the bomb
ebenso   just so, equally
entfernt   distant, away
fast   almost
das Flüßchen, -s, -   the rivulet,
  stream
füllen   to fill
der Fürst, -en, -en   the prince
gehorchen (+ dat.)   to obey
geschnitzt   carved
gotisch   gothic
der Graben, -s, ⸚   the ditch,
  moat
das Gras, -es, ⸚er   the grass
herum   around
hinab   down, downwards
hinauf-steigen, stieg hinauf, ist
  hinaufgestiegen   to mount,
  ascend
das Innere, -n   the interior,
  inside
das Interes'se, n, n   the interest
das Leben, -s, -   the life
der Maler, -s, -   the painter
die Mauer, -, -n   the wall
nah(e)   near
(das) Nürnberg, -s   (city of)
  Nuremberg
Nürnberger   Nuremberg (adj.)

passie'ren (sein)   to pass
der Rand, -es, ⸚er   the edge,
  brink
die Reichsstadt, -, ⸚e   the imperial city
der Reichtum, -(e)s, ⸚er   the
  wealth
der Renaissancestil, -(e)s   the
  Renaissance style
(das) Rothenburg ob der
  Tauber, -s   (city of) Rothenburg-on-the-Tauber
die St. Jakobskirche, -   the
  Church of St. Jacob
schauen   to look, gaze
die Schönheit, -   the beauty
selten   seldom, rare(ly)
das Stadtbild, -es, -er   the
  view of the city
stammen (sein)   to stem from,
  date back to
die Tauber, -   the Tauber
  (river on which Rothenburg is
  situated)
das Tor, -(e)s, -e   the gateway,
  gate
die Tradition', -, -nen   the
  tradition
verarmen (sein)   to become
  poor
verlieren, verlor, hat verloren
  to lose
verschieden   different, various
vollständig   complete(ly)
das Wasser, -s, -   the water
wiederentdecken   to discover
  again (insep.)

Aufgabe Einundzwanzig

Modal Auxiliaries

I. READING SELECTION

Der fleißige Student

Ein junger Mann, den wir Fritz Müller nennen **wollen** und der in einer kleinen Stadt in Deutschland lebte, **wollte** in der großen Stadt Berlin studieren, aber er **konnte** das nicht, weil er arm war und kein Geld hatte. Also **mußte** er zu Hause bleiben und arbeiten. Das gefiel ihm gar nicht. Eines Tages dachte er an einen Onkel und eine Tante, die in einer anderen Stadt lebten und ziemlich reich waren. Also schrieb er an seinen Onkel: ,,Ich **möchte** gern in Berlin auf der Universität studieren, aber seit mein Vater gestorben ist, **muß** ich arbeiten. **Kannst** Du[1] mir nicht helfen? Du **sollst** mit mir zufrieden sein.`` Der Onkel schickte ihm dreihundert Mark und schrieb: ,,Ich **will** Dir gerne helfen. Jeden Monat werde ich Dir dreihundert Mark schicken, aber Du **darfst** nicht faul sein, sondern Du **mußt** fleißig studieren, sonst bekommst Du kein Geld mehr.``

Fritz Müller war sehr glücklich. Er reiste sogleich nach Berlin, wo er das Leben sehr angenehm fand, besonders da er Geld hatte. Es gab so viel Neues und Interessantes zu sehen. Fritz war selten zu Hause. Er ging fleißig ins Theater, ins Kino, in Cafés und Restaurants, aber zur Universität ging er nicht.

Eines Tages kam sein Onkel nach Berlin, um ihn zu besuchen. Fritz erzählte viel von der Universität, den Professoren und Studenten. Der Onkel sagte: ,,Ich freue mich, daß du so fleißig bist, aber jetzt **will** ich selber etwas von der

[1] In letters the familiar pronouns are capitalized.

Stadt sehen, denn ich bin das erste Mal hier. **Kannst** du mir nicht etwas von der Stadt zeigen?" Also machten sie einen langen Spaziergang und Fritz zeigte seinem Onkel allerlei Sehenswürdigkeiten. Als sie an einem großen Gebäude vorbeikamen, fragte der Onkel: „Weißt du, was dieses Gebäude ist?" „Nein," antwortete Fritz, „das kenne ich nicht, denn ich bin noch nicht in dieser Gegend gewesen. Aber der Schutzmann dort wird es wissen." Also fragte er den Schutzmann: „**Können** Sie uns vielleicht sagen, was dieses Gebäude ist?" „Gewiß," antwortete der Schutzmann, „das ist die Universität."

II. VOCABULARY

*Idioms {
es gefällt mir (dir, ihm, usw.) I (you, he, etc.) like it
denken an (+ acc.) to think of (someone)
(einen Brief) schreiben an (+ acc.) to write (a letter) to
kein Geld (Brot, usw.) mehr no more money (bread, etc.)
}

allerlei all sorts of (things)
angenehm agreeable
das Café, -s, -s the café
*denken, dachte, hat gedacht to think
*dürfen, durfte, hat gedurft, er darf to be permitted
*sich freuen to be pleased
Fritz Fred
das Gebäu'de, -s, - the building
gefallen, gefiel, hat gefallen, er (es) gefällt (+ dat.) to please
die Gegend, -, -en the region, district
*glücklich happy
*helfen, half, hat geholfen, er hilft (+ dat.) to help
*kennen, kannte, hat gekannt to know, be acquainted with

das Ki'no, -s, -s the moving-picture theatre
*können, konnte, hat gekonnt, er kann to be able, can
das Leben, -s, - the life
*das Mal, -(e)s, -e or mal time(s); das erste Mal or das erstemal the first time
*mögen, mochte, hat gemocht, er mag to care for, to like, may; er möchte he would like
*müssen, mußte, hat gemußt, er muß to be obliged, must
*nennen, nannte, hat genannt to name, call
*der Onkel, -s, - the uncle
der Schutzmann, -(e)s, ̈er or die Schutzleute the policeman

die Se'henswürdigkeit, -, -en
thing worth seeing, object of
interest
*selten seldom, rare
sogleich' at once
*sollen, sollte, hat gesollt, er
soll shall, ought, to be to,
to be said to
*sonst otherwise, usually,
formerly
*die Tante, -, -n the aunt

das Thea'ter, -s, - the theatre
vorbei-kommen, kam vorbei,
ist vorbeigekommen an
(+ dat.) to pass
*weil (conj.) because
*wissen, wußte, hat gewußt, er
weiß to know (a fact)
*wollen, wollte, hat gewollt, er
will will, wish, want, be
about to, try to, claim to
*zeigen to show

III. GRAMMAR

A. Modal Auxiliaries

dürfen	können	mögen	müssen	sollen	wollen

PRESENT TENSE

	dürfen	können	mögen	müssen	sollen	wollen
Sing.	ich darf du darfst er darf	ich kann du kannst er kann	ich mag du magst er mag	ich muß du mußt er muß	ich soll du sollst er soll	ich will du willst er will
Plural	Regular					

PAST TENSE

ich durfte	ich konnte	ich mochte	ich mußte	ich sollte	ich wollte

FUTURE

ich werde dürfen, können, etc.

PRESENT PERFECT

ich habe gedurft or dürfen, gekonnt or können, etc.

PAST PERFECT

ich hatte gedurft or dürfen, gekonnt or können, etc.

1. All the modal auxiliaries except **sollen** change their stem vowels in the singular of the present indicative. The plural, however, is formed from the infinitive stem.
2. In the past tense all the modals have the regular endings of the weak conjugation, but none of them has Umlaut. In addition the **g** in the stem of **mögen** is changed to **ch**.
3. There are two possibilities of forming the present perfect and past perfect tenses, one with the regular past participle of the weak conjugation without Umlaut, the other with a past participle that is identical with the infinitive. The latter is used only with a dependent infinitive.

Er hat es gedurft.
He was allowed to.

Er hat gehen dürfen.
He was allowed to go.

4. When a modal auxiliary has a dependent infinitive the latter is used without **zu**.

Er muß nach Hause gehen.
He must go home.
He has to go home.

5. The verbs **helfen, hören, sehen** and **lassen** (*let*) resemble the modals in two respects. They take a dependent infinitive without **zu**, and they substitute the infinitive form for the past participle when they have a dependent infinitive without **zu**.

Ich habe ihn singen hören.
I heard him sing(ing)

6. The fundamental meaning of the modal auxiliaries is fairly definite and can be more or less clearly defined. The chief difficulty arises from the fact that, whereas in German they have a full conjugation, their English cognates are extremely defective in inflections. Consequently numerous paraphrases must be used to render the German forms adequately into English.

(a) **Dürfen** implies permission. The negative **nicht dür-fen** is rendered by *must not.*

Er darf hier bleiben.
He is permitted to stay here.
He may stay here.

Sie dürfen hier nicht rauchen.
You are not permitted to smoke here.
You must not smoke here.

(b) **Können** implies ability or possibility.

Er kann gut lesen.
He can read well.
He is able to read well.

Das kann wahr sein.
That may be true.
It is possible that that is true.

(c) **Mögen** expresses inclination, liking, and also possibility or concession.

Ich mag das nicht tun.
I don't care to do that.

Ich mag dieses Buch nicht.
I don't like this book.
I don't care for this book.

Das mag sein.
That may be (so).

(d) **Müssen** expresses necessity or moral obligation and is usually translated by *must* or *have to.*

Ich muß jetzt nach Hause gehen.
I must go home now.
I have to go home now.

Ich muß das tun.
I must do that.
I have to do that.
I am obliged to do that.

(e) **Sollen** implies an obligation imposed by an outside agency, such as a commandment, or an assertion.

Du sollst nicht stehlen.
Thou shalt not steal.
You are commanded not to steal.

Ich soll um neun Uhr zu Hause sein.
I am (expected, told, commanded) to be home at nine o'clock.

Herr Braun soll sehr reich sein.
Mr. Braun is said to be very rich.

(f) **Wollen** expresses volition, intention, determination; it also translates *to claim* and *to be about to*.

Ich will morgen früh aufstehen.
I want (intend, am determined) to get up early tomorrow.

Er will das gesehen haben.
He claims to have seen that.

Ich wollte eben einen Brief an Sie schreiben.
I was just about to write a letter to you.
I was just on the point of writing a letter to you.

B. Wissen, kennen, können

1. **Wissen** means to know a fact.

    Weißt du das?
    Do you know that?

    Weißt du, wann er kommt?
    Do you know when he is coming?

2. **Kennen** means to be acquainted with.

    Kennen Sie Herrn Braun?
    Do you know Mr. Braun?

3. **Können** is also used to express knowledge of a language, the verbs *to speak, read, write* being understood.

    Ich kann Deutsch und Englisch.
    I know German and English.

C. Conjugation of wissen

Wissen is conjugated like the modal auxiliaries in the present tense and like a weak verb in all other tenses according to the principal parts given in the vocabulary.

ich weiß	wir wissen
du weißt	ihr wißt
er weiß	sie wissen

IV. QUESTIONS

1. Wo lebte Fritz Müller? 2. Was wollte er tun? 3. Warum konnte er das nicht? 4. Was mußte er also tun? 5. Wie gefiel ihm das? 6. An wen dachte er eines Tages? 7. Wie war dieser Onkel? 8. Was tat Fritz eines Tages? 9. Was versprach ihm der Onkel? 10. Wie durfte Fritz nicht sein? 11. Was bekam er sonst nicht? 12. Wie war Fritz, als er den Brief bekam? 13. Wohin reiste er? 14. Was gab es dort zu sehen? 15. Wo war Fritz selten? 16. Wohin ging er aber nicht? 17. Was tat sein Onkel eines Tages? 18. Wovon erzählte Fritz viel? 19. Welches Gebäude kannte Fritz nicht?

V. GRAMMATICAL EXERCISES

(a) Supply the present and past tenses of the modal auxiliaries given in parentheses:

1. Ich (dürfen) das Fenster nicht aufmachen. 2. Du (wollen) nicht früh aufstehen. 3. Annas Freundin (mögen) nicht allein gehen. 4. Ich (können) die Geschichte erzählen. 5. Wir (müssen) fleißig arbeiten. 6. Er (sollen) seinem Freunde einen Brief schicken.

(b) Change the following sentences to the past, future, and perfect tenses:

1. Er muß das Gedicht auswendig lernen. 2. Der Gast will eine Weile schlafen. 3. Niemand darf in diesem Zimmer rauchen. 4. Das Kind mag die Katze nicht. 5. Ich kann keinen Platz finden. 6. Der Schüler soll immer laut und deutlich lesen.

(c) Supply correct forms for the English words in parentheses:

1. Er (wanted to) schlafen, aber er (could) nicht. 2. Das (must) nicht wieder geschehen. 3. (Shall) ich dieses Gedicht auswendig lernen? 4. (May) ich einen Augenblick hier bleiben? 5. Der Gast (had to) seine Rechnung bezahlen. 6. Er (may) recht haben. 7. Sie (must) nicht lachen, wenn ich das sage. 8. Es (is said to) dort im Winter viel regnen. 9. Er (claims to) es gesehen haben. 10. Das Kind (was to) um drei Uhr zu Hause sein. 11. Ich (know) Deutsch. 12. (Do you know), wer heute hier war? 13. Der Doktor (knows) viele Leute. 14. Er (intends to) fleißig studieren. 15. Sie (was permitted) ihren Großvater und ihre Großmutter besuchen. 16. Der Lehrer hat dem Schüler die Aufgabe schreiben (helped). 17. Fritz hat in Berlin auf der Universität studieren (was permitted).

VI. TRANSLATION EXERCISES

1. One day a young man thought of his uncle. 2. He wanted to study at the university, but he had no money. 3. He had to work, which he did not like at all. 4. Fred was happy, because he received a letter from his uncle. 5. He does not know what time it is. 6. Do you know many people here? 7. I do not care for this picture. 8. He could not read the letter. 9. The poor student had no more money. 10. The parents named their son Fred. 11. He was to get up early, but he didn't (did it not). 12. I am sorry that I cannot help you. 13. The uncle was pleased that Fred was so diligent. 14. Can you show me the university? 15. You must not smoke here.

VII. VOCABULARY BUILDING

Both simple and compound forms of the infinitive may be used as neuter nouns. They are always capitalized. They denote the activity itself rather than the result of the activity.

das **Aufstehen**   the getting up
das **Bezahlen**   the paying
das **Erzählen**   the telling
das **Fragen**   the asking
das **Geben**   the giving
das **Lachen**   the laughing (laughter)
das **Lesen**   the reading
das **Rauchen**   the smoking
das **Reisen**   the traveling
das **Schlafen**   the sleeping
das **Schreiben**   the writing
das **Singen**   the singing

VIII. SUPPLEMENTARY READING

Maulbronn

Ein anderer Ausflug führte die Familie Braun nach Maulbronn. „Was ist Maulbronn?" fragten Karl und Anna. „Wartet nur," antwortete Herr Braun. Nach einigen Stunden Autofahrt kamen sie nach Maulbronn. „Ich kann nicht verstehen," sagte Frau Braun, „warum du uns in dieses kleine Dorf führst. Es ist nicht so malerisch wie Rothenburg." „Warte nur," erwiderte Herr Braun, „dieser Marktplatz ist nicht weniger hübsch." In diesem Augenblick begann ein starkes Gewitter, und die Familie Braun mußte schnell in ein Gasthaus gehen. Dort fanden sie viele Bauern, die den Sonntag genoßen, Wein tranken und lustig waren. Schließlich begannen sie Lieder zu singen. Nach dem Gewitter ging die Familie über den großen Platz. „Dies ist das Kloster, das ich euch zeigen wollte," sagte Herr Braun. „Es wurde im 12. Jahrhundert gebaut und ist einer der schönsten gotischen Klosterbauten des Mittelalters." Sie gingen in die Kirche und bewunderten das spätgotische Kreuzgewölbe und die

Blumen, die an der Decke gemalt waren. Sie sehen noch heute so neu und frisch aus, wie vor sechshundert Jahren. Dann sahen sie den Kreuzgang und den schönen Brunnen. Jeden Morgen um zwei Uhr, wenn die Mönche in die Kirche gehen mußten, wuschen sie ihr Gesicht darin. Ihr Leben war sehr hart, ihre Zellen waren im Winter kalt, ihre Mahlzeiten frugal. Im frühen Mittelalter waren die Klöster der Mittelpunkt der Kultur; nur hier fanden Künstler und Gelehrte den Frieden, den sie brauchten, um ihre Aufgabe zu erfüllen. In der Reformation wurde das Land Württemberg, in dem Maulbronn liegt, protestantisch. Das Kloster wurde eine Schule, und hier wurden junge Leute erzogen, die später protestantische Pastoren werden sollten. Nicht immer geschah das. Der klassizistische Dichter Hölderlin (1770–1843) und der moderne Dichter Hermann Hesse (geboren 1877) waren Schüler in Maulbronn, aber sie sind niemals Pastoren geworden.

IX. SUPPLEMENTARY VOCABULARY

aus-sehen, sah aus, hat aus-gesehen, er sieht aus   to appear, look
die Autofahrt, -, -en   the motor trip
bewundern   to admire
die Blume, -, -n   the flower
der Brunnen, -s, -   the fountain; spring
die Decke, -, -n   the ceiling
erfüllen   to fulfil
erwidern   to return; reply
erziehen, erzog, hat erzogen   to bring up, educate
der Friede, -ns   the peace
frisch   fresh
frugal'   frugal
der Gelehrte, -n, -n   the learned person, scholar

genießen, genoß, hat genossen   to enjoy
das Gesicht, -(e)s, -er   the face, visage
hart   hard
klassizistisch   classicist (adj.)
das Kloster, -s, ÷   the monastery, cloister
der Klosterbau, -es, -e or -ten   the monastery building
der Kreuzgang, -(e)s, ÷e   the cloisters (in a monastery)
das Kreuzgewölbe, -s, -   the groined vault
die Kultur', -, -en   the culture, civilization
lustig   jolly, gay, merry
die Mahlzeit, -, -en   the meal, meal-time

malen   to paint
(das) Maulbronn, -s (village of) Maulbronn
der Mittelpunkt, -(e)s, -e   the middle point, center
modern′ modern
der Mönch, -es, -e   the monk
niemals   at no time, never
noch heute   even today

der Pastor, -s, -en   the pastor
protestan′tisch   Protestant
die Reformation′, -   the Reformation
spätgotisch   late Gothic
waschen, wusch, hat gewaschen, er wäscht   to wash
weniger   less
die Zelle, -, -n   the cell

Aufgabe Zweiundzwanzig

The Passive Voice

I. READING SELECTION

Der Brief und das Paket

Der deutsche Dichter Joseph Viktor von Scheffel **wurde** im Jahre 1826 **geboren** und starb im Jahre 1886. Die folgende Geschichte **wird** über ihn **erzählt**. Er **wurde** einmal, als er krank war, von seinem Arzte nach der Insel Capri **geschickt**. Scheffel machte sich sogleich auf den Weg. Zuerst **wurde** die lange Reise mit der Post **gemacht**, denn es gab damals noch keine Eisenbahn nach Italien, und dann fuhr er mit einem kleinen Schiff nach der Insel. Hier gefiel es ihm sehr. Er hatte reichlich frische Luft, und oft saß er auf einer Bank in einem Garten mit vielen Bäumen und schönen Blumen, aber er war oft einsam.

Eines Tages kam der Briefträger und fragte nach ihm. Von einem Freunde in Deutschland **war** ihm ein dicker Brief **geschickt worden**, aber es waren keine Briefmarken darauf. Scheffel konnte sogleich sehen, daß der Brief von einem guten Freunde war, und darum bezahlte er gern das teure Postgeld. Er war sehr erstaunt, als er nichts darin fand als die Worte: ,,Es geht mir sehr gut." Aber er hatte ein gutes Herz. Anstatt böse zu werden, lachte er. An demselben Tage schickte er ein großes Paket an seinen Freund in Deutschland, aber er vergaß auch die Briefmarken. Sein Freund mußte viel mehr für das Paket bezahlen als Scheffel für den Brief bezahlt hatte. Aber er tat es gerne, denn er dachte: ,,Dies ist ein Geschenk von Scheffel, das viel mehr wert ist als die Briefmarken." Aber als er das Paket aufmachte, fand er nichts darin als einen Stein und einen Brief mit den Worten: ,,Dieser Stein ist mir vom Herzen gefallen, als ich Deinen Brief bekam."

Sprichwörter

Wer A sagt, muß auch B sagen.
Wie der Vater, so der Sohn.
Besser heute als morgen.
Kein Jahr hat zwei Sommer.
Keine Antwort ist auch eine Antwort.

II. VOCABULARY

*Idioms
{
fragen nach (+ *dat.*)   to ask for, inquire for (about)
sich auf den Weg machen   to start out
schicken an (+ *acc.*)   to send to
(viel) mehr wert   worth (much) more; nichts wert
   not worth anything
}

*anstatt (+ *gen.* or *inf. with* zu)
   instead of
*die Bank, -, ⸚e   the bench
*der Baum, -(e)s, ⸚e   the tree
*die Blume, -, -n   the flower
*die Briefmarke, -, -n   the
   postage stamp
der Briefträger, -s, -   the mail
   carrier, postman
(das) Capri, -s   Capri (*island
   off the coast of Italy*)
damals   at that time
*darum   therefore
*derselbe, dieselbe, dasselbe
   the same
dick   thick; fat
einsam   lonesome
*die Eisenbahn, -, -en   the
   railroad
*fallen, fiel, ist gefallen, er
   fällt   to fall
*frisch   fresh
*der Garten, -s, ⸚   the garden
*geboren   born

das Geschenk, -(e)s, -e   the
   present, gift
*das Herz, -ens, -en   the heart
die Insel, -, -n   the island
(das) Ita′lien, -s   Italy
*mehr   more
*die Luft, -, ⸚e   the air
*das Paket′, -(e)s, -e   the package
die Post, -, -en   the post, mail;
   mail-coach
das Postgeld, -(e)s, -er   the
   postage
reichlich   plenty
*das Schiff, -(e)s, -e   the ship,
   boat
sogleich′   at once
das Sprichwort, -(e)s, ⸚er
   the proverb
*der Stein, -(e)s, -e   the stone
teuer   dear, expensive
*wert   worth
*das Wort, -(e)s, -e *or* ⸚er   the
   word

III. GRAMMAR

A. The Passive Voice

1. Synopsis of a sentence in the active voice.

Pres.		schreibt		
Past		schrieb		
Fut.	**Der Schüler**	wird	**den Brief**	schreiben
Pres. Perf.		hat		geschrieben
Past Perf.		hatte		geschrieben
Fut. Perf.		wird		geschrieben haben

2. Synopsis of the same sentence in the passive voice.

Pres.		wird		geschrieben		*is (being) written*
Past		wurde		geschrieben		*was (being) written*
Fut.	**Der Brief** *The letter*	wird	**von dem Schüler** *by the pupil*	geschrieben	werden	*will be written*
Pres. Perf.		ist		geschrieben	worden	*has been written*
Past Perf.		war		geschrieben	worden	*had been written*
Fut. Perf.		wird		geschrieben	worden sein	*will have been written*

(a) The passive is formed by conjugating the auxiliary **werden** with the past participle of the respective verb. The regular form **geworden,** however, loses the prefix **ge-.**

(b) The object of the active sentence becomes the subject in the passive voice. Generally the agent, i.e., the doer of the action, is indicated by the preposition **von** (+ *dat.*). The means by which the action is done is usually introduced by the preposition **durch** (+ *acc.*).

> **Er wurde durch die Medizin kuriert.**
> *He was cured by the medicine.*

There are, however, exceptions and borderline cases.

> **Der Brief wurde mit einem Bleistift geschrieben.**

The English *by* is never rendered by the preposition **bei.**

(c) The passive is far less frequently used in German than in English. There are, however, various substitutes. The most common of these is the impersonal **man.**

> **Man sagt, daß er faul ist.**
> *It is said that he is lazy.*
> *He is said to be lazy.*

A reflexive construction may also be employed.

> **Die Tür öffnete sich.**
> *The door was opened.*

3. True and apparent passive.

Since the passive voice in English is formed by conjugating the auxiliary *to be*, an occasional ambiguity may arise. This is not the case in German. A true passive in German, i.e., an action taking place, is always rendered by the auxiliary **werden.** An *apparent* passive, i.e., a condition or the result of a completed action, is rendered by the auxiliary **sein.**

> **Die Türen des Museums wurden um fünf Uhr geschlossen.**
> *The doors of the museum were (being) closed at five o'clock.*

In the above example the closing of the doors actually took place at five o'clock.

> **Die Türen des Museums waren um fünf Uhr geschlossen.**
> *The doors of the museum were closed at five o'clock.*

The latter sentence merely states that the person arriving there at five o'clock found the doors closed. There is no indication when the actual closing took place.

B. *Declension of* derselbe

	MASC.	FEM.	NEUTER
Singular	derselbe desselben demselben denselben	dieselbe derselben derselben dieselbe	dasselbe desselben demselben dasselbe
Plural		dieselben derselben denselben dieselben	

The declension of **derselbe** is identical with the declension of the definite article + an adjective (**selb-**) with weak endings, except that these two form one compound word.

C. *Plural Forms of* das Wort

The noun **das Wort** has two plurals. **Die Worte** is used to indicate connected words in a sentence. **Die Wörter** is used when referring to words as separate items.

D. *Auxiliary with* geboren

The regular passive auxiliary **werden** is used with the past participle **geboren** when referring to people who are dead. With living people the auxiliary **sein** is used.

Wann wurde Goethe geboren?
Wann sind Sie geboren?
Ich bin im November geboren.

IV. QUESTIONS

1. In welchem Jahre wurde Scheffel geboren? 2. Wann starb er? 3. Von wem wurde er einmal nach der Insel Capri geschickt? 4. Warum wurde er nach Capri geschickt? 5. Was tat Scheffel sogleich? 6. Womit wurde die Reise nicht gemacht? 7. Womit fuhr er nach der Insel? 8. Wie gefiel es ihm hier? 9. Wo saß er oft? 10. Was war in dem Garten? 11. Was tat der Briefträger eines Tages? 12. Von wem war ihm ein Brief geschickt worden? 13. Was war nicht auf dem Brief? 14. Was schrieb der Freund in dem Brief? 15. Was für ein Herz hatte Scheffel? 16. Was tat er an demselben Tage? 17. Was vergaß er auch? 18. Was mußte der Freund tun? 19. Was fand er in dem Paket, als er es aufmachte? 20. Was hatte Scheffel geschrieben?

V. GRAMMATICAL EXERCISES

(a) Change the following sentences to the past, future, and perfect tenses:

1. Das Gedicht wird von dem Studenten gelernt. 2. Der Hut wird von dem Gast abgenommen. 3. Brot und Butter werden dem Gast von dem Kellner gebracht. 4. Das Fleisch wird von der Katze gegessen. 5. Die Kuh wird von dem Bauer geholt. 6. Das Paket wird von der Tante geschickt.

(b) Change the above sentences to the active voice in the past, future, and perfect tenses.

(c) Change the following sentences to the corresponding tenses of the active voice:

1. Von den Kindern ist über die Geschichte gelacht worden. 2. Das Bier wird von dem Gast getrunken werden. 3. Der Name war von der Dame vergessen worden. 4. Die Briefmarken wurden von dem Dichter vergessen. 5. Es ist von den Leuten darüber gesprochen worden. 6. Der linke Schuh wurde von diesem Manne gefunden.

(d) Substitute active sentences with **man** as the subject for the following:

1. Nichts ist vergessen worden. 2. Es wurde fleißig studiert. 3. Es ist viel versprochen worden. 4. Es war an die Tür geklopft worden. 5. Eine richtige Antwort wurde selten gegeben. 6. Es durfte hier nicht geraucht werden.

VI. TRANSLATION EXERCISES

1. The friend who sent a letter to Scheffel forgot the stamps. 2. Scheffel did not become angry because he had a good heart. 3. The bench was placed under the tree. 4. The man was sent to the country by the doctor. 5. He was sick and needed more fresh air. 6. Many beautiful flowers can be found in the garden. 7. The journey will be made by railroad. 8. Instead of going to bed the boy read a story. 9. The package was not worth anything. 10. Goethe was born in the year 1749. 11. When were you born? 12. Many people were on the ship that went (fahren) to Europe. 13. A stone fell out of the same package. 14. We started out early. 15. The man knocked on the door and asked for Mr. Braun.

VII. VOCABULARY BUILDING

Feminine nouns may be formed from masculine nouns denoting rank, position, occupation, or nationality by adding the suffix **-in**. Such feminine nouns usually take Umlaut.

der **Amerikaner** the American	die **Amerikanerin** the American (woman)
der **Bauer** the peasant	die **Bäuerin** the peasant woman
der **Engländer** the Englishman	die **Engländerin** the English woman
der **Freund** the friend	die **Freundin** the (woman) friend
der **Gott** God	die **Göttin** the goddess
der **Herr** the master	die **Herrin** the mistress
der **Kellner** the waiter	die **Kellnerin** the waitress

der König the king	die Königin the queen
der Lehrer the teacher	die Lehrerin the (woman) teacher
der Schüler the pupil	die Schülerin the (girl) pupil
der Student the student	die Studentin the (girl) student
der Wirt the host, landlord	die Wirtin the hostess, landlady

VIII. SUPPLEMENTARY READING

Heidelberg

Von Baden-Baden reiste die Familie Braun nach Heidelberg. Diese Stadt wird von vielen Reisenden für die romantischste aller deutschen Städte gehalten. Sie liegt am linken Ufer des Neckars, im Norden und Süden von hohen Bergen und grünen Wäldern umgeben. Nach Osten sieht man in das enge Neckartal, nach Westen öffnet sich die Ebene des Oberrheins. Heidelberg ist am bekanntesten durch seine Universität, die im Jahre 1386 gegründet wurde. Sie ist die älteste deutsche Universität nach Prag und Wien. Die Bibliothek besteht aus ungefähr 400 000 Bänden und enthält viele wertvolle Handschriften. Die schönste davon ist die sogenannte Manessische Handschrift. Sie ist um 1300 geschrieben und enthält die Lieder der mittelalterlichen Minnesänger, darunter die Walthers von der Vogelweide. Primitive, aber sehr hübsche Miniaturen illustrieren sie.

Viele bedeutende Gelehrte haben in Heidelberg gelebt. Noch bekannter aber wurde die Universität durch das lustige Studentenleben mit seiner Tradition des Trinkens und des Duellierens. Die Universitätsstudenten in Deutschland sind ganz frei und niemand kontrolliert sie, ob sie studieren oder nicht. Kein Professor gibt ihnen eine Aufgabe, ein Semesterexamen oder eine Note. Wenn sie wollen, können sie jedes Semester auf eine andere Universität gehen, aber das ist natürlich unpraktisch, denn einmal, am Ende ihrer Studien, müssen sie ein großes Examen machen, und da ist es besser, wenn man die Professoren schon längere Zeit kennt.　In früheren Zeiten gab es viele Studenten, die nie in der Universität gesehen wurden, weil sie das romantische Leben in Heidelberg zu sehr genossen.　Heute haben nicht viele junge Menschen genug Geld, um solch ein müßiges Leben zu führen.　Aber wenn man abends durch Heidelberg geht, kann man noch oft aus den Studentenhäusern und Gartenrestaurants Scheffels Lied hören:

> Alt Heidelberg, du feine,
> Du Stadt an Ehren reich,
> Am Neckar und am Rheine
> Kein' andre kommt dir gleich.

Großartig ist auch die Ruine des Heidelberger Schlosses, die über der Stadt am Walde liegt.　Das Schloß wurde 1689 und 1693 von den Franzosen zerstört.　In seinem Keller zeigt man das große Faß, das acht und einhalb Meter lang, und sieben Meter breit ist.　Es fasst mehr als 220 000 Liter Wein. Daneben steht die Statue des Zwerges Perkeo, der im Lauf seines Lebens das Faß ausgetrunken haben soll.

IX. SUPPLEMENTARY VOCABULARY

abends in the evening

aus-trinken, trank aus, hat ausgetrunken to empty by drinking, drain (a glass, etc.)

der Band, -(e)s, ⸚e the volume

beste'hen, bestand, hat bestanden to exist; (**aus** + *dat.*) consist of

daneben near it, next to it

darunter among them; under it

das Duellie'ren, -s the dueling

einhalb one-half

eng narrow

enthalten, enthielt, hat ent-

halten, er enthält to contain

das Examen, -s, Examina the examination; **ein Examen machen** to take an examination

das Faß, -sses, ⸚sser the cask, keg, barrel

fassen to hold

das Gartenrestaurant, -s, -s the garden restaurant

gleich equal, like; immediately

großartig grand, magnificent

gründen to found

halten, hielt, hat gehalten, er hält to hold; keep; **halten für** to hold to be

die Handschrift, -, -en the manuscript

(das) Heidelberg, -s (city of) Heidelberg

Heidelberger Heidelberg (*adj.*)

illustrie'ren to illustrate

kontrollie'ren to control

das (*or* **der**) **Liter, -s, -** the liter

die Miniatur', -, -en the miniature

der Minnesänger, -s, - the minnesinger (*German lyric poet of the 12th or 13th century*)

mittelalterlich medieval

müßig idle

der Neckar, -s the Neckar (river)

das Neckartal, -(e)s the Neckar valley

die Note, -, -n the note, report, mark

der Oberrhein, -s the upper Rhine

sich öffnen to open (oneself)

(das) Prag, -(e)s (city of) Prague

primitiv' primitive

romantisch romantic

das Semester, -s, - the university term, semester

das Semesterexamen, -s, -examina the term examination

die Statue, -, -n the statue

das Studen'tenhaus, -es, ⁼er the students' house

das Studen'tenleben, -s the student life

die Studie, -, -n the study, studies

das Trinken, -s the drinking

der Universitätsstudent, -en, -en the university student

un'praktisch unpractical; impracticable

wertvoll valuable

Aufgabe Dreiundzwanzig

The Subjunctive. The Conditional. Unreal Conditions

I. READING SELECTION

Der unhöfliche Bauer

Ein Bauer, der in einem kleinen Dorfe wohnte, hatte viele Eier zu verkaufen, aber er verkaufte sie immer in dem Dorfe, wo die Eier billig waren, während sie in der Stadt ziemlich teuer waren. Eines Tages sagte seine Frau zu ihm: „Wenn du in die Stadt **gingest** und deine Eier dort **verkauftest, würdest** du einen besseren Preis dafür **bekommen.**" Der Bauer antwortete: „Ja, du hast recht. **Hätte** ich nur früher daran **gedacht!**" Also zog er seine besten Kleider an und machte sich sogleich auf den Weg. Der Bauer war noch nie mit der Eisenbahn gefahren und freute sich auf die Reise. Aber er kam zu früh zum Bahnhof und mußte eine Stunde auf den Zug warten. Er dachte: „Wenn ich das **gewußt hätte, hätte** ich zu Hause **gewartet.**" Er ging zuerst eine Weile hin und her. Endlich wurde er ungeduldig, und da es ein kalter Tag war, ging er in ein Restaurant und trank eine Tasse heißen Kaffee. Dann kam er wieder zurück, setzte sich in eine Ecke des Wartezimmers, nahm eine Pfeife aus der Tasche und fing an zu rauchen. Etwas später kam eine Frau in das Wartezimmer und setzte sich neben ihn. Als der Bauer ruhig weiterrauchte, sagte sie zu ihm: „Wenn Sie höflich **wären, würden** Sie hier nicht **rauchen.**" Der Bauer war ärgerlich und antwortete: „Wenn es Ihnen nicht gefällt, können Sie hinausgehen." Nun wurde die Frau böse und sagte: „Wenn Sie mein Mann **wären, würde** ich Sie sogleich **vergiften.**" Der Bauer antwortete ruhig: „**Wären** Sie meine Frau, **würde** ich das Gift **nehmen.**"

Sprichwörter

Wer zuletzt lacht, lacht am besten.
Kalte Hände, warmes Herz.
Wer nicht hören will, muß fühlen.
Eine Hand wäscht die andere.
Der gerade Weg ist der beste.
Geben ist seliger als Nehmen.

II. VOCABULARY

*Idioms { **hin und her** back and forth, to and fro
sich freuen auf (+ *acc.*) to look forward to
warten auf (+ *acc.*) to wait for }

ärgerlich annoyed, angry, peeved
*besser better
*billig cheap
*das Dorf, -(e)s, ̈er the village
*die Ecke, -, -n the corner
*das Ei, -(e)s, -er the egg
fühlen to feel
*gefallen, gefiel, hat gefallen, es (er) gefällt to please; like
gerade straight
das Gift, -(e)s, -e the poison
*heiß hot
*her here, hither (*direction toward the speaker*)
*hin thither, there, to, toward (*direction away from the speaker*)
*hinaus-gehen, ging hinaus, ist hinausgegangen to go out
höflich polite, courteous
*der Kaffee, -s the coffee
*kalt cold

*neben (+ *dat.* or *acc.*) next to, near, beside
*der Preis, -es, -e the price
*ruhig quiet(ly), calm(ly)
selig blessed, happy
*sogleich' (*or* **gleich**) at once, immediately
*die Tasse, -, -n the cup
*teuer dear, expensive
ungeduldig impatient
unhöflich impolite
vergiften to poison
*verkaufen to sell
das Wartezimmer, -s, - the waiting room
waschen, wusch, hat gewaschen, er wäscht to wash
weiter-rauchen, rauchte weiter, hat weitergeraucht to continue smoking
*ziemlich rather, fairly
zuletzt last
zurück-kommen, kam zurück, ist zurückgekommen to come back

III. GRAMMAR

A. *The Subjunctive Mood*

		haben	sein	werden	nehmen	fragen
		PRESENT TENSE				
Sing.	1.	ich habe	ich **sei**	ich werde	ich nehme	ich frage
	2.	du **habest**	du **sei(e)st**	du **werdest**	du **nehmest**	du **fragest**
		Sie haben	Sie **seien**	Sie werden	Sie nehmen	Sie fragen
	3.	er **habe**	er **sei**	er **werde**	er **nehme**	er **frage**
Plural	1.	wir haben	wir **seien**	wir werden	wir nehmen	wir fragen
	2.	ihr **habet**	ihr **seiet**	ihr **werdet**	ihr **nehmet**	ihr **fraget**
		Sie haben	Sie **seien**	Sie werden	Sie nehmen	Sie fragen
	3.	sie haben	sie **seien**	sie werden	sie nehmen	sie fragen
		PAST TENSE				
Sing.	1.	ich **hätte**	ich **wäre**	ich **würde**	ich **nähme**	ich **fragte**
	2.	du **hättest**	du **wärest**	du **würdest**	du **nähmest**	du **fragtest**
		Sie **hätten**	Sie **wären**	Sie **würden**	Sie **nähmen**	Sie **fragten**
	3.	er **hätte**	er **wäre**	er **würde**	er **nähme**	er **fragte**
Plural	1.	wir **hätten**	wir **wären**	wir **würden**	wir **nähmen**	wir **fragten**
	2.	ihr **hättet**	ihr **wäret**	ihr **würdet**	ihr **nähmet**	ihr **fragtet**
		Sie **hätten**	Sie **wären**	Sie **würden**	Sie **nähmen**	Sie **fragten**
	3.	sie **hätten**	sie **wären**	sie **würden**	sie **nähmen**	sie **fragten**

FUTURE

er werde nehmen, fragen, etc.

PRESENT PERFECT

er habe genommen, gefragt, etc.
er sei gekommen, gegangen, etc.

PAST PERFECT

er hätte genommen, gefragt, etc.
er wäre gekommen, gegangen, etc.

FUTURE PERFECT

er werde genommen haben
er werde gekommen sein

1. There is only one set of endings for all tenses of the subjunctive. These are identical with the endings of the past tense of weak verbs minus the **t-**.

SING.	PLURAL
1. ich frag- (t) **e**	1. wir frag- (t) **en**
2. du frag- (t) **est** Sie frag- (t) **en**	2. ihr frag- (t) **et** Sie frag- (t) **en**
3. er sie } frag- (t) **e** es	3. sie frag- (t) **en**

2. The present tense of the subjunctive is regularly formed from the infinitive stem, without any vowel changes, by adding the above endings. **Sein** is an exception.
3. Strong verbs take Umlaut in the past tense of the subjunctive whenever possible.

ich nähme, etc.

4. The past subjunctive of weak verbs is identical with the past indicative.

ich fragte, etc.

5. The compound tenses of the subjunctive are formed by changing the auxiliary verbs to the corresponding forms of the subjunctive.

B. *The Conditional Mood*

PRESENT CONDITIONAL

ich würde nehmen
I would (should) take
er würde gehen
he would go

PERFECT CONDITIONAL

ich würde genommen haben
I would (should) have taken
er würde gegangen sein
he would have gone

In form the two conditionals resemble the two future tenses, except that the past subjunctive of **werden** is used as the auxiliary. In usage they closely resemble the English and should cause little practical difficulty.

C. *Unreal or Contrary to Fact Conditions*

PRESENT TIME

Wenn er hier wäre,
Wäre er hier,
If he were here,
{(so) **sähe ich ihn.**
{(so) **würde ich ihn sehen.**
I would (should) see him.

PAST TIME

Wenn er hier gewesen wäre,
Wäre er hier gewesen,
If he had been here,
{(so) **hätte ich ihn gesehen.**
{(so) **würde ich ihn gesehen**
   haben.
I would (should) have seen him.

1. Unreal or contrary to fact conditions imply that the condition is not, or was not, being fulfilled.

If he were here, I should see him (but he isn't here).

2. To express present time the past subjunctive is used, to express past time the past perfect subjunctive is used, in both the condition and the conclusion.   In the conclusion the cor-

responding form of the conditional may be substituted for the subjunctive. This is generally done when the subjunctive of a weak verb is identical with the indicative. It is also the more common practice in colloquial German.

3. The conjunction **wenn** may be omitted if inverted word order is substituted. This corresponds to English usage.

If he had been here ⎫
Had he been here ⎬ *I should have seen him.*

4. A real condition, i.e., one that leaves an open question, is rendered in the indicative.

Wenn es heute nicht regnet, gehen wir auf das Land.

D. *The Optative Subjunctive*

1. The conditional clause in an unreal condition is frequently used independently to express a wish impossible of fulfillment at the moment, generally with the addition of **nur.**

Wenn er nur hier wäre!
If only he were here (but alas he isn't).

Wenn er nur hier gewesen wäre!
If only he had been here.

2. To express a wish possible of fulfillment the present subjunctive is used, chiefly in set phrases and formal wishes.

Gott sei mit uns!
God be with us.

E. *The Potential Subjunctive*

The conclusion of an unreal condition may be used independently to express a possibility.

Das wäre sehr schön.
That would be very nice.

Courtesy of the German Tourist Information Office

Mainz: der Kaiserdom

Das Bundeshaus in Bonn

Der Rhein bei Kaub

F. Als wenn, als ob

1. The past or past perfect subjunctive is generally used after **als wenn**, and **als ob**   *as if*, to express the unreal condition.

Er ging, als ob er müde wäre.
He walked as if he were tired.

2. The **ob**, like the **wenn**, may be omitted if inverted word order is used.

Er ging, als wäre er müde.

IV. QUESTIONS

1. Von wem handelt diese Geschichte? 2. Wo wohnte dieser Bauer? 3. Was hatte er zu verkaufen? 4. Wo verkaufte er die Eier immer? 5. Wo waren die Eier billig? 6. Wie waren die Eier in der Stadt? 7. Was sagte seine Frau eines Tages zu dem Bauer? 8. Was antwortete der Bauer? 9. Was tat der Bauer sogleich? 10. Womit war der Bauer noch nie gefahren? 11. Worauf freute er sich? 12. Wohin kam er zu früh? 13. Wie lange mußte er auf den Zug warten? 14. Was tat er zuerst? 15. Wohin ging er dann? 16. Was tat er in dem Restaurant? 17. Was tat er, als er wieder in dem Bahnhof war? 18. Wer kam etwas später in das Wartezimmer? 19. Wohin setzte sich die Frau?

V. GRAMMATICAL EXERCISES

(a) In the following sentences substitute the present conditional for the subjunctive in the conclusion:

1. Wenn es nicht regnete, ginge ich auf das Land. 2. Wenn er die Eier in der Stadt verkaufte, bekäme er einen besseren Preis dafür. 3. Wenn Sie mehr in der frischen Luft wären, ginge es Ihnen besser. 4. Wenn ich das glaubte, wäre ich sehr dumm. 5. Wenn der Stein nicht so schwer wäre, höbe ich ihn auf. 6. Wenn ich einen Bleistift hätte, schriebe ich den Brief. 7. Wenn wir das Fenster aufmachten, hätten

wir mehr frische Luft. 8. Wenn der Kaffee nicht so kalt wäre, tränke ich ihn.

(b) Change the above sentences to past time, using the subjunctive in the conclusion.

(c) Change the above sentences to past time, using the conditional in the conclusion.

(d) Begin the above sentences with the conclusion, changing the inverted order to normal order.

(e) Change the following sentences to present time:

1. Wenn ich genug Geld gehabt hätte, wäre ich nach Europa gefahren. 2. Wenn er das gewünscht hätte, hätte er es getan. 3. Wenn er Zeit gehabt hätte, wäre er gekommen. 4. Wenn er Geld gebraucht hätte, hätte ich es ihm gegeben.

(f) In the above sentences substitute the conditional for the subjunctive in the conclusion.

VI. TRANSLATION EXERCISES

1. If I were hungry, I would go into a restaurant. 2. If the eggs were cheaper, we would buy more. 3. If the peasant had sold the eggs in the city, he would have received more money. 4. Oh, if only I had more time! 5. If it rains tomorrow, we shall stay home. 6. I am looking forward to the journey. 7. If this book belonged to me, I would read it. 8. If he had known that, he would have remained at home. 9. I have to wait for a friend. 10. A woman sat down beside the peasant. 11. When I heard that, I started out at once. 12. If we had only known that! 13. I would never do that. 14. If it were not so cold, I would take a walk. 15. If the books had not been so expensive, we would have bought them.

VII. VOCABULARY BUILDING

By adding the suffix **-er** to verbal stems, masculine nouns denoting the agent may be formed. Some of these nouns also take Umlaut.

anfangen — der Anfänger the beginner
arbeiten — der Arbeiter the worker, laborer
besuchen — der Besucher the visitor
denken — der Denker the thinker
erzählen — der Erzähler the narrator
finden   — der Finder the finder
hören   — der Hörer the hearer, auditor
kaufen — der Käufer the buyer
laufen   — der Läufer the runner
rauchen — der Raucher the smoker
schlafen — der Schläfer the sleeper
sprechen — der Sprecher the speaker

Feminine nouns may be formed from the above by adding the suffix -in (cf. Lesson XXII).

VIII. SUPPLEMENTARY READING

Frankfurt

Von Heidelberg ist es nur 88 Kilometer nördlich nach Frankfurt, und da die Familie Braun viel von dieser alten, bekannten Stadt gehört hatte, beschloßen sie, über Frankfurt nach Hause zu reisen und sich dort einige Tage aufzuhalten.

Frankfurt hat über eine halbe Million Einwohner und liegt in einer fruchtbaren Ebene am rechten Ufer des Mains.

Der Name der Stadt stammt aus der Zeit Karls des Großen (742–814), von dem sie gegründet wurde. Ehe Karl römischer Kaiser wurde (800), war er König der Franken. Einmal wurden er und seine Soldaten von einem Feinde verfolgt. Sie kamen bis an den Main, konnten aber das andere Ufer nicht erreichen, weil der Fluß sehr tief war. Endlich entdeckten sie eine Furt und dadurch wurden sie gerettet, denn die Feinde konnten die Furt nicht finden. Deshalb nannte Karl der Große diesen Ort die Franken-Furt.

Seit dem 14. Jahrhundert wurden viele deutsche Kaiser in Frankfurt gewählt und seit dem 16. Jahrhundert auch gekrönt. Im 16. Jahrhundert wurde Frankfurt eine freie Reichsstadt.

Eines der bekanntesten Gebäude in Frankfurt war der

Römer, das Rathaus der Stadt. Hier wurden die Kaiser gewählt und gekrönt. In dem Kaisersaal speiste der neugewählte Kaiser mit den Kurfürsten, von denen er gewählt worden war. Im Jahre 1944 wurde der Römer durch Bomben zerstört, ebenso wie der größte Teil der alten Stadt. Darunter war auch das Haus, in dem Goethe, der größte deutsche Dichter, seine Jugend verlebte. Er war am 28. August 1749 geboren; als er sechzehn Jahre alt war, verließ er Frankfurt und ging nach Leipzig auf die Universität. Das Haus seiner Eltern ist 1949 wieder aufgebaut worden und das Innere ist so wiederhergestellt, wie es im Jahre 1755 war.

IX. SUPPLEMENTARY VOCABULARY

sich auf-halten, hielt sich auf, hat sich aufgehalten, er hält sich auf to stop, sojourn, stay

beschließen, beschloß, hat beschlossen to decide

dadurch thereby

entdecken to discover

erreichen to reach

der Feind, -(e)s, -e the enemy

der Franke, -n, -n the Frank

(das) Frankfurt, -s (city of) Frankfort

fruchtbar fruitful, fertile

die Furt, -, -en the ford

der Kaisersaal, -(e)s, die Kaisersäle the imperial hall

Karl der Große, Karls des Großen Charles the Great, Charlemagne

krönen to crown

der Kurfürst, -en, -en the electoral prince

(das) Leipzig, -s (city of) Leipzig

der Main, -(e)s the Main (river)

neugewählt newly elected

der Ort, -(e)s, -e *and* **⸚er** the place, locality

das Rathaus, -es, ⸚er the city hall

retten to save

der Römer, -s *name of the city hall in Frankfort*

verfolgen to pursue

verleben to pass, spend (time)

wählen to elect

wiederher'-stellen, stellte wiederher, hat wiederhergestellt to restore

Aufgabe Vierundzwanzig

The Subjunctive. Indirect Discourse

I. READING SELECTION

Der König und der Bauer

Ein Bauer, der nicht weit von Paris wohnte, machte sich
'eines Tages auf den Weg nach der Stadt. Das Wetter war
herrlich. Die Sonne schien hell und der Himmel war blau.
Der Bauer ritt auf einem alten Pferde. Auf dem Wege
begegnete er einem Herrn, der sehr feine Kleider hatte und
auf einem sehr feinen Pferde ritt. Der fremde Herr fragte den
Bauern, wo er **geboren sei** und wo er **wohne.** Der Bauer
antwortete, daß er in dem kleinen Dorfe dort **geboren sei** und
immer noch dort **wohne.** Der fremde Herr fragte weiter, wo
er jetzt **hinreite.** Der Bauer antwortete, daß er nach Paris
reite, um dort seine Eier und Butter zu verkaufen, und daß er
hoffe, auch den König dort zu sehen. Der Herr fragte ihn, ob
er den König noch nie **gesehen habe.** Der Bauer antwortete,
nein, er **sei** noch nicht so glücklich **gewesen.** Dann lächelte
der fremde Herr und sagte, das **sei** schade, aber er **glaube,** der
Bauer **werde** heute den König sicher **sehen.** Der Bauer
sagte, er **hoffe** das auch, aber er **werde** so viele Menschen
sehen. Wie **könne** er wissen, wer der König **sei?** Der Herr
antwortete, der Bauer **solle** mit ihm nach Paris **reiten** und die
Augen gut offen **halten.** Alle Leute in Paris **würden** den
Hut **abnehmen,** nur ein Mann **würde** es nicht **tun,** und das
sei der König.

Also ritten sie beide durch eine lange Straße langsam in die
Stadt. Der Bauer ritt nicht hinter dem Herrn, sondern neben
ihm. Viele Leute, die in der Straße wohnten, machten die
Fenster auf und grüßten den Herrn, und alle Leute auf der
Straße nahmen den Hut ab. Nach und nach merkte der

Bauer, daß sein Freund immer noch den Hut auf dem Kopf hatte, und sagte zu ihm: „Entweder bist du der König oder ich bin es selber, denn wir zwei sind die einzigen Leute, die den Hut noch auf dem Kopfe haben." Da lachte der fremde Herr und sagte, er **sei** der König, und wenn der Bauer noch weiter mit ihm reiten **wolle,** dann **würde** er ihm sein Schloß und seine Gärten **zeigen.**

II. VOCABULARY

*Idioms {
es ist schade   it is a pity, it is too bad
auf der Straße   on (in) the street (*people walking, children playing*)
in der Straße   on the street (*to live on a certain street*)
nach und nach   by and by, gradually
}

*das Auge, -s, -n   the eye
*blau   blue
einzig   sole, only
*entweder   either; **entweder
... oder**   either ... or
*fein   fine
*fremd   strange
*grüßen   to greet
*halten, hielt, hat gehalten, er hält   to hold; keep
*hell   bright(ly)
*herrlich   glorious, wonderful
*der Himmel, -s, -   the heaven, sky
hin-reiten, ritt hin, ist hingeritten   to ride to
*hinter   (+ *dat.* or *acc.*) behind

*der König, -(e)s, -e   the king
*langsam   slow(ly)
*der Mensch, -en, -en   man, human being, person; *pl.* people
*merken   to notice
*offen   open
(das) **Paris'**   (city of) Paris
reiten, ritt, ist geritten (*intransitive verb*) or hat geritten (*transitive verb*)   to ride (horseback)
*scheinen, schien, hat geschienen   to shine; seem
*das Schloß, -sses, ⸚sser   the castle
*sicher   safe(ly); sure(ly)
*die Sonne, -, -n   the sun

III. GRAMMAR

A. The Subjunctive in Indirect Discourse

1. The use of the subjunctive in indirect discourse, i.e., in reporting the words or thoughts of some other person, not as

a direct quotation but in substance only, implies that the person reporting assumes no responsibility for the statement reported.

2. The chief difficulty in using the subjunctive in indirect discourse is the selection of the proper tense.

	DIRECT	INDIRECT	FORM I	FORM II
	(Der Mann sagte:)	(Der Mann sagte,)		
Present:	„Ich bin arm."	daß er arm	sei	wäre
Past:	„Ich war arm."			
Perfect:	„Ich bin arm gewesen."	daß er arm gewesen	sei	wäre
Past P.:	„Ich war arm gewesen."			
Future:	„Ich werde arm sein."	daß er arm sein	werde	würde
	(Die Studenten sagten:)	(Die Studenten sagten,)		
Present:	„Wir haben kein Buch."	daß sie kein Buch	(haben)	hätten
Past:	„Wir hatten kein Buch."			
Perfect:	„Wir haben kein Buch gehabt."	daß sie kein Buch gehabt	(haben)	hätten
Past P.:	„Wir hatten kein Buch gehabt."			
Future:	„Wir werden kein Buch haben."	daß sie kein Buch haben	(werden)	würden

(a) Note that *all* past times in direct discourse, whether past, perfect, or past perfect tense, are expressed by the perfect or past perfect tense in indirect discourse.

(b) There is no difference in meaning between Form I and

Form II in indirect discourse. The former is preferable in formal speech, the latter is more common in colloquial German.

(c) Form II is used exclusively when the subjunctive of Form I is identical with the indicative.

3. The same rules as to tense apply also to indirect questions, introduced by an interrogative pronoun (**wer, was**), a prepositional compound with **wo-** (**womit, worin, worauf,** etc.), an interrogative adverb (**wo, wohin, warum, wann, wie, wieviel,** etc.), or the conjunction **ob** *if, whether.*

4. The conjunction **daß** may be omitted as in English, but normal word order must then be used.

> **Er sagte, daß er das Buch gelesen habe.**
> **Er sagte, er habe das Buch gelesen.**

5. An imperative in direct discourse is expressed in indirect discourse by the present or past subjunctive of **sollen** with the infinitive of the respective verb.

> **Der Lehrer sagte zu dem Schüler: „Schreiben Sie die Aufgabe!"**
> *The teacher said to the pupil, "Write the lesson."*

> **Der Lehrer sagte dem Schüler, daß er die Aufgabe schreiben solle (sollte).**

The teacher told the pupil { *that he should write the lesson.* / *to write the lesson.* / *that he was to write the lesson.* }

NOTE: The dative noun object after **sagen** is governed by the preposition **zu** when followed by direct discourse. When **sagen** introduces indirect discourse, the **zu** is omitted.

B. *The Indicative in Indirect Discourse*

The indicative is used:

1. After verbs expressing certainty, such as **sehen, wissen,** etc.

> **Der Lehrer sieht, daß der Schüler kein Buch hat.**
> **Sie wußten, daß der Mann arm war.**

2. When the introductory verb is in the first person, present tense.

Ich sage, daß er gestern nicht hier war.

3. Generally also when the introductory verb is in some other person of the present tense.

Er sagt, daß sein Bruder heute kommt (komme).

4. When the speaker himself vouches for the statement of another.

Man hat mir gesagt, daß er nach Berlin gereist ist.

IV. QUESTIONS

1. Wo wohnte einmal ein Bauer? 2. Was tat er eines Tages? 3. Wie war das Wetter? 4. Wie war der Himmel? 5. Wem begegnete der Bauer? 6. Was für Kleider hatte dieser Herr? 7. Was fragte der fremde Herr den Bauern? 8. Warum ging der Bauer nach der Stadt? 9. Wen hoffte er auch zu sehen? 10. Was fragte ihn der fremde Herr? 11. Was glaubte der Herr? 12. Was fürchtete der Bauer? 13. Mit wem sollte der Bauer in die Stadt reiten? 14. Was würden alle Leute in Paris tun? 15. Wer würde den Hut nicht abnehmen? 16. Was taten viele Leute, die in der Straße wohnten? 17. Was taten alle Leute auf der Straße? 18. Was merkte der Bauer nach und nach? 19. Was sagte er zu dem Herrn? 20. Was antwortete der Herr?

V. GRAMMATICAL EXERCISES

(a) In the reading selection above, change all indirect discourse to direct.

(b) Make the following sentences dependent on „Er sagte, daß:"

1. Der Bauer hat seine Eier verkauft. 2. Er saß in einer Ecke des Bahnhofs. 3. Heute ist herrliches Wetter. 4. Meine Tante wohnt in einem Dorf. 5. Das Schiff ist langsam

gefahren. 6. Die Bank steht unter einem Baum. 7. Der Bauer dankte dem fremden Herrn. 8. Karl, falle nicht von der Bank! 9. Herr Braun, trinken Sie eine Tasse Kaffee! 10. Ich habe den König noch nie gesehen.

(c) Make the above sentences dependent on „Er sagte" (without daß).

(d) Make the following questions dependent on „Er fragte:"
1. Wieviel Uhr ist es? 2. Wer hat die Briefmarke vergessen? 3. Warum lachen die Kinder? 4. Womit schreibt er den Brief? 5. Wer klopfte an die Tür? 6. Ist das Tier tot? 7. Was wünscht der König? 8. Wem ist der Bauer begegnet? 9. Wo hat er das gehört? 10. Wann kaufte er das Pferd?

VI. TRANSLATION EXERCISES

1. The peasant did not know that it was the king. 2. It is too bad that he cannot come. 3. The peasant said that he had sold his eggs. 4. Many people lived on this street. 5. He told me to open the window. 6. The teacher asked the pupil whether he had learned his lesson. 7. He said he had no money. 8. He saw that I had no pencil. 9. They said that she had blue eyes. 10. I say that he is not here. 11. The student says that he is sick. 12. I did not walk behind him but beside him. 13. The king said to the peasant: I shall show you my castle. 14. The strange gentleman said that he spoke German. 15. This man said that he wrote the letter.

VII. VOCABULARY BUILDING

Diminutives may be formed from nouns by adding the suffixes **-chen** and (or) **-lein**. Sometimes such nouns express the idea of endearment. Many nouns may take either suffix, but with certain nouns one or the other suffix is preferable or even imperative. The grammatical gender of such nouns is always neuter, no matter what the real gender is. They take Umlaut where possible.

der Baum	—das Bäumchen, das Bäumlein the little tree
die Blume	—das Blümchen, das Blümlein the little flower
das Brot	—das Brötchen the roll (of bread)
der Bruder	—das Brüderchen, das Brüderlein the little brother
das Buch	—das Büchlein the little book
das Fenster	—das Fensterchen, das Fensterlein the little window
die Frau	—das Fräulein the young lady; Miss
das Haus	—das Häuschen, das Häuslein the little house
die Katze	—das Kätzchen, das Kätzlein the (dear) little cat
die Maid	—das Mädchen the girl
die Mutter	—das Mütterchen, das Mütterlein the dear mother
die Schwester	—das Schwesterchen, das Schwesterlein the little sister

VIII. SUPPLEMENTARY READING

Die Rheinreise

Die Familie Braun hatte nur noch einige Tage in Deutschland, ehe sie von Bremen nach Amerika abfuhr. Aber sie wollten auf jeden Fall die berühmte Rheinreise machen. Deshalb fuhren sie zuerst mit der Eisenbahn nach Mainz, wo im 15. Jahrhundert Johann Gutenberg, der Erfinder der Buchdruckerkunst lebte. Dort gingen sie auf einen Dampfer, da man von ihm aus viel mehr als von der Eisenbahn aus sehen kann.

Der schönste Teil des Rheines ist zwischen Bingen und Bonn. Die hohen Berge kommen hier nah ans Ufer, so daß das Tal sehr eng wird. Auf beiden Seiten sieht man grüne Wiesen und Weinberge, und auf beinahe jedem Berg ist ein altes Schloß oder eine Ruine. Viele bekannte Sagen sind mit diesen Schlössern verknüpft.

Nach einigen Stunden sahen sie am rechten Ufer die Lorelei. Das ist ein steiler Felsen, der 132 Meter hoch ist und weit in den Rhein hineinreicht, so daß der Fluß hier sehr eng wird. Die Fahrt an diesem Felsen vorbei war früher sehr gefährlich und viele Schiffer haben hier ihr Leben verloren. Dadurch

entstand die Sage von der schönen Zauberin auf dem Gipfel
des Berges, die durch ihr süßes Singen die Schiffer bezauberte.
Später fuhren sie an der Stadt Koblenz vorbei, wo die Mosel
in den Rhein fließt, und kamen nach Bonn, wo Beethoven
geboren wurde. Bonn war früher nur eine Universitätsstadt
wie Heidelberg. Seit 1949 ist es aber die Hauptstadt der
Bundesrepublik Deutschland. Hier sind alle Ministerien und
das Parlament der Republik, dessen schönes Gebäude man
vom Rhein aus sieht. Daher ist Bonn größer geworden, und
mehr neue Häuser sind hier nach dem zweiten Weltkrieg
gebaut worden als in anderen Städten. 30 Kilometer nördlich von Bonn liegt Köln, die bedeutendste Handelsstadt in
Westdeutschland. Große Teile von Köln liegen seit dem
Krieg in Ruinen, aber der berühmte Dom steht noch. Nachdem die Familie Braun sich den Dom angesehen hatte, fuhren
sie mit der Eisenbahn nach Bremen und übernachteten dort.
Am nächsten Morgen fuhren sie nach Bremerhaven und einige
Stunden später waren sie wieder auf dem Dampfer, der sie
nach Amerika zurückbrachte.

IX. SUPPLEMENTARY VOCABULARY

bezaubern to bewitch,
  enchant
(das) Bingen, -s (city of) Bingen
(das) Bremerhaven, -s (city
  of) Bremerhaven
die Buchdruckerkunst, - the
  art of printing
der Erfinder, -s, - the inventor
der Fall, -(e)s, ⸚e the case;
  auf jeden Fall in any case,
  by all means
gefährlich dangerous
der Gipfel, -s, - the peak, summit, top
die Handelsstadt, -, ⸚e the
  commercial city

hinein-reichen to reach in,
  extend
(das) Koblenz (city of)
  Coblenz
(das) Köln, -s (city of)
  Cologne
die Lorelei, - the Lorelei
(das) Mainz (city of) Mayence
das Ministe'rium, -s, Ministe'-
  rien the ministry, government office
die Mo'sel, - the Moselle
  (river)
das Parlament', -(e)s, -e the
  parliament
die Rheinreise, -, -n the
  Rhine journey

die Sage, -, -n the legend
der Schiffer, -s, - the boatman
das Singen, -s the singing
süß sweet
übernachten to spend the
  night
die Universitätsstadt, -, ⁼e the
  university town
verknüpfen to connect
vorbei past; an dem Felsen
vorbei past the cliff

vorbei-fahren, fuhr vorbei, ist
  vorbeigefahren, er fährt
  vorbei to ride past, to sail
  past
die Wiese, -, -n the meadow
die Zauberin, -, -nen the enchantress, witch
zurück-bringen, brachte zurück, hat zurückgebracht
  to bring back

POEMS

Heidenröslein

Sah ein Knab' ein Röslein stehn,
Röslein auf der Heiden,
War so jung und morgenschön,
Lief er schnell, es nah zu sehn,
Sah's mit vielen Freuden.
Röslein, Röslein, Röslein rot,
Röslein auf der Heiden.

Knabe sprach: Ich breche dich,
Röslein auf der Heiden!
Röslein sprach: Ich steche dich,
Daß du ewig denkst an mich,
Und ich will's nicht leiden.
Röslein, Röslein, Röslein rot,
Röslein auf der Heiden.

Und der wilde Knabe brach
's Röslein auf der Heiden;
Röslein wehrte sich und stach,
Half ihm doch kein Weh und Ach,
Mußt' es eben leiden.
Röslein, Röslein, Röslein rot,
Röslein auf der Heiden.

JOHANN WOLFGANG VON GOETHE (1749–1832).

Gefunden

Ich ging im Walde
So für mich hin,
Und nichts zu suchen,
Das war mein Sinn.

Im Schatten sah ich
Ein Blümchen stehn,
Wie Sterne leuchtend,
Wie Äuglein schön.

Ich wollt' es brechen,
Da sagt' es fein:
Soll ich zum Welken
Gebrochen sein?

Ich grub's mit allen
Den Würzlein aus,
Zum Garten trug ich's
Am hübschen Haus.

Und pflanzt' es wieder
Am stillen Ort;
Nun zweigt es immer
Und blüht so fort.

JOHANN WOLFGANG VON GOETHE.

Harfenspieler

Wer nie sein Brot mit Tränen aß,
Wer nie die kummervollen Nächte
Auf seinem Bette weinend saß,
Der kennt euch nicht, ihr himmlischen Mächte.

Ihr führt ins Leben uns hinein,
Ihr laßt den Armen schuldig werden,
Dann überlaßt ihr ihn der Pein:
Denn alle Schuld rächt sich auf Erden.

JOHANN WOLFGANG VON GOETHE.

Der gute Kamerad

Ich hatt' einen Kameraden,
Einen bessern findst du nit.
Die Trommel schlug zum Streite,
Er ging an meiner Seite
In gleichem Schritt und Tritt.

Eine Kugel kam geflogen;
Gilt's mir oder gilt es dir?
Ihn hat es weggerissen,
Er liegt mir vor den Füßen,
Als wär's ein Stück von mir.

Will mir die Hand noch reichen,
Derweil ich eben lad':
„Kann dir die Hand nicht geben;
Bleib du im ew'gen Leben
Mein guter Kamerad!"

LUDWIG UHLAND (1787–1862).

Der Wirtin Töchterlein

Es zogen drei Bursche wohl über den Rhein,
Bei einer Frau Wirtin, da kehrten sie ein:

„Frau Wirtin, hat sie gut Bier und Wein?
Wo hat sie ihr schönes Töchterlein?"

„Mein Bier und Wein ist frisch und klar.
Mein Töchterlein liegt auf der Totenbahr'."

Und als sie traten zur Kammer hinein,
Da lag sie in einem schwarzen Schrein.

Der erste, der schlug den Schleier zurück
Und schaute sie an mit traurigem Blick:

„Ach, lebtest du noch, du schöne Maid!
Ich würde dich lieben von dieser Zeit."

Der zweite deckte den Schleier zu
Und kehrte sich ab und weinte dazu:

„Ach, daß du liegst auf der Totenbahr'!
Ich hab' dich geliebet so manches Jahr."

Der dritte hub ihn wieder sogleich
Und küßte sie an den Mund so bleich:

,Dich liebt' ich immer, dich lieb' ich noch heut
Und werde dich lieben in Ewigkeit."

LUDWIG UHLAND.

Der frohe Wandersmann

Wem Gott will rechte Gunst erweisen,
Den schickt er in die weite Welt;
Dem will er seine Wunder weisen
In Berg und Wald und Strom und Feld.

Die Trägen, die zu Hause liegen,
Erquicket nicht das Morgenrot;
Sie wissen nur von Kinderwiegen,
Von Sorgen, Last und Not um Brot.

Die Bächlein von den Bergen springen,
Die Lerchen schwirren hoch vor Lust,
Was sollt' ich nicht mit ihnen singen
Aus voller Kehl' und frischer Brust?

Den lieben Gott lass' ich nur walten;
Der Bächlein, Lerchen, Wald und Feld
Und Erd' und Himmel will erhalten,
Hat auch mein Sach' aufs best' bestellt!

JOSEPH FREIHERR VON EICHENDORFF (1788–1857).

Aus der Jugendzeit

Aus der Jugendzeit, aus der Jugendzeit
Klingt ein Lied mir immerdar;
O wie liegt so weit, o wie liegt so weit,
Was mein einst war!

Was die Schwalbe sang, was die Schwalbe sang,
Die den Herbst und Frühling bringt;
Ob das Dorf entlang, ob das Dorf entlang
Das jetzt noch klingt?

„Als ich Abschied nahm, als ich Abschied nahm,
Waren Kisten und Kasten schwer;
Als ich wieder kam, als ich wieder kam,
War alles leer."

O du Kindermund, o du Kindermund,
Unbewußter Weisheit froh,
Vogelsprachekund, vogelsprachekund
Wie Salomo!

O du Heimatflur, o du Heimatflur,
Laß zu deinem heil'gen Raum
Mich noch einmal nur, mich noch einmal nur
Entfliehn im Traum!

Als ich Abschied nahm, als ich Abschied nahm,
War die Welt mir voll so sehr;
Als ich wieder kam, als ich wieder kam,
War alles leer.

Wohl die Schwalbe kehrt, wohl die Schwalbe kehrt,
Und der leere Kasten schwoll,
Ist das Herz geleert, ist das Herz geleert,
Wird's nie mehr voll.

Keine Schwalbe bringt, keine Schwalbe bringt,
Dir zurück, wonach du weinst;
Doch die Schwalbe singt, doch die Schwalbe singt
Im Dorf wie einst:

„Als ich Abschied nahm, als ich Abschied nahm,
Waren Kisten und Kasten schwer;
Als ich wieder kam, als ich wieder kam,
War alles leer."

FRIEDRICH RÜCKERT (1788–1866).

Du bist wie eine Blume

Du bist wie eine Blume
So hold und schön und rein;
Ich schau' dich an, und Wehmut
Schleicht mir ins Herz hinein.

Mir ist, als ob ich die Hände
Aufs Haupt dir legen sollt',
Betend, daß Gott dich erhalte
So rein und schön und hold.

HEINRICH HEINE (1797–1856).

Ein Fichtenbaum

Ein Fichtenbaum steht einsam
Im Norden auf kahler Höh'.
Ihn schläfert; mit weißer Decke
Umhüllen ihn Eis und Schnee.

Er träumt von einer Palme,
Die fern im Morgenland
Einsam und schweigend trauert
Auf brennender Felsenwand.

HEINRICH HEINE.

Die Lorelei

Ich weiß nicht, was soll es bedeuten,
Daß ich so traurig bin;
Ein Märchen aus alten Zeiten,
Das kommt mir nicht aus dem Sinn.

Die Luft ist kühl und es dunkelt,
Und ruhig fließt der Rhein;
Der Gipfel des Berges funkelt
Im Abendsonnenschein.

Die schönste Jungfrau sitzet
Dort oben wunderbar,
Ihr goldnes Geschmeide blitzet,
Sie kämmt ihr goldenes Haar.

Sie kämmt es mit goldenem Kamme,
Und singt ein Lied dabei;
Das hat eine wundersame,
Gewaltige Melodei.

Den Schiffer im kleinen Schiffe
Ergreift es mit wildem Weh;
Er schaut nicht die Felsenriffe,
Er schaut nur hinauf in die Höh'.

Ich glaube, die Wellen verschlingen
Am Ende Schiffer und Kahn;
Und das hat mit ihrem Singen
Die Lorelei getan.

HEINRICH HEINE.

Das verlassene Mägdlein

Früh, wann die Hähne krähn,
Eh' die Sternlein verschwinden,
Muß ich am Herde stehn,
Muß Feuer zünden.

Schön ist der Flammen Schein,
Es springen die Funken;
Ich schaue so drein,
In Leid versunken.

Plötzlich, da kommt es mir,
Treuloser Knabe,
Daß ich die Nacht von dir
Geträumet habe.

Träne auf Träne dann
Stürzet hernieder;
So kommt der Tag heran—
O ging' er wieder!

EDUARD MÖRIKE (1804–1875).

Lebewohl

„Lebe wohl!"—Du fühlest nicht,
Was es heißt, dies Wort der Schmerzen;
Mit getrostem Angesicht
Sagtest du's und leichtem Herzen.

Lebe wohl!—Ach, tausendmal
Hab' ich mir es vorgesprochen,
Und in nimmersatter Qual
Mir das Herz damit gebrochen!

EDUARD MÖRIKE.

Die Stadt

Am grauen Strand, am grauen Meer
Und seitab liegt die Stadt;
Der Nebel drückt die Dächer schwer,
Und durch die Stille braust das Meer
Eintönig um die Stadt.

Es rauscht kein Wald, es schlägt im Mai
Kein Vogel ohn' Unterlaß;
Die Wandergans mit hartem Schrei
Nur fliegt in Herbstesnacht vorbei,
Am Strande weht das Gras.

Doch hängt mein ganzes Herz an dir,
Du graue Stadt am Meer;
Der Jugend Zauber für und für
Ruht lächelnd doch auf dir, auf dir,
Du graue Stadt am Meer.

THEODOR STORM (1817–1888).

Der Arbeitsmann

Wir haben ein Bett, wir haben ein Kind,
    mein Weib!
Wir haben auch Arbeit, und gar zu zweit,
und haben die Sonne und Regen und Wind,
und uns fehlt nur eine Kleinigkeit,
um so frei zu sein, wie die Vögel sind:
    Nur Zeit.

Wenn wir Sonntags durch die Felder gehn,
    mein Kind,
und über den Ähren weit und breit
das blaue Schwalbenvolk blitzen sehn,
oh, dann fehlt uns nicht das bißchen Kleid,
um so schön zu sein, wie die Vögel sind:
    Nur Zeit.

Nur Zeit! wir wittern Gewitterwind,
    wir Volk.
Nur eine kleine Ewigkeit;
uns fehlt ja nichts, mein Weib, mein Kind,
als all das, was durch uns gedeiht,
um so kühn zu sein, wie die Vögel sind.
    Nur Zeit!

RICHARD DEHMEL (1863–1920).

APPENDIX

APPENDIX

1. The Definite Article

	SINGULAR			PLURAL
	Masculine	Feminine	Neuter	All Genders
Nom.	der	die	das	die
Gen.	des	der	des	der
Dat.	dem	der	dem	den
Acc.	den	die	das	die

2. The der-words: dieser, jener, jeder, welcher, mancher, solcher

	SINGULAR			PLURAL
	Masculine	Feminine	Neuter	All Genders
Nom.	dieser	diese	dies(es)	diese
Gen.	dieses	dieser	dieses	dieser
Dat.	diesem	dieser	diesem	diesen
Acc.	diesen	diese	dies(es)	diese

3. The Indefinite Article

	SINGULAR		
	Masculine	Feminine	Neuter
Nom.	ein	eine	ein
Gen.	eines	einer	eines
Dat.	einem	einer	einem
Acc.	einen	eine	ein

4. The ein-words: kein, mein, dein, sein, unser, euer, ihr, Ihr

	SINGULAR			PLURAL
	Masculine	Feminine	Neuter	All Genders
Nom.	mein	meine	mein	meine
Gen.	meines	meiner	meines	meiner
Dat.	meinem	meiner	meinem	meinen
Acc.	meinen	meine	mein	meine

5. *Strong Declension of Nouns*
A. Class I

SINGULAR

Nom.	der Vater	die Mutter	das Mädchen
Gen.	des Vaters	der Mutter	des Mädchens
Dat.	dem Vater	der Mutter	dem Mädchen
Acc.	den Vater	die Mutter	das Mädchen

PLURAL

Nom.	die Väter	die Mütter	die Mädchen
Gen.	der Väter	der Mütter	der Mädchen
Dat.	den Vätern	den Müttern	den Mädchen
Acc.	die Väter	die Mütter	die Mädchen

To this class belong

(a) Masculine and neuter nouns ending in **-el, -en, -er,** except **der Bauer.**

(b) Diminutives formed by adding **-chen** or **-lein,** which are always neuter.

(c) Neuter nouns with the prefix **Ge-** and the ending **-e.**

(d) Two feminine nouns, **die Mutter** and **die Tochter.**

(e) No nouns of one syllable belong to Class I.

The following nouns belonging to Class I are designated as active in *Beginning German* and should be thoroughly mastered by students. Parentheses indicate that the plural forms are relatively rare.

SINGULAR	PLURAL	MEANING
der Amerikaner	die Amerikaner	*the American*
der Bruder	die Brüder	*the brother*
der Dampfer	die Dampfer	*the steamer*
der Dichter	die Dichter	*the poet*
das Dienstmädchen	die Dienstmädchen	*the maid*
das Fenster	die Fenster	*the window*
das Feuer	(die Feuer)	*the fire*
der Garten	die Gärten	*the garden*
das Gemüse	(die Gemüse)	*the vegetable(s)*
die Großmutter	die Großmütter	*the grandmother*
der Großvater	die Großväter	*the grandfather*

SINGULAR	PLURAL	MEANING
der Himmel	(die Himmel)	*the heaven, sky*
der Kellner	die Kellner	*the waiter*
der Lehrer	die Lehrer	*the teacher*
das Mädchen	die Mädchen	*the girl*
das (*or* der) Meter	die Meter	*the meter*
das Mittagessen	(die Mittagessen)	*the dinner*
der Morgen	(die Morgen)	*the morning*
die Mutter	die Mütter	*the mother*
der Onkel	die Onkel	*the uncle*
der Schüler	die Schüler	*the pupil*
der Sommer	(die Sommer)	*the summer*
die Tochter	die Töchter	*the daughter*
der Vater	die Väter	*the father*
das Viertel	die Viertel	*the quarter*
das Wetter	(die Wetter)	*the weather*
der Winter	(die Winter)	*the winter*
das Zimmer	die Zimmer	*the room*

B. Class II

SINGULAR

Nom.	der Stuhl	die Stadt	das Heft
Gen.	des Stuhl(e)s	der Stadt	des Heft(e)s
Dat.	dem Stuhl(e)	der Stadt	dem Heft(e)
Acc.	den Stuhl	die Stadt	das Heft

PLURAL

Nom.	die Stühle	die Städte	die Hefte
Gen.	der Stühle	der Städte	der Hefte
Dat.	den Stühlen	den Städten	den Heften
Acc.	die Stühle	die Städte	die Hefte

To this class belong

(a) Most masculine nouns of one syllable.
(b) Some feminine nouns of one syllable.
(c) A few neuter nouns of one syllable.

The following nouns belonging to Class II are designated as active in *Beginning German.*

Singular	Plural	Meaning
der Abend	die Abende	*the evening*
die Angst	(die Ängste)	*the fear*
der Arm	die Arme	*the arm*
der Arzt	die Ärzte	*the physician*
der Augenblick	(die Augenblicke)	*the moment*
das Automobil	die Automobile	*the automobile*
der Bahnhof	die Bahnhöfe	*the railroad station*
die Bank	die Bänke	*the bench*
der Baum	die Bäume	*the tree*
das Beispiel	die Beispiele	*the example*
das Bier	(die Biere)	*the beer*
der Bleistift	die Bleistifte	*the lead-pencil*
der Brief	die Briefe	*the letter*
das Brot	(die Brote)	*the bread, loaf*
der Dienstag	(die Dienstage)	*Tuesday*
das Ding	die Dinge	*the thing*
der Donnerstag	(die Donnerstage)	*Thursday*
der Freitag	(die Freitage)	*Friday*
der Freund	die Freunde	*the friend*
der Frühling	(die Frühlinge)	*the spring*
das Frühstück	(die Frühstücke)	*the breakfast*
der Fuß	die Füße	*the foot*
der Gast	die Gäste	*the guest*
das Gedicht	die Gedichte	*the poem*
die Hand	die Hände	*the hand*
das Heft	die Hefte	*the notebook*
der Herbst	die Herbste	*the autumn*
der Hund	die Hunde	*the dog*
der Hut	die Hüte	*the hat*
das Jahr	die Jahre	*the year*
der König	die Könige	*the king*
der Kopf	die Köpfe	*the head*
die Kuh	die Kühe	*the cow*
die Luft	die Lüfte	*the air*
das Mal	(die Male)	*time*
der Mittag	(die Mittage)	*the noon*
der Mittwoch	(die Mittwoche)	*Wednesday*
der Monat	die Monate	*the month*
der Montag	(die Montage)	*Monday*
der Nachmittag	die Nachmittage	*the afternoon*

SINGULAR	PLURAL	MEANING
die Nacht	die Nächte	*the night*
das Paar	die Paare	*the pair, couple*
das Paket	die Pakete	*the package*
der Park	(die Parke)	*the park*
das Pferd	die Pferde	*the horse*
der Platz	die Plätze	*the place*
der Preis	die Preise	*the price, prize*
der Regenschirm	die Regenschirme	*the umbrella*
das Schiff	die Schiffe	*the ship*
der Schuh	die Schuhe	*the shoe*
der Sonnabend	(die Sonnabende)	*Saturday*
der Sonntag	(die Sonntage)	*Sunday*
der Spaziergang	die Spaziergänge	*the walk*
die Stadt	die Städte	*the city*
der Stein	die Steine	*the stone*
der Stuhl	die Stühle	*the chair*
der Tag	die Tage	*the day*
das Tier	die Tiere	*the animal*
der Tisch	die Tische	*the table*
der Vormittag	die Vormittage	*the forenoon*
die Wand	die Wände	*the wall*
der Weg	die Wege	*the road, path, way*
der Wein	die Weine	*the wine*
das Werk	die Werke	*the work*
der Wirt	die Wirte	*the innkeeper*
der Zug	die Züge	*the train*

C. Class III

SINGULAR

Nom.	der Mann	das Haus
Gen.	des Mannes	des Hauses
Dat.	dem Mann(e)	dem Haus(e)
Acc.	den Mann	das Haus

PLURAL

Nom.	die Männer	die Häuser
Gen.	der Männer	der Häuser
Dat.	den Männern	den Häusern
Acc.	die Männer	die Häuser

To this class belong
(a) Most neuter nouns of one syllable.
(b) A few masculine nouns of one syllable.
(c) There are no feminine nouns in this class.

The following nouns belonging to Class III are designated as active in *Beginning German*.

SINGULAR	PLURAL	MEANING
das Buch	die Bücher	*the book*
das Dorf	die Dörfer	*the village*
das Ei	die Eier	*the egg*
das Geld	(die Gelder)	*the money*
das Glas	die Gläser	*the glass*
das Haus	die Häuser	*the house*
das Kind	die Kinder	*the child*
das Kleid	die Kleider	*the dress*
das Land	die Länder	*the land, country*
das Lied	die Lieder	*the song*
der Mann	die Männer	*the man*
das Schloß	die Schlösser	*the castle*
das Streichholz	die Streichhölzer	*the match*
der Wald	die Wälder	*the forest*

6. *Weak Declension of Nouns*

SINGULAR

Nom.	der Knabe	die Schule
Gen.	des Knaben	der Schule
Dat.	dem Knaben	der Schule
Acc.	den Knaben	die Schule

PLURAL

Nom.	die Knaben	die Schulen
Gen.	der Knaben	der Schulen
Dat.	den Knaben	den Schulen
Acc.	die Knaben	die Schulen

To this class belong
(a) Almost all feminine nouns, except **die Mutter** and **die Tochter.**
(b) A few masculine nouns.
(c) There are no neuter nouns in this class.

The following nouns belonging to the weak declension are designated as active in *Beginning German.*

SINGULAR	PLURAL	MEANING
die Amerikanerin	die Amerikanerinnen	*the American* (woman)
die Antwort	die Antworten	*the answer*
die Aufgabe	die Aufgaben	*the lesson*
die Blume	die Blumen	*the flower*
die Briefmarke	die Briefmarken	*the postage stamp*
die Dame	die Damen	*the lady*
die Ecke	die Ecken	*the corner*
die Eisenbahn	die Eisenbahnen	*the railroad*
die Fahrkarte	die Fahrkarten	*the ticket*
die Familie	die Familien	*the family*
die Farbe	die Farben	*the color*
die Feder	die Federn	*the feather, pen*
die Frage	die Fragen	*the question*
die Frau	die Frauen	*the woman, Mrs.*
die Geschichte	die Geschichten	*the story*
der Herr	die Herren	*the gentleman, Mr.*
der Junge	die Jungen	*the boy*
die Karte	die Karten	*the card*
die Kartoffel	die Kartoffeln	*the potato*
die Katze	die Katzen	*the cat*
die Klasse	die Klassen	*the class*
der Knabe	die Knaben	*the boy*
die Kreide	(die Kreiden)	*the chalk*
die Lehrerin	die Lehrerinnen	*the teacher* (fem.)
die Medizin	(die Medizinen)	*the medicine*
der Mensch	die Menschen	*the man, human being*
die Million	die Millionen	*the million*
die Minute	die Minuten	*the minute*
die Rechnung	die Rechnungen	*the bill*
die Reise	die Reisen	*the journey*
die Schule	die Schulen	*the school*
die Schülerin	die Schülerinnen	*the pupil* (fem.)
die Schwester	die Schwestern	*the sister*
die Seite	die Seiten	*the side, page*
die Sekunde	die Sekunden	*the second*
die Sonne	(die Sonnen)	*the sun*
die Straße	die Straßen	*the street*

SINGULAR	PLURAL	MEANING
die Straßenbahn	die Straßenbahnen	*the street car*
der Student	die Studenten	*the student*
die Stunde	die Stunden	*the hour*
die Tafel	die Tafeln	*the blackboard*
die Tante	die Tanten	*the aunt*
die Tasche	die Taschen	*the pocket*
die Tasse	die Tassen	*the cup*
die Tür	die Türen	*the door*
die Uhr	die Uhren	*the clock, watch*
die Universität	die Universitäten	*the university*
die Weihnachten	(die Weihnachten)	*Christmas*
die Welt	(die Welten)	*the world*
die Woche	die Wochen	*the week*
die Wohnung	die Wohnungen	*the house, apartment*
die Zeit	die Zeiten	*the time*

7. *Mixed Declension*

SINGULAR

Nom.	der See	das	Auge
Gen.	des Sees	des	Auges
Dat.	dem See	dem	Auge
Acc.	den See	das	Auge

PLURAL

Nom.	die Seen	die	Augen
Gen.	der Seen	der	Augen
Dat.	den Seen	den	Augen
Acc.	die Seen	die	Augen

To this class belong only a small number of masculine and neuter nouns, but no feminines. The following nouns in this class are designated as active in *Beginning German*.

SINGULAR	GENITIVE	PLURAL	MEANING
das Auge	des Auges	die Augen	*the eye*
das Bett	des Bettes	die Betten	*the bed*
der Doktor	des Doktors	die Doktoren	*the doctor*
das Ende	des Endes	die Enden	*the end*
der Professor	des Professors	die Professoren	*the professor*

8. *Irregular Declension*

The following irregular and defective nouns are designated as active in *Beginning German*.

SINGULAR	GENITIVE	PLURAL	MEANING
das Auto	des Autos	die Autos	*the auto*
der Bauer	des Bauers *or* Bauern	die Bauern	*the peasant*
die Butter	der Butter	————	*the butter*
————	————	die Eltern	*the parents*
————.	————	die Ferien	*the vacation*
das Fleisch	des Fleisches	————	*the meat*
das Herz	des Herzens	die Herzen	*the heart*
————	————	die Leute	*the people*
der Name	des Namens	die Namen	*the name*
das Restaurant	des Restaurants	die Restaurants	*the restaurant*
die Weile	der Weile	————	*the while*
das Wort	des Wort(e)s	die Worte *or* Wörter	*the word*

9. *Declension of Adjectives*

A. Strong declension

MASCULINE	FEMININE	NEUTER
alter Mann	große Tür	kleines Fenster
alten Mannes	großer Tür	kleinen Fensters
altem Mann(e)	großer Tür	kleinem Fenster
alten Mann	große Tür	kleines Fenster
alte Männer	große Türen	kleine Fenster
alter Männer	großer Türen	kleiner Fenster
alten Männern	großen Türen	kleinen Fenstern
alte Männer	große Türen	kleine Fenster

Note that in the genitive singular, masculine and neuter, the weak ending **-en** is now generally used instead of the strong ending **-es**.

B. Weak declension

MASCULINE	FEMININE	NEUTER
dieser alte Mann	diese große Tür	dieses kleine Fenster
dieses alten Mannes	dieser großen Tür	dieses kleinen Fensters
diesem alten Mann(e)	dieser großen Tür	diesem kleinen Fenster
`diesen alten Mann	diese große Tür	dieses kleine Fenster
diese alten Männer	diese großen Türen	diese kleinen Fenster
dieser alten Männer	dieser großen Türen	dieser kleinen Fenster
diesen alten Männern	diesen großen Türen	diesen kleinen Fenstern
diese alten Männer	diese großen Türen	diese kleinen Fenster

C. Mixed declension

MASCULINE	FEMININE	NEUTER
ein alter Mann	eine große Tür	ein kleines Fenster
eines alten Mannes	einer großen Tür	eines kleinen Fensters
einem alten Mann(e)	einer großen Tür	einem kleinen Fenster
einen alten Mann	eine große Tür	ein kleines Fenster
alte Männer	große Türen	kleine Fenster
alter Männer	großer Türen	kleiner Fenster
alten Männern	großen Türen	kleinen Fenstern
alte Männer	große Türen	kleine Fenster

10. *Comparison of Adjectives and Adverbs*
The comparative is formed by adding **-er,** the superlative
by adding **-(e)st** to the adjective stem.   Adjectives ending in
a **t** or **s** sound add **-est** to form the superlative.   Constructions
corresponding to the English *more* and *most* are not used.

POSITIVE	COMPARATIVE	SUPERLATIVE	
breit	breiter	der, die, das breiteste	am breitesten
faul	fauler	der, die, das faulste	am faulsten
heiß	heißer	der, die, das heißeste	am heißesten
interessant	interessanter	der, die, das interessanteste	am interessantesten
klein	kleiner	der, die, das kleinste	am kleinsten

Certain adjectives in addition take Umlaut in the comparative and superlative. Such forms must be memorized. However, it is well to note that only adjectives of one syllable can take such an Umlaut, and the majority of these do. The following adjectives, designated as active in *Beginning German*, require Umlaut in the comparative and superlative.

alt	dumm	kalt	kurz	schwarz
arm	jung	krank	lang	warm

NOTE: **rot** may be used either with or without Umlaut.

The following adjectives and adverbs, designated as active in *Beginning German*, are irregular.

POSITIVE	COMPARATIVE	SUPERLATIVE	
bald	eher		am ehesten
gern	lieber		am liebsten
groß	größer	der, die, das größte	am größten
gut	besser	der, die, das beste	am besten
hoch	höher	der, die, das höchste	am höchsten
viel	mehr	der, die, das meiste	am meisten

11. Personal Pronouns

		1ST PERSON		2ND PERSON		3RD PERSON		
Sing.	Nom.	ich	I	du	Sie	er	sie	es
	Gen.	(meiner)	(of me)	(deiner)	(Ihrer)	(seiner)	(ihrer)	(seiner)
	Dat.	mir	to me	dir	Ihnen	ihm	ihr	ihm
	Acc.	mich	me	dich	Sie	ihn	sie	es

		1ST PERSON		2ND PERSON		3RD PERSON
Plural	Nom.	wir	we	ihr	Sie	sie
	Gen.	(unser)	(of us)	(euer)	(Ihrer)	(ihrer)
	Dat.	uns	to us	euch	Ihnen	ihnen
	Acc.	uns	us	euch	Sie	sie

12. *Relative Pronouns*

		MASCULINE		FEMININE	NEUTER
Sing.	Nom.	der	*who*	die	das
	Gen.	dessen	*whose*	deren	dessen
	Dat.	dem	*whom, to whom*	der	dem
	Acc.	den	*whom*	die	das

		FEMININE
Plural	Nom.	die
	Gen.	deren
	Dat.	denen
	Acc.	die

		MASCULINE	FEMININE	NEUTER
Sing.	Nom.	welcher	welche	welches
	Gen.	(dessen)	(deren)	(dessen)
	Dat.	welchem	welcher	welchem
	Acc.	welchen	welche	welches

Plural	Nom.	welche
	Gen.	(deren)
	Dat.	welchen
	Acc.	welche

13. *Interrogative Pronouns*

Nom.	wer	*who*	was	*what*
Gen.	wessen	*whose*	wessen	*of what*
Dat.	wem	*whom, to whom*	————	
Acc.	wen	*whom*	was	*what*

14. *Prepositions*

The following prepositions govern the genitive case. Except for **wegen** they have been designated as active in *Beginning German*.

anstatt (statt)	*instead of*
während	*during*
wegen	*on account of*

The following prepositions governing the dative have all been designated as active.

aus	*out, of, from*
außer	*besides, except*
bei	*by, at, near, with, at the house of*
mit	*with, by, at*
nach	*toward, to, for, after, according to*
seit	*since*
von	*from, of, by*
zu	*to, at, for, in, with*

The following prepositions governing the accusative have all been designated as active.

bis	*to, as far as, until*
durch	*through, by, by means of*
für	*for*
gegen	*against, towards, compared with, about*
ohne	*without*
um	*about, around, by, after, at, for*

The following prepositions govern either the dative or the accusative. They require the dative when the verb expresses rest or action not directed towards somebody or something. They govern the accusative when the verb expresses action directed toward somebody or something. All of the following have been designated as active, with the exception of **unter.**

an	*on, at, by, along, in, to, near*
auf	*on, upon, at, in, to, for*
hinter	*behind*
in	*in, at, into, to, within*
neben	*next to, near, beside*
über	*over, at, above, concerning*
unter	*under, below, among*
vor	*before, in front of, from, for, ago*
zwischen	*between*

15. *Numerals*

	CARDINALS	ORDINALS
1	ein(s)	der, die das **erste**
2	zwei	zweite
3	drei	**dritte**
4	vier	vierte
5	fünf	fünfte
6	sechs	sechste
7	sieben	sieb(en)te
8	acht	**achte**
9	neun	neunte
10	zehn	zehnte
11	elf	elfte
12	zwölf	zwölfte
13	dreizehn	dreizehnte
14	vierzehn	vierzehnte
15	fünfzehn	fünfzehnte
16	**sechzehn**	sechzehnte
17	**siebzehn**	siebzehnte
18	achtzehn	achtzehnte
19	neunzehn	neunzehnte
20	**zwanzig**	**zwanzigste**
21	einundzwanzig	einundzwanzigste
22	zweiundzwanzig	zweiundzwanzigste
23	dreiundzwanzig	dreiundzwanzigste
30	**dreißig**	dreißigste
40	vierzig	vierzigste
50	fünfzig	fünfzigste
60	**sechzig**	sechzigste
70	**siebzig**	siebzigste
80	achtzig	achtzigste
90	neunzig	neunzigste
100	hundert	hundertste
101	hundertundeins	hundertunderste
102	hundertundzwei	hundertundzweite
200	zweihundert	zweihundertste
1000	tausend	tausendste
1 000 000	eine Million	million(s)te
1 000 000 000	eine Milliarde	

16. *Conjugation of* **haben**

<table>
<tr><td colspan="2" align="center">INDICATIVE</td><td colspan="2" align="center">SUBJUNCTIVE</td></tr>
</table>

Present

INDICATIVE	SUBJUNCTIVE
ich habe	ich habe
du hast	du habest
er hat	er habe
wir haben	wir haben
ihr habt	ihr habet
sie haben	sie haben

Past

ich hatte	ich hätte
du hattest	du hättest
er hatte	er hätte
wir hatten	wir hätten
ihr hattet	ihr hättet
sie hatten	sie hätten

Future

ich werde haben	ich werde haben
du wirst haben	du werdest haben
er wird haben	er werde haben
wir werden haben	wir werden haben
ihr werdet haben	ihr werdet haben
sie werden haben	sie werden haben

Present Perfect

ich habe gehabt	ich habe gehabt
etc.	*etc.*

Past Perfect

ich hatte gehabt	ich hätte gehabt
etc.	*etc.*

Future Perfect

ich werde gehabt haben	ich werde gehabt haben
etc.	*etc.*

PRESENT CONDITIONAL	PERFECT CONDITIONAL
ich würde haben	ich würde gehabt haben
etc.	*etc.*

IMPERATIVE	PARTICIPLES	INFINITIVES
habe	*Present:* habend	*Present:* haben
habt	*Past:* gehabt	*Perfect:* gehabt haben
haben Sie		

17. *Conjugation of* sein

<table>
<tr><td align="center">INDICATIVE</td><td align="center">SUBJUNCTIVE</td></tr>
<tr><td colspan="2" align="center">*Present*</td></tr>
<tr><td>ich bin</td><td>ich sei</td></tr>
<tr><td>du bist</td><td>du sei(e)st</td></tr>
<tr><td>er ist</td><td>er sei</td></tr>
<tr><td>wir sind</td><td>wir seien</td></tr>
<tr><td>ihr seid</td><td>ihr seiet</td></tr>
<tr><td>sie sind</td><td>sie seien</td></tr>
<tr><td colspan="2" align="center">*Past*</td></tr>
<tr><td>ich war</td><td>ich wäre</td></tr>
<tr><td>du warst</td><td>du wärest</td></tr>
<tr><td>er war</td><td>er wäre</td></tr>
<tr><td>wir waren</td><td>wir wären</td></tr>
<tr><td>ihr wart</td><td>ihr wäret</td></tr>
<tr><td>sie waren</td><td>sie wären</td></tr>
<tr><td colspan="2" align="center">*Future*</td></tr>
<tr><td>ich werde sein</td><td>ich werde sein</td></tr>
<tr><td>du wirst sein</td><td>du werdest sein</td></tr>
<tr><td>er wird sein</td><td>er werde sein</td></tr>
<tr><td>wir werden sein</td><td>wir werden sein</td></tr>
<tr><td>ihr werdet sein</td><td>ihr werdet sein</td></tr>
<tr><td>sie werden sein</td><td>sie werden sein</td></tr>
<tr><td colspan="2" align="center">*Present Perfect*</td></tr>
<tr><td>ich bin gewesen
etc.</td><td>ich sei gewesen
etc.</td></tr>
<tr><td colspan="2" align="center">*Past Perfect*</td></tr>
<tr><td>ich war gewesen
etc.</td><td>ich wäre gewesen
etc.</td></tr>
<tr><td colspan="2" align="center">*Future Perfect*</td></tr>
<tr><td>ich werde gewesen sein
etc.</td><td>ich werde gewesen sein
etc.</td></tr>
</table>

PRESENT CONDITIONAL

ich würde sein
etc.

PERFECT CONDITIONAL

ich würde gewesen sein
etc.

IMPERATIVE	PARTICIPLES	INFINITIVES
sei	*Present:* seiend	*Present:* sein
seid	*Past:* gewesen	*Perfect:* gewesen sein
seien Sie		

18. *Conjugation of* **werden.**

INDICATIVE   SUBJUNCTIVE

Present

ich werde	ich werde
du wirst	du werdest
er wird	er werde

wir werden	wir werden
ihr werdet	ihr werdet
sie werden	sie werden

Past

ich wurde	ich würde
du wurdest	du würdest
er wurde	er würde

wir wurden	wir würden
ihr wurdet	ihr würdet
sie wurden	sie würden

Future

ich werde werden   ich werde werden
etc.   *etc.*

Present Perfect

ich bin geworden   ich sei geworden
etc.   *etc.*

Past Perfect

ich war geworden   ich wäre geworden
etc.   *etc.*

Future Perfect

ich werde geworden sein   ich werde geworden sein
etc.   *etc.*

PRESENT CONDITIONAL	PERFECT CONDITIONAL
ich würde werden	ich würde geworden sein
etc.	*etc.*

IMPERATIVE	PARTICIPLES	INFINITIVES
werde	*Present:* werdend	*Present:* werden
werdet	*Past:* geworden	*Perfect:* geworden sein
werden Sie		

19. Conjugation of a Weak Verb

INDICATIVE	SUBJUNCTIVE

Present

ich frage	ich frage
du fragst	du fragest
er fragt	er frage
wir fragen	wir fragen
ihr fragt	ihr fraget
sie fragen	sie fragen

Past

ich fragte	ich fragte
du fragtest	du fragtest
er fragte	er fragte
wir fragten	wir fragten
ihr fragtet	ihr fragtet
sie fragten	sie fragten

Future

ich werde fragen	ich werde fragen
etc.	*etc.*

Present Perfect

ich habe gefragt	ich habe gefragt
etc.	*etc.*

Past Perfect

ich hatte gefragt	ich hätte gefragt
etc.	*etc.*

Future Perfect

ich werde gefragt haben	ich werde gefragt haben
etc.	*etc.*

PRESENT CONDITIONAL	PERFECT CONDITIONAL
ich würde fragen	ich würde gefragt haben
etc.	*etc.*

IMPERATIVE	PARTICIPLES	INFINITIVES
frage	*Present:* fragend	*Present:* fragen
fragt	*Past:* gefragt	*Perfect:* gefragt haben
fragen Sie		

20. Conjugation of a Strong Verb

INDICATIVE	SUBJUNCTIVE
	Present
ich singe	ich singe
du singst	du singest
er singt	er singe
wir singen	wir singen
ihr singt	ihr singet
sie singen	sie singen
	Past
ich sang	ich sänge
du sangst	du sängest
er sang	er sänge
wir sangen	wir sängen
ihr sangt	ihr sänget
sie sangen	sie sängen
	Future
ich werde singen	ich werde singen
etc.	*etc.*
	Present Perfect
ich habe gesungen	ich habe gesungen
etc.	*etc.*
	Past Perfect
ich hatte gesungen	ich hätte gesungen
etc.	*etc.*
	Future Perfect
ich werde gesungen haben	ich werde gesungen haben
etc.	*etc.*

PRESENT CONDITIONAL	PERFECT CONDITIONAL
ich würde singen	ich würde gesungen haben
etc.	*etc.*

IMPERATIVE	PARTICIPLES	INFINITIVES
singe	*Present:* singend	*Present:* singen
singt	*Past:* gesungen	*Past:* gesungen haben
singen Sie		

21. Conjugation of Reflexive Verbs

DATIVE

ACCUSATIVE

Sing.

1. ich kaufe mir ein Buch

1. ich fürchte mich

2. du kaufst dir ein Buch
   Sie kaufen sich ein Buch

2. du fürchtest dich
   Sie fürchten sich

3. er ⎫
   sie ⎬ kauft sich ein Buch
   es ⎭

3. er ⎫
   sie ⎬ fürchtet sich
   es ⎭

Plural

1. wir kaufen uns ein Buch

1. wir fürchten uns

2. ihr kauft euch ein Buch
   Sie kaufen sich ein Buch

2. ihr fürchtet euch
   Sie fürchten sich

3. sie kaufen sich ein Buch

3. sie fürchten sich

22. Conjugation of Impersonal Verbs

Sing.

1. es geht mir gut

1. es freut mich

2. es geht dir gut
   es geht Ihnen gut

2. es freut dich
   es freut Sie

3. es geht ⎧ihm⎫
            ⎨ihr⎬ gut
            ⎩ihm⎭

3. es freut ⎧ihn
            ⎨sie
            ⎩es

Plural

1. es geht uns gut

1. es freut uns

2. es geht euch gut
   es geht Ihnen gut

2. es freut euch
   es freut Sie

3. es geht ihnen gut

3. es freut sie

23. Modal Auxiliaries

dürfen   können   mögen   müssen   sollen   wollen

PRESENT INDICATIVE

ich darf	ich kann	ich mag	ich muß	ich soll	ich will
du darfst	du kannst	du magst	du mußt	du sollst	du willst
er darf	er kann	er mag	er muß	er soll	er will

Sing.

Plural   Regular

PAST INDICATIVE

ich durfte ich konnte ich mochte ich mußte ich sollte ich wollte

PRESENT SUBJUNCTIVE

ich dürfe ich könne ich möge ich müsse ich solle ich wolle

PAST SUBJUNCTIVE

ich dürfte ich könnte ich möchte ich müßte ich sollte ich wollte

FUTURE

ich werde dürfen, können, *etc.*

PRESENT PERFECT

ich habe gedurft *or* dürfen, gekonnt *or* können, *etc.*

PAST PERFECT

ich hatte gedurft *or* dürfen, gekonnt *or* können, *etc.*

FUTURE PERFECT

ich werde gedurft haben, gekonnt haben, *etc.*

or

ich werde haben gehen dürfen, ich werde haben sehen dürfen,

etc.

PRESENT CONDITIONAL

ich würde dürfen, können, *etc.*

PERFECT CONDITIONAL

ich würde gedurft haben, gekonnt haben, **etc.**

or

ich würde haben gehen dürfen,
ich würde haben sehen dürfen,

etc.

24. *The Passive Voice*

<table>
<tr><td align="center">INDICATIVE</td><td align="center">SUBJUNCTIVE</td></tr>
</table>

Present

ich werde gesehen	ich werde gesehen
du wirst gesehen	du werdest gesehen
etc.	*etc.*

Past

ich wurde gesehen	ich würde gesehen
du wurdest gesehen	du würdest gesehen
etc.	*etc.*

Future

ich werde gesehen werden	ich werde gesehen werden
du wirst gesehen werden	du werdest gesehen werden
etc.	*etc.*

Present Perfect

ich bin gesehen worden	ich sei gesehen worden
du bist gesehen worden	du sei(e)st gesehen worden
etc.	*etc.*

Past Perfect

ich war gesehen worden	ich wäre gesehen worden
du warst gesehen worden	du wärest gesehen worden
etc.	*etc.*

Future Perfect

ich werde gesehen worden sein
du wirst gesehen worden sein
etc.

ich werde gesehen worden sein
du werdest gesehen worden sein
etc.

PRESENT CONDITIONAL

ich würde gesehen werden
du würdest gesehen werden
etc.

PERFECT CONDITIONAL

ich würde gesehen worden sein
du würdest gesehen worden sein
etc.

INFINITIVES

gesehen werden
gesehen worden sein

25. Irregular Weak Verbs

NOTE: Verbs marked with an asterisk are designated as active in *Beginning German.*

INFINITIVE	PAST	PAST PARTICIPLE	3RD SING.	MEANING
brennen	brannte	hat gebrannt		*to burn*
*kennen	kannte	hat gekannt		*to know*
*nennen	nannte	hat genannt		*to name*
rennen	rannte	ist gerannt		*to run*
senden	sandte	hat gesandt		*to send*
wenden	wandte	hat gewandt		*to turn*
*bringen	brachte	hat gebracht		*to bring*
*denken	dachte	hat gedacht		*to think*

26. Modal Auxiliaries and wissen

*dürfen	durfte	hat gedurft	er darf	*to be allowed*
*können	konnte	hat gekonnt	er kann	*to be able*
*mögen	mochte	hat gemocht	er mag	*to like; may*
*müssen	mußte	hat gemußt	er muß	*must; have to*
*sollen	sollte	hat gesollt	er soll	*shall; to be to*
*wollen	wollte	hat gewollt	er will	*to want to*
*wissen	wußte	hat gewußt	er weiß	*to know*

27. Strong and Irregular Verbs

backen	buk	hat gebacken	er bäckt	*to bake*
befehlen	befahl	hat befohlen	er befiehlt	*to command*
beginnen	begann	hat begonnen	er beginnt	*to begin*
beißen	biß	hat gebissen		*to bite*
bergen	barg	hat geborgen	er birgt	*to hide*
betrügen	betrog	hat betrogen		*to deceive*
bewegen	bewog	hat bewogen		*to induce*
biegen	bog	hat gebogen		*to bend*
bieten	bot	hat geboten		*to bid; offer*
binden	band	hat gebunden		*to bind; tie*
*bitten	bat	hat gebeten		*to ask; request*
blasen	blies	hat geblasen	er bläst	*to blow*
*bleiben	blieb	ist geblieben		*to remain*
braten	briet	hat gebraten	er brät	*to roast; fry*
brechen	brach	hat gebrochen	er bricht	*to break*
dringen	drang	ist gedrungen		*to press*

Infinitive	Past	Past Participle	3rd Sing.	Meaning
empfehlen	empfahl	hat empfohlen	er empfiehlt	*to recommend*
erlöschen	erlosch	ist erloschen	er erlischt	*to be extinguished*
erschrecken	erschrak	ist erschrocken	er erschrickt	*to be frightened*
*essen	aß	hat gegessen	er ißt	*to eat*
*fahren	fuhr	ist gefahren	er fährt	*to drive; ride*
*fallen	fiel	ist gefallen	er fällt	*to fall*
fangen	fing	hat gefangen	er fängt	*to catch*
fechten	focht	hat gefochten	er ficht	*to fight*
*finden	fand	hat gefunden		*to find*
fliegen	flog	ist geflogen		*to fly*
fliehen	floh	ist geflohen		*to flee*
fließen	floß	ist geflossen		*to flow*
fressen	fraß	hat gefressen	er frißt	*to eat* (of animals)
frieren	fror	hat gefroren		*to freeze*
*geben	gab	hat gegeben	er gibt	*to give*
gedeihen	gedieh	ist gediehen		*to thrive*
*gehen	ging	ist gegangen		*to go*
gelingen	gelang	ist gelungen		*to succeed*
gelten	galt	hat gegolten	er gilt	*to be worth*
genesen	genas	ist genesen		*to recover*
genießen	genoß	hat genossen		*to enjoy*
*geschehen	geschah	ist geschehen	es geschieht	*to happen*
gewinnen	gewann	hat gewonnen		*to win; gain*
gießen	goß	hat gegossen		*to pour*
gleichen	glich	hat geglichen		*to resemble*
gleiten	glitt	ist geglitten		*to glide*
graben	grub	hat gegraben	er gräbt	*to dig*
greifen	griff	hat gegriffen		*to seize; grip*
*halten	hielt	hat gehalten	er hält	*to hold*
hangen	hing	hat gehangen	er hängt	*to hang*
hauen	hieb	hat gehauen		*to hew; hit*
heben	hob	hat gehoben		*to lift*
*heißen	hieß	hat geheißen		*to be called*
*helfen	half	hat geholfen	er hilft	*to help*
klingen	klang	hat geklungen		*to sound*
*kommen	kam	ist gekommen		*to come*
kriechen	kroch	ist gekrochen		*to creep*
laden	lud	hat geladen	er ladet (lädt)	*to load*
lassen	ließ	hat gelassen	er läßt	*to let*
*laufen	lief	ist gelaufen	er läuft	*to run*
leiden	litt	hat gelitten		*to suffer*
leihen	lieh	hat geliehen		*to lend*
*lesen	las	hat gelesen	er liest	*to read*
liegen	lag	hat gelegen		*to lie*
lügen	log	hat gelogen		*to tell a lie*
meiden	mied	hat gemieden		*to avoid*
messen	maß	hat gemessen	er mißt	*to measure*

Infinitive	Past	Past Participle	3rd Sing.	Meaning
*nehmen	nahm	hat genommen	er nimmt	to take
pfeifen	pfiff	hat gepfiffen		to whistle
preisen	pries	hat gepriesen		to praise
quellen	quoll	ist gequollen	er quillt	to well up
raten	riet	hat geraten	er rät	to guess; advise
reiben	rieb	hat gerieben		to rub
reißen	riß	hat gerissen		to tear
reiten	ritt	ist geritten		to ride
riechen	roch	hat gerochen		to smell
rufen	rief	hat gerufen		to call
saufen	soff	hat gesoffen	er säuft	to drink (of animals)
schaffen	schuf	hat geschaffen		to create
scheiden	schied	hat (ist) geschieden		to part
*scheinen	schien	hat geschienen		to shine; seem
schelten	schalt	hat gescholten	er schilt	to scold
schieben	schob	hat geschoben		to shove
schießen	schoß	hat geschossen		to shoot
*schlafen	schlief	hat geschlafen	er schläft	to sleep
schlagen	schlug	hat geschlagen	er schlägt	to strike
schleichen	schlich	ist geschlichen		to sneak
schließen	schloß	hat geschlossen		to close
schleifen	schliff	hat geschliffen		to grind
schmelzen	schmolz	hat (ist) geschmolzen	er schmilzt	to melt
schneiden	schnitt	hat geschnitten		to cut
*schreiben	schrieb	hat geschrieben		to write
schreien	schrie	hat geschrien		to cry
schreiten	schritt	ist geschritten		to stride
schweigen	schwieg	hat geschwiegen		to be silent
schwellen	schwoll	ist geschwollen	er schwillt	to swell
schwimmen	schwamm	ist geschwommen		to swim
schwinden	schwand	ist geschwunden		to vanish
schwingen	schwang	hat geschwungen		to swing
schwören	schwor	hat geschworen		to swear
*sehen	sah	hat gesehen	er sieht	to see
*sein	war	ist gewesen	er ist	to be
sieden	sott	hat gesotten		to boil
*singen	sang	hat gesungen		to sing
sinken	sank	ist gesunken		to sink
sinnen	sann	hat gesonnen		to think
*sitzen	saß	hat gesessen		to sit
speien	spie	hat gespien		to spit
spinnen	spann	hat gesponnen		to spin
*sprechen	sprach	hat gesprochen	er spricht	to speak
sprießen	sproß	ist gesprossen		to sprout
stechen	stach	hat gestochen	er sticht	to prick
*stehen	stand	hat gestanden		to stand
stehlen	stahl	hat gestohlen	er stiehlt	to steal

INFINITIVE	PAST	PAST PARTICIPLE	3RD SING.	MEANING
steigen	stieg	ist gestiegen		to climb
*sterben	starb	ist gestorben	er stirbt	to die
stoßen	stieß	hat gestoßen	er stößt	to push
streichen	strich	hat gestrichen		to stroke
streiten	stritt	hat gestritten		to contend
tragen	trug	hat getragen	er trägt	to carry
*treffen	traf	hat getroffen	er trifft	to hit; meet
treiben	trieb	hat getrieben		to drive
treten	trat	ist getreten	er tritt	to step
*trinken	trank	hat getrunken		to drink
*tun	tat	hat getan		to do
verderben	verdarb	hat (ist) verdorben	er verdirbt	to spoil; ruin
*vergessen	vergaß	hat vergessen	er vergißt	to forget
verlieren	verlor	hat verloren		to lose
verzeihen	verzieh	hat verziehen		to pardon
wachsen	wuchs	ist gewachsen	er wächst	to grow
waschen	wusch	hat gewaschen	er wäscht	to wash
weichen	wich	ist gewichen		to yield
weisen	wies	hat gewiesen		to show
werben	warb	hat geworben	er wirbt	to woo
*werden	wurde	ist geworden	er wird	to become
werfen	warf	hat geworfen	er wirft	to throw
wiegen	wog	hat gewogen		to weigh
winden	wand	hat gewunden		to wind
ziehen	zog	hat gezogen		to pull
zwingen	zwang	hat gezwungen		to force

28. German Type

ROMAN TYPE		GERMAN TYPE		ROMAN TYPE		GERMAN TYPE	
A	a	𝔄	a	N	n	𝔑	n
B	b	𝔅	b	O	o	𝔒	o
C	c	ℭ	c	P	p	𝔓	p
D	d	𝔇	d	Q	q	𝔔	q
E	e	𝔈	e	R	r	𝔑	r
F	f	𝔉	f	S	s	𝔖 ſ s	
G	g	𝔊	g	T	t	𝔗	t
H	h	𝔥	h	U	u	𝔘	u
I	i	𝔍	i	V	v	𝔙	v
J	j	𝔍	j	W	w	𝔚	w
K	k	𝔎	k	X	x	𝔛	x
L	l	𝔏	l	Y	y	𝔜	y
M	m	𝔐	m	Z	z	𝔷	z

Modified Vowels (Umlaute)

Ä ä 𝔄 ä   Ö ö 𝔒 ö   Ü ü 𝔘 ü

Compound Consonants

ch	ch	ss	ſſ	tz	tz
sch	ſch	ß, sz, ss	ß	ph	ph
ck	ck	st	ſt		

Distinguish carefully between 𝔅 and 𝔙, ℭ and ℭ, 𝔑 and 𝔑, ſ and ſ, n and u, r and r.

The German capital form 𝔍 stands for both I and J. When followed by a vowel it is read as J; when followed by a consonant, as I: der Juli, der Junge; die Jdee, die Jnſel.

The so-called final ß is used only at the end of words or syllables.

IDIOMS AND VOCABULARIES

NOTE.—The genitive singular and the nominative plural of nouns are indicated as follows: **der Mann, -es, ⸚er = der Mann, des Mannes, die Männer; die Frau, -, -en = die Frau, der Frau, die Frauen.** The principal parts of strong and irregular verbs are given with the auxiliary in the perfect tense, and the third person of the present indicative when it has a vowel change or is irregular: **nehmen, nahm, hat genommen, er nimmt.** When the auxiliary of weak verbs is **sein,** it is indicated in parentheses after the infinitive: **folgen (sein).** Separable compound verbs have a hyphen between the prefix and the verb: **ab-fahren.**

The accent is indicated where it might be helpful to the student.

The following abbreviations are used:

acc.	accusative	*inf.*	infinitive
adj.	adjective	*intr.*	intransitive
adv.	adverb	*masc.*	masculine
conj.	conjunction	*neut.*	neuter
dat.	dative	*pl.*	plural
fam.	familiar	*prep.*	preposition
fem.	feminine	*sing.*	singular
gen.	genitive	*trans.*	transitive

LIST OF ACTIVE IDIOMS

Abend: guten Abend good evening
alle beide both
Angst haben vor (+ *dat.*) to be afraid of
aus: die Schule ist aus school is over
auswendig lernen (können, wissen) to learn (know) by heart
Beispiel: zum Beispiel for example; *abbrev.* **z.B.**
bitte please
bitten um (+ *acc.*) to ask for, request
bleiben: stehenbleiben to stop
danke (schön) thanks, thank you (very much)
denken an (+ *acc.*) to think of
deutsch: auf deutsch in German
einmal: auf einmal suddenly, all at once
Ende: am Ende at the end
  zu Ende at an end, over
Frage: eine Frage stellen to ask a question
fragen nach (+ *dat.*) to ask for, inquire for (about)
freuen: sich freuen auf (+ *acc.*) to look forward to
fürchten: sich fürchten vor (+ *dat.*) to be afraid of
Fuß: zu Fuß on foot
gar nicht (nichts) not (nothing) at all; **gar kein Geld** no money at all
geben: es gibt (+ *acc.*) there is, there are (*general existence only*)
gefallen: es gefällt mir (dir, ihm, usw.) I (you, he, etc.) like
gehen: es geht mir (dir, ihm, usw.) gut I (you, he, etc.) am well
  wie geht es Ihnen? how are you?
  das geht nicht that won't do, that's out of the question
gern lesen (schreiben, usw.) to like to read (write, etc.)
gestern abend (morgen, usw.) last evening, yesterday morning, etc.
Hand: die Hand geben to shake hands
handeln von (+ *dat.*) to treat of, deal with
Haus: nach Hause home (*direction*)
  zu Hause at home
heißen: er heißt he is called, his name is
  wie heißt er? what is his name?
  das heißt (d.h.) that is (i.e.)
heute abend (morgen, usw.) this evening (morning, etc.)
hin und her to and fro, back and forth
immer noch still
immer später (länger, usw.) later and later (longer and longer, etc.)
immer wieder again and again
Jahr: vor einem Jahr a year ago; **vor Jahren** years ago

Land: auf das Land   to the country
   auf dem Lande   in the country
leid tun: es tut mir (dir, ihm, usw.) leid   I (you, he, etc.) am sorry
los: was ist los?   what is the matter?
machen: das macht nichts   that does not matter
machen Sie schnell (*fam.* **mach' schnell)**   make haste, hurry (up)
mehr: kein Geld mehr   no more money
Mittagessen: zum Mittagessen   for (to) dinner
Morgen: guten Morgen   good morning
nach und nach   by and by, gradually
noch ein   another
noch ein paar   a few more
noch immer   still
noch nicht(s)   not yet (anything); **noch nie**   never yet
paar: ein paar   a few, several
Platz nehmen   to take a seat, be seated
Reise: eine Reise machen   to take a trip
recht haben   to be right
schade: es ist schade   it is too bad, it is a pity
schicken an (+ *acc.*)   to send to
so groß wie   as large as
schreiben an (+ *acc.*)   to write to
Schule: in die Schule   to school
Stadt: in die Stadt gehen   to go down town
stehenbleiben   to stop; **er bleibt stehen**   he stops
Spaziergang: einen Spaziergang machen   to take a walk
Straße: auf der Straße   on (in) the street (*walking, playing*)
   in der Straße   on the street (*residing*)
Tag: guten Tag   good day, how do you do? good-bye
   heute (morgen) über acht Tage   a week from today (tomorrow)
   heute (gestern) vor acht Tagen   a week ago today (yesterday)
Uhr: wieviel Uhr ist es?   what time is it?
   um ein (zwei, drei) Uhr   at one (two, three) o'clock
usw. (und so weiter)   etc. (et cetera, and so forth)
Universität: an der Universität   at the university (*faculty*)
   auf der Universität   at the university (*students*)
vor fünf (zehn, vielen, usw.) Jahren   five (ten, many, etc.) years ago
vor kurzem   a short time ago, recently
wahr: nicht wahr?   isn't that so?
warten auf (+ *acc.*)   to wait for
was für ein   what kind of; what a
Weg: sich auf den Weg machen   to start out
wert: (viel) mehr wert   worth (much) more; **nichts wert**   not worth
   anything
wie ist?   how is?
wiedersehen: auf Wiederseh(e)n   au revoir, good-bye

GERMAN-ENGLISH VOCABULARY

A

*der Abend, -s, -e the evening; abends in the evening; zu Abend in the evening

der Abendsonnenschein, -s the evening sunshine

*aber but, however

*ab-fahren, fuhr ab, ist abgefahren, er fährt ab to leave, depart

die Abfahrt, -, -en the departure

sich ab-kehren to turn away

*ab-nehmen, nahm ab, hat abgenommen, er nimmt ab to take off

der Abschied, -(e)s, -e the farewell, departure; Abschied nehmen to take leave, depart

ab-schneiden, schnitt ab, hat abgeschnitten to cut off

das (or der) Abteil, -(e)s, -e the compartment

ab-wischen to wipe off, wipe away

*ach ah, oh, alas

*acht eight

achtzehn eighteen

(das) Afrika, -s Africa

ähnlich similar, like

die Ähre, -, -n the ear of grain

(das) Albany, -s Albany

Alexander der Große, Alexanders des Großen Alexander the Great

*allein' alone

*aller, alle, alles all, every; alles everything

allerlei all kinds of; das Allerlei, -s, -s miscellaneous things; miscellany

die Alpen (pl.) the Alps

*als as, when; (after comparative) than; als ob as if

*also so, therefore, accordingly

die Alster, - the Alster (river flowing through Hamburg)

*alt old, ancient

der Altar', -s, ⁻e the altar

*(das) Amē'rika, -s America

*der Amērika'ner, -s, - the American

*die Amērika'nerin, -, -nen the American (woman)

amērika'nisch American (adj.)

*an (+ dat. or acc.) on, at, by, along, in, to, near

*ander other

die Anekdo'te, -, -n the anecdote

der Anfang, -(e)s, ⁻e the beginning

*an-fangen, fing an, hat angefangen, er fängt an to begin

angenehm pleasant, agreeable

das Angesicht, -(e)s, -e the countenance, face

an-grenzen, grenzte an, ist angegrenzt to border upon

*die Angst, -, ⁻e the fear

*an-kommen, kam an, ist angekommen to arrive

die Ankunft, -, ⁻e the arrival

an-schauen to look at

an-sehen, sah an, hat angesehen, er sieht an to look at

*anstatt (+ gen. or inf. with zu) instead of

267

*die Antwort, -, -en   the answer
*antworten   to answer
*an-ziehen, zog an, hat ange-
  zogen   to put on, to dress
der Appetit', -s   the appetite
der April', - or -s, -e   April
der Äqua'tor, -s   the equator
die Arbeit, -, -en   the work
*arbeiten   to work
der Arbeitsmann, -(e)s, ⸚er   the
  workingman, laborer
der Architekt', -s, -en   the
  architect
ärgerlich   annoyed, angry, peeved
aristokra'tisch   aristocratic
Aristo'teles   Aristotle
*arm   poor
*der Arm, -es, -e   the arm
die Armee', -, -n   the army
*der Arzt, -es, ⸚e   the physician,
  doctor
(das) Asien, -s   Asia
der Atlan'tische Ozean, des
  Atlantischen Ozeans   the Atlantic Ocean
die Atmosphä're, -, -n   the atmosphere
*auch   also, too
*auf (+ dat. or acc.)   on, upon, at,
  in, to, for
auf-bauen   to erect, build up;
  rebuild; aufgebaut   built up
auf-führen   to perform
die Aufführung, -, -en   the performance, production
*die Aufgabe, -, -n   the lesson,
  task
aufgeregt   excited
sich auf-halten, hielt sich auf,
  hat sich aufgehalten, er hält
  sich auf   to stop, sojourn, stay
*auf-heben, hob auf, hat aufge-
  hoben   to pick up; to raise
*auf-machen   to open

die Aufrichtigkeit, -, -en   the
  uprightness, sincerity
auf-sehen, sah auf, hat auf-
  gesehen, er sieht auf   to look
  upon, observe
auf-setzen   to set on, put up
*auf-stehen, stand auf, ist auf-
  gestanden   to stand up, get up,
  rise
auf-steigen, stieg auf, ist aufge-
  stiegen   to ascend, rise
*das Auge, -s, -n   the eye
*der Augenblick, -(e)s, -e   the
  moment
das Äuglein, -s, -   the little eye
der August', - or -(e)s, -e   August
*aus (+ dat.)   out, of, from
der Ausflug, -(e)s, ⸚e   the outing,
  picnic; einen Ausflug machen
  to take a trip (for pleasure)
aus-gehen, ging aus, ist ausgegangen   to go out
aus-graben, grub aus, hat aus-
  gegraben, er gräbt aus   to dig
  out
die Ausnahme, -, -n   the exception
aus-sehen, sah aus, hat aus-
  gesehen, er sieht aus   to appear, look
*außer (+ dat.)   except, besides
außerdem   besides
die Aussicht, -, -en   the view
(das) Austra'lien, -s   Australia
aus-trinken, trank aus, hat ausgetrunken   to empty by drinking, drain (a glass, etc.)
*auswendig   by heart
*das Auto(mobil'), -s, die Autos,
  die Automobile   the automobile
die Autobahn, -, -en   the super
  highway
der Autobus, -ses, -se   the motor-
  bus

die Autofahrt, -, -en the motor trip

B

das Bächlein, -s, - the little brook

das Bad, -es, ⁼er the bath

(das) Baden-Baden, -s (city of) Baden-Baden

das Badezimmer, -s, - the bathroom

*der Bahnhof, -(e)s, ⁼e the railway station

*bald soon

das Baltische Meer, des Baltischen Meeres the Baltic Sea

der Band, -es, ⁼e the volume

*die Bank, -, ⁼e the bench; bank

das Barock', -s the baroque (*style*)

der Barockstil, -(e)s the baroque style (*architecture of the 17th century, coming between Renaissance and Rococo*)

der Bart, -es, ⁼e the beard

(das) Basel, -s (city of) Basle

bauen to build

*der Bauer, -s *or* -n, -n the peasant

die Bäuerin, -, -nen the peasant woman

bäuerlich peasant (*adj.*); country, rural

das Bauernhaus, -es, ⁼er the peasant's house

der Bauernhof, -es, ⁼e the farm

*der Baum, -(e)s, ⁼e the tree

(das) Bayern, -s Bavaria

bayrisch Bavarian

das Becken, -s, - the basin

bedeckt covered

bedeu'ten to signify, mean

bedeu'tend significant, important

die Bedeu'tung, -, -en the significance, importance

beenden to terminate

sich befin'den, befand sich, hat sich befunden to be, feel; to be found

sich begeben, begab sich, hat sich begeben, er begibt sich to betake (oneself), go, set out

*begeg'nen (sein) (+ *dat.*) to meet

begin'nen, begann, hat begonnen to begin

beherrschen to command

*bei (+ *dat.*) by, at, near, with, at the house of

*beide both

*beina'h(e) almost

*das Beispiel, -(e)s, -e the example

*bekannt' well known

*bekom'men, bekam, hat bekommen to get, receive

(das) Belgien, -s Belgium

benutzen to use

der Berg, -(e)s, -e the hill, mountain

(das) Berlin', -s Berlin

der Berli'ner, -s the inhabitant (or native) of Berlin

berühmt' famous

beschädigen to damage, injure

beschließen, beschloß, hat beschlossen to decide

besetzen to occupy, put, lay on

beson'der special

beson'ders especially

*besser better

beste'hen, bestand, hat bestanden to exist; (aus + *dat.*) consist of

*bestel'len to order

*besu'chen to visit

beten to pray

*das Bett, -es, -en the bed

bevor before

bewundern to admire

*bezah'len to pay
die Bezah'lung, -, -en the payment
bezau'bern to bewitch, enchant
die Bibliothek', -, -en the library
*das Bier, -(e)s, -e the beer
das Bild, -es, -er the picture
bilden to form
der Bildhauer, -s, - the sculptor
*billig cheap, inexpensive
(das) Bingen, -s (city of) Bingen
*bis (+ acc.) to, as far as, until; **bis an, bis auf, bis zu,** etc. to, up to, as far as; conj. until
der Bischof, -s, ⁼e the bishop
das bißchen the little bit
bitte please
*bitten, bat, hat gebeten um (+ acc.) to beg, plead, ask for
bitter bitter
bitterlich bitterly
*blau blue
*bleiben, blieb, ist geblieben to remain, stay
bleich pale
*der Bleistift, -(e)s, -e the lead pencil
der Blick, -(e)s, -e the view; glance, look
*blitzen to lighten, emit lightning; flash, gleam
die Blocka'de, -, -n the blockade
blühen to bloom, flourish
das Blümchen, -s, - the little flower
*die Blume, -, -n the flower
der Bodensee, -s the Lake of Constance
der Böhmer Wald, -(e)s the Bohemian Forest
die Bombe, -, -n the bomb
(das) Bonn (city of) Bonn
das Boot, -(e)s, -e the boat

der Bord, -(e)s, -e the shipboard; **an Bord** on board, aboard
*böse bad; angry
(das) Bozen, -s (city of) Bolzano
das Brandenburger Tor, des Brandenburger Tor(e)s the Brandenburg Gate
*brauchen to need
*braun brown
brausen to roar
brechen, brach, hat gebrochen, er bricht to break; pick (a flower)
*breit wide
(das) Bremen, -s (city of) Bremen
(das) Bremerhaven, -s (city of) Bremerhaven
der Brenner-Paß, -Passes the Brenner Pass
*der Brief, -(e)s, -e the letter
*die Briefmarke, -, -n the postage stamp
der Briefträger, -s, - the postman, mail carrier
*bringen, brachte, hat gebracht to bring
der Brocken, -s the Brocken (highest peak of the Harz Mountains)
*das Brot, -(e)s, -e the bread
die Brücke, -, -n the bridge
*der Bruder, -s, ⁼ the brother
der Brunnen, -s, - the fountain; spring
die Brust, -, ⁼e the breast
*das Buch, -es, ⁼er the book
die Buchdruckerkunst, - the art of printing
(das) Budapest, -s (city of) Budapest
die Bühne, -, -n the stage
(das) Bulga'rien, -s Bulgaria

das Bundeshaus, -es, ¨er the federal parliament building
die Bundesrepublik, -, -en the federal republic
bunt gay-colored
die Burg, -, -en the castle
das Burgtheater, -s the Burg (castle) Theater (*principal theater of Vienna*)
das Burgtor, -(e)s, -e the castle gate
der Bursche, -n, -n(*or* -e) youth, fellow
*die Butter, - the butter

C

das Café, -s, -s the café
der Charak'ter, -s, -e the character
charakteris'tisch characteristic
der Chauffeur', -s, -e the chauffeur
(das) Chika'go, -s Chicago
(das) China, -s China
der Columbia-Distrikt', -s the District of Columbia
(das) Cuxhaven, -s (city of) Cuxhaven

D

*da there, here, then; *conj*. as, since, when
das Dach, -(e)s, ¨er the roof
das Dachl, -s, - the little roof (*Austrian colloquial*)
dadurch thereby
dafür for it
daher thence, from that place; *conj*. therefore
damals at that time
*die Dame, -, -n the lady
damit therewith, with it; *conj*. in order that, so that

*der Dampfer, -s, - the steamer
daneben near it, next to it
(das) Dänemark, -s Denmark
die Dankbarkeit, - the gratitude
*danken (+ *dat*.) to thank
*dann then
darauf thereupon, on it
daraus out of it, from it
darin therein, in it
darüber about it
*darum therefore
darunter under it; among them
*das the (*neuter article*); that
*daß (*conj*.) that
*dauern to last; take
davon of that, therefrom
das Deck, -(e)s, -e the deck
die Decke, -, -n covering, blanket; ceiling, roof
*dein your (*fam. sing.*)
demokratisch democratic
*denken, dachte, hat gedacht (an + *acc*.) to think
*denn for
*der the (*masc. article*); that
*derselbe, dieselbe, dasselbe the same
derweil' while
deshalb therefore
deutlich clear, distinct
*deutsch German; das Deutsch the German language
*(das) Deutschland, -s Germany
der Dezem'ber, - *or* -s, - December
*der Dichter, -s, - the poet
die Dichterin, -, -nen the poetess
dick thick, fat
*die the (*fem. article*); that
*der Dienstag, -s, -e Tuesday
*das Dienstmädchen, -s, - the servant girl
*dieser, diese, dieses this, this one
*das Ding, -(e)s, -e the thing

direkt' direct(ly)

doch nevertheless, yet

*der Doktor, -s, die Dokto'ren the doctor

die Dolomiten (*pl*.) the Dolomites (*Alps of the Southern Tyrol*)

der Dom, -(e)s, -e the cathedral

die Donau, - the Danube (river)

*donnern to thunder

*der Donnerstag, -s, -e Thursday

doppelt double; twice

*das Dorf, -(e)s, ⸗er the village

die Dorfstraße, -, -n the village street

*dort there

(das) Dortmund (city of) Dortmund

*drei three

drein-schauen to look on

*dreißig thirty

dreizehn thirteen

(das) Dresden, -s (city of) Dresden

*dritt third

drittgrößt third largest

drücken to press

*du you (*fam. sing.*)

das Duellie'ren, -s the dueling

*dumm stupid

*dunkel dark

dunkeln to grow dark

*durch (+ *acc*.) through, by, by means of

*dürfen, durfte, hat gedurft, er darf to be allowed, be permitted, may

(das) Düsseldorf (city of) Düsseldorf

E

eben even, smooth; *adv.* just, just now, then

ebenso just so, equally

die Ebene, -, -n the plain

*die Ecke, -, -n the corner

edel noble

*ehe before

die Ehre, -, -n the honor

*das Ei, -(e)s, -er the egg

*ein a, an, one; eins one (*in counting*)

einfach simple, easy

der Einfluß, -sses, ⸗sse the influence

einhalb one-half

*einige several, some

ein-kehren to enter, turn in

*einmal once

einsam lonesome

einst sometime, once upon a time

ein-steigen, stieg ein, ist eingestiegen to get in

eintönig monotonous

der Eintritt, -(e)s, -e the entrance, admission; beginning

der Einwohner, -s, - the inhabitant

einzig only, sole

das Eis, -es the ice

*die Eisenbahn, -, -en the railroad

der Eisenbahnzug, -(e)s, ⸗e the (railway) train

die Elbe, - the Elbe (river)

elegant' elegant

*elf eleven

*die Eltern the parents

*das Ende, -s, -n the end

*endlich finally

eng narrow

(das) England, -s England

der Engländer, -s, - the Englishman

die Engländerin, -, -nen the English woman

englisch English

entdecken to discover

entfernt distant, away

entflie'hen, entfloh, ist entflohen to escape

enthal'ten, enthielt, hat enthalten, er enthält to contain

entlang' along; am Ufer entlang along the shore

entste'hen, entstand, ist entstanden to originate, arise

*entwe'der either

*er he; it

die Erde, -, -n the earth

der Erfinder, -s, - the inventor

erfüllen to fulfil

ergrei'fen, ergriff, hat ergriffen to seize, grasp

ergriffen (adj.) deeply stirred

erhal'ten, erhielt, hat erhalten, er erhält to preserve, keep; receive

erklä'ren to explain

der Ernst, -es the earnestness, seriousness

erquicken to refresh

errei'chen to reach

*erst first; only, not until

*erstaunt' astonished

erwei'sen, erwies, hat erwiesen to bestow upon

erwidern to return; reply

*erzäh'len to relate, tell

das Erzbistum, -s, ⸗er the archbishopric

das Erzgebirge, -s Ore Mountains

erziehen, erzog, hat erzogen to bring up, educate

*es it; she

der Esel, -s, - the donkey, ass; fool

(das) Essen (city of) Essen

*essen, aß, hat gegessen, er ißt to eat

*etwas something, anything

*euer your (pl. fam.)

*das Euro'pa, -s Europe

der Europä'er, -s, - the European

europä'isch European

ewig eternal

die Ewigkeit, -, -en eternity

das Examen, -s, Examina the examination; ein Examen machen to take an examination

existieren to exist

F

*fahren, fuhr, ist gefahren, er fährt to drive, go, ride, travel

*die Fahrkarte, -, -n the ticket

die Fahrt, -, -en the journey, trip, ride

der Fall, -(e)s, ⸗e the case; auf jeden Fall in any case, by all means

*fallen, fiel, ist gefallen, er fällt to fall

*falsch wrong

*die Fami'lie, -, -n the family

*die Farbe, -, -n the color

das Faß, -sses, ⸗sser the cask, keg, barrel

fassen to hold

fast almost

*faul lazy

der Februar, - or -s, -e February

*die Feder, -, -n the feather; pen

fehlen to lack; uns fehlt we lack

*fein fine

der Feind, -(e)s, -e the enemy

das Feld, -(e)s, -er the field

der Fels, -en, -en or der Felsen, -s, - the rock, cliff

das Felsenriff, -(e)s, -e the reef

die Felsenwand, -, ⸗e the wall of rock, precipice

*das Fenster, -s, - the window

*die Ferien (*pl. only*) the vacation
fern far, distant
die Ferne, -, -n the distance
fertig finished, ready
das Fest, -es, -e the festival, fête
das Festspielhaus, -es, =er the festival playhouse
das Festungswerk, -(e)s, -e the fortification
*das Feuer, -s, - the fire
die Fichte, -, -n the fir, spruce
der Fichtenbaum, -(e)s, =e the fir tree
der Film, -(e)s, -e the film
*finden, fand, hat gefunden to find
sich finden, fand sich, hat sich gefunden to find oneself
flach flat, level
die Flamme, -, -n the flame
die Flasche, -, -n the bottle
*das Fleisch, -es the meat
*fleißig diligent, industrious
fliegen, flog, ist geflogen to fly
fließen, floß, ist geflossen to flow
die Flugkarte, -, -n the air ticket
der Flugplatz, -es, =e the airport
das Flugzeug, -(e)s, -e the airplane
der Fluß, -sses, =sse the river
das Flüßchen, -s, - the rivulet, stream
*folgen (sein) (+ *dat.*) to follow
folgend following, next, subsequent
fort-blühen to continue to blossom, bloom
*die Frage, -, -n the question
*fragen to ask
der Franke, -n, -n the Frank
(das) Frankfurt, -s (city of) Frankfort
(das) Frankreich, -s France

der Franzo'se, -n, -n the Frenchman
*die Frau, -, -en the woman; Mrs.
frei free
*der Freitag, -(e)s, -e Friday
*fremd strange
die Freude, -, -n the joy
*sich freuen to be pleased
*der Freund, -(e)s, -e the friend
die Freundin, -, -nen the friend (*fem.*)
freundlich friendly
der Friede, -ns the peace; **Frieden schließen** to make peace
Friedrich der Große, Friedrichs des Großen Frederick the Great
(das) Friedrichshafen, -s (town of) Friedrichshafen
*frisch fresh
froh happy, glad, merry
fromm pious
fruchtbar fruitful, fertile
frugal' frugal
*früh early
früher formerly
*der Frühling, -s, -e the spring
*das Frühstück, -s, -e the breakfast
fühlen to feel
führen to lead, bring
füllen to fill
*fünf five
fünfzehn fifteen
der Funke, -n, -n *or* **der Funken, -s, -** the spark
funkeln to sparkle
*für (+ *acc.*) for; **für und für** forever and ever
*fürchten to fear; **sich fürchten** to be afraid; **sich fürchten vor** (+ *dat.*) to be afraid of
die Furt, -, -en the ford
der Fürst, -en, -en the prince

das Fürstentum, -(e)s, ⸗er the principality

*der Fuß, -es, ⸗e the foot

G

die Galerie', -, -n the gallery

*ganz whole, entire

gar very; at all; even

*der Garten, -s, ⸗ the garden

das Gartenrestaurant, -s, -s the garden restaurant

*der Gast, -(e)s, ⸗e the guest

das Gasthaus, -es, ⸗er the inn

das Gebäude, -s, - the building

*geben, gab, hat gegeben, er gibt to give

das Gebiet, -(e)s, -e the district

das Gebir'ge, -s, - the mountain range

gebir'gig mountainous

*gebo'ren born

das Geburtshaus, -es, ⸗er the house where a person was born

der Geburts'tag, -(e)s, -e the birthday

die Gedächtniskirche, -, -n the memorial church

gedei'hen, gedieh, ist gediehen to prosper, thrive, grow

*das Gedicht', -(e)s, -e the poem

gefähr'lich dangerous

*gefal'len, gefiel, hat gefallen, er (es) gefällt to please; like

*gegen (+ acc.) against, toward, compared with, about

die Gegend, -, -en the region, district

*gehen, ging, ist gegangen to go

gehorchen (+ dat.) to obey

*gehö'ren (+ dat.) to belong

*gelb yellow

*das Geld, -es, -er the money

der Geldbeutel, -s, - the money bag, purse

geleert' (see leeren)

der Gelehrte, -n, -n the learned person, scholar

geloben to vow

gelten, galt, hat gegolten, er(es) gilt be valid, be worth, concern; es gilt mir it is meant for me

*das Gemü'se, -s, - the vegetable(s)

genau' exact

genießen, genoß, hat genossen to enjoy

*genug' enough

die Geographie', -, -n the geography

das Gepäck', -(e)s, -e the baggage

der Gepäck'träger, -s, - the baggage carrier, porter

gepol'stert upholstered

gera'de straight; just

*gern(e) gladly

*gesche'hen, geschah, ist geschehen, es geschieht to happen

das Geschenk', -(e)s, -e the present, gift

*die Geschich'te, -, -n the story; history

das Geschmei'de, -s, - the jewelry

geschnitzt carved

das Gesicht, -(e)s, -er the face, visage

das Gespräch', -(e)s, -e the conversation

*gestern yesterday

getrost' confident

gewal'tig powerful, mighty

*gewiß' certain, sure

das Gewitter, -s, - the thunder storm

der Gewit'terregen, -s, - the thunder shower

der Gewit′terwind, -(e)s, -e   the wind of a thunder storm
*gewöhn′lich   usual
das Gift, -(e)s, -e   the poison
der Gipfel, -s, -   the summit, peak, top
*das Glas, -es, ″er   the glass
*glauben   to believe
gleich   immediately; equal, like
*glücklich   happy
golden   golden
der Golfstrom, -(e)s   the gulf stream
gotisch   gothic
der Gott, -es, ″er   God
der Graben, -s, ″   the ditch, moat
graben, grub, hat gegraben, er gräbt   to dig
das Gras, -es, ″er   the grass
grau   gray
greifen, griff, hat gegriffen   to grasp, seize; reach
die Grenze, -, -n   the boundary
Gretchen   *diminutive of* Margaret
das Griechenland, -(e)s   Greece
*groß   large, great
großartig   grand, magnificent
das Großherzogtum, -s, ″er   the grand duchy
*die Großmutter, -, ″   the grandmother
die Großstadt, -, ″e   the metropolis
*der Großvater, -s, ″   the grandfather
grün   green
gründen   to found
die Gründung, -, -en   the founding
der Gruß, -es, ″e   the greeting
*grüßen   to greet
die Gunst, -   the favor
*gut   good

H

das Haar, -(e)s, -e   the hair
*haben, hatte, hat gehabt, er hat   to have
der Hafen, -s, ″   the harbor
die Hafenstadt, -, ″e   the harbor city, seaport
der Hahn, -(e)s, ″e   the rooster
halb   half
die Hälfte, -, -n   half
*halten, hielt, hat gehalten, er hält   to hold; keep; halten für   to hold to be
(das) Hamburg, -s   (city of) Hamburg
die Hamburg-Amerika Linie   the Hamburg-American Line
*die Hand, -, ″e   the hand
*handeln   to act; von   (+ *dat.*) deal with, treat of
die Handelsstadt, -, ″e   the commercial city
die Handschrift, -, -en   the manuscript
die Handvoll, -, -   the handful
der Handwerker, -s, -   the artisan
hangen, hing, hat gehangen, er hängt   to hang (*intr.*)
hängen   to hang (*trans.*)
(das) Hannover, -s   (city of) Hanover
hart   hard
der Harz, -es   the Harz Mountains
das Haupt, -(e)s, ″er   the head
die Hauptstadt, -, ″e   the capital
*das Haus, -es, ″er   the house
der Hausdiener, -s, -   the servant, porter
heben, hob *or* hub, hat gehoben   to raise
das Heer, -(e)s, -e   the army
*das Heft, -(e)s, -e   the notebook

der Hegereiter, -s, - the gamekeeper
das Hegereiterhaus, -es, ⸗er the
gamekeeper's house
die Heide, -, -n the heath
(das) Heidelberg, -s (city of)
Heidelberg
Heidelberger Heidelberg (adj.)
heilig holy, sacred
die Heimatflur, -, -en the home,
native fields
heimlich secretly
*heiß hot
*heißen, hieß, hat geheißen to
be called
*helfen, half, hat geholfen, er
hilft to help
*hell bright
*her hither, here (direction toward
the speaker)
heran-kommen, kam heran, ist
herangekommen to approach
*der Herbst, -(e)s, -e the fall,
autumn
die Herbstesnacht, -, ⸗e the
autumn night
der Herd, -(e)s, -e the hearth,
stove
hernieder-stürzen (sein) to fall
down, plunge down
*der Herr, -n, -en the gentleman;
Mr.; the Lord God
*herrlich glorious, wonderful
herum around
*das Herz, -ens, -en the heart
herzlich hearty
das Herzogtum, -(e)s, ⸗er the
duchy
(das) Hessen, -s Hesse
die Heuernte, -, -n the hay-
harvest
*heute today
*hier here
*der Himmel, -s, - the heaven,
sky

himmlisch heavenly
*hin there, thither (direction away
from the speaker)
hinab down, downwards
hinauf-schauen to look up
hinauf-steigen, stieg hinauf, ist
hinaufgestiegen to mount,
ascend
*hinaus-gehen, ging hinaus, ist
hinausgegangen to go out
hinein' in, into
hinein-führen to lead in
hinein-reichen to reach in, extend
hinein-schleichen, schlich hinein, ist hineingeschlichen to
sneak in
hinein-treten, trat hinein, ist
hineingetreten, er tritt hinein
to step in
hin-reiten, ritt hin, ist hingeritten to ride to
*hinter (+ dat. or acc.) behind
der Hintergrund, -es, ⸗e the
background
hinunter-tragen, trug hinunter,
hat hinuntergetragen, er trägt
hinunter to carry down
*hoch high; höher, höchst
higher, highest
die Hochzeit, -, -en the wed-
ding, marriage, festivity
der Hof, -es, ⸗e the court, court-
yard
*hoffen to hope
höflich courteous, polite
die Höhe, -, -n the height
die Hohenzollern the Hohen-
zollerns
hold charming, fair, sweet
*holen to fetch, go and get
(das) Holland, -s Holland
die Hölle, -, -n hell, infernal
regions

das Höllental, -(e)s the Höllental (*name of a valley in the
Black Forest*)
das Holz, -es, ⸗er the wood
*hören to hear
das Hotel', -s, -s the hotel
hübsch pretty
der Hudson, -s the Hudson
der Hügel, -s, - the hill
hügelig hilly
*der Hund, -(e)s, -e the dog
*hundert hundred
*hungrig hungry
*der Hut, -(e)s, ⸗e the hat

I

*ich I
*ihr you (*pl. fam.*)
*ihr her; their; Ihr your (*conventional*)
illustrie'ren to illustrate
*immer always
immerdar always, forever
*in (+ *dat.* or *acc.*) in, at, into, to,
within
(das) Indien, -s India
die Industrie', -, -en the industry
die Industrie'stadt, -, ⸗e the industrial city
das Inland, -(e)s the interior,
inland
der Inn, -s the Inn (*river flowing
through Innsbruck*)
das Innere, -n the interior, inside
(das) Innsbruck, -s (city of)
Innsbruck
die Insel, -, -n the island
die Inselstadt, -, ⸗e the insular
town
inspizie'ren to inspect
*interessant' interesting
das Interes'se, -s, -n the interest

die Isar, - the Isar (*river flowing
through Munich*)
(das) Ita'lien, -s Italy
der Italie'ner, -s - the Italian
italie'nisch Italian

J

*ja yes, indeed
*das Jahr, -(e)s, -e the year
die Jahreszeit, -, -en the time of
year, season
das Jahrhun'dert, -s, -e the
century
-jährig years old
der Januar, - *or* -s, -e January
(das) Ja'pan, -s Japan
*jeder, jede, jedes each, every
jedesmal every time
*jener, jene, jenes that, that one
(das) Jena, -s (city of) Jena
*jetzt now
der Jubel, -s the jubilation, rejoicing
die Jugend, -, -en the youth
die Jugendzeit, -, -en the time
of youth
der Ju'li, - *or* -s, -s July
*jung young
*der Junge, -n, -n the boy
die Jungfrau, -, -en the maiden
der Juni, - *or* -s, -s June

K

die Kabine, -, -n the cabin
*der Kaffee, -s the coffee
kahl bare
der Kahn, -(e)s, ⸗e the boat
der Kaiser, -s, - the emperor
der Kaiserdom, -(e)s, -e the
imperial cathedral
die Kaiserin, -, -nen the empress
der Kaisersaal, -(e)s, die Kaisersäle the imperial hall

*kalt cold
der Kamerad', -en, -en the comrade
der Kamm, -(e)s, ⸗e the comb
kämmen to comb
die Kammer, -, -n chamber, room
(das) Kanada, -s Canada
der Kanal', -(e)s, ⸗e the canal, channel
der Kandidat', -en, -en the candidate
die Kapelle, -, -n the band, choir; chapel
Karl der Große, Karls des Großen Charles the Great, Charlemagne
*die Karte, -, -n the card; map
*die Kartof'fel, -, -n the potato
der Kasta'nienbaum, -(e)s, ⸗e the chestnut tree
der Kasten, -s, - the box
*die Katze, -, -n the cat
*kaufen to buy
der Kavalier', -s, -e the cavalier, courtier
die Kehle, -, -n the throat
kehren (sein) to return
*kein no, not a
der Keller, -s, - the cellar, basement
*der Kellner, -s, - the waiter
*kennen, kannte, hat gekannt to know, be acquainted with
die Kette, -, -n the chain, range
das (or der) Ki'lome'ter, -s, - the kilometer
*das Kind, -(e)s, -er the child
der Kindermund, -(e)s the mouth of a child
das Kinderwiegen, -s the rocking of a child (in a cradle)
das Kino, -s, -s the moving picture theatre
die Kirche, -, -n the church

die Kiste, -, -n the chest, box
das Klappern, -s, - the clatter, click
klar clear
*die Klasse, -, -n the class
klassisch classical
klassizistisch classicist (adj.)
das Klavier', -s, -e the piano
*das Kleid, -(e)s, -er the dress; pl. dresses or clothes
*klein small
die Kleinigkeit, -, -en the trifle
klettern to climb
das Klima, -s, -s or -te the climate
klingeln to ring
klingen, klang, hat geklungen to sound, resound
*klopfen to knock
das Kloster, -s, ⸗ the monastery, cloister
der Klosterbau, -es, -e or -ten the monastery building
*der Knabe, -n, -n the boy
der Knabenchor, -(e)s, ⸗e the boys' choir
(das) Koblenz (city of) Coblenz
der Koffer, -s, - the trunk; suitcase
die Kohle, -, -n the coal
(das) Köln, -s (city of) Cologne
*kommen, kam, ist gekommen to come
kommerzialisiert commercialized
der Kommunist', -en, -en the Communist
komponie'ren to compose
der Komponist', -en, -en the composer
*der König, -(e)s, -e the king
das Königreich, -(e)s, -e the kingdom
*können, konnte, hat gekonnt, er kann can, to be able, may

(das) Konstanz (town of) Constance
der Kontinent', -(e)s, -e the continent
kontrollie'ren to control
das Konzert', -(e)s, -e the concert
die Konzertreise, -, -n the concert tour
*der Kopf, -(e)s, ⸗e the head
das Kopfweh, -s the headache
*kosten to cost
das Kostüm', -s, -e the costume
krähen to crow
*krank sick
*die Kreide, -, -n the chalk
der Kreuzgang, -(e)s, ⸗e the cloisters (in a monastery)
das Kreuzgewölbe, -s, - the groined (cross-shaped) vault
der Krieg, -(e)s, -e the war
krönen to crown
die Kugel, -, -n the bullet
*die Kuh, -, ⸗e the cow
kühl cool
kühn bold
die Kultur', -, -en the culture, civilization
kummervoll filled with care
die Kunst, -, ⸗e the art
der Künstler, -s, - the artist
künstlerisch artistic
die Kunstschule, -, -n the art school
die Kunststadt, -, ⸗e the art city
das Kunstwerk, -(e)s, -e the work of art
der Kurfürst, -en, -en the electoral prince
der Kurort, -(e)s, -e or ⸗er the watering-place, spa
*kurz short
der Kuß, Kusses, Küsse the kiss
küssen to kiss

L

*lächeln to smile
*lachen to laugh
laden, lud, hat geladen, er lädt to load
die Lage, -, -n the situation, site
*das Land, -(e)s, ⸗er the land; country
landen to land
die Landschaft, -, -en the landscape
der Landungsplatz, -es, ⸗e the landing place, dock, pier
*lang(e) long
*langsam slow
lassen, ließ, hat gelassen, er läßt to let
die Last, -, -en the burden
der Lauf, -(e)s, ⸗e the course, career
*laufen, lief, ist gelaufen, er läuft to run
*laut loud
*leben to live; lebe wohl farewell
das Leben, -s, - the life
das Lebensjahr, -(e)s, -e the year of one's life
das Lebensmittel, -s, - the food, provisions
leer empty
leeren to empty
legen to lay
die Legen'de, -, -n the legend
lehren to teach
*der Lehrer, -s, - the teacher
*die Lehrerin, -, -nen the teacher (fem.)
*leicht light, easy
das Leid, -(e)s, -en grief, sorrow
leiden, litt, hat gelitten to suffer, endure
leider unfortunately

(das) **Leipzig, -s** (city of) Leipzig
*__leise__ softly, in a low voice
die **Lerche, -, -n** the lark
*__lernen__ to learn
*__lesen, las, hat gelesen, er liest__ to read
*__letzt__ last
leuchten to shine, glow, gleam
*__die Leute__ (*pl.*) the people
das **Licht, -(e)s, -er** the light
*__lieb__ dear
lieben to love
*__das Lied, -(e)s, -er__ the song
liegen, lag, hat gelegen to lie, be situated
die **Limona'de, -, -n** the lemonade
(das) **Lindau, -s** (city of) Lindau
*__link__ left
das (*or* der) **Liter, -s, -** the liter
die **Literatur', -** the literature
loben to praise
der **Lohn, -(e)s, ⸗e** the pay, wages
die **Lorelei, -** the Lorelei
los loose
lösen to buy, loosen, untie; **eine Aufgabe lösen** to accomplish a task
(das) **Lübeck, -s** (city of) Lübeck
*__die Luft, -, ⸗e__ the air
die **Luftbrücke, -, -n** the air bridge, airlift
das **Luftschiff, -(e)s, -e** the airship
die **Lust, -, ⸗e** joy; desire
lustig jolly, gay, merry

M

*__machen__ to make
die **Macht, -, ⸗e** the might, power
mächtig mighty, huge
*__das Mädchen, -s, -__ the girl

das **Mägdlein, -s, -** the maiden, girl
die **Mahlzeit, -, -en** the meal, meal-time
der **Mai, -** *or* **-(e)s, -e** May
die **Maid, -** (*poetic*) the maiden
der **Main, -s** the Main (river)
(das) **Mainz** (city of) Mayence
die **Majestät', -, -en** the majesty
*__das Mal, -(e)s, -e__ time; **mal** times; **dreimal,** *etc.* three times
malen to paint
der **Maler, -s, -** the painter
die **Malerei, -, -en** the painting
malerisch picturesque
*__man__ one, people, they
*__mancher, manche, manches__ many a; *pl.* some
manchmal sometimes
*__der Mann, -es, ⸗er__ the man
das **Märchen, -s, -** the fairy tale
Maria Theresia, -s Maria Theresa
die **Maria-Theresienstraße, -** Maria Theresa Street (*in Innsbruck*)
*__die Mark, -__ the mark
markiert' marked
der **Marktplatz, -es, ⸗e** the market place
der **März, -en** *or* **-es, -e** March
die **Mauer, -, -n** the wall
(das) **Maulbronn, -s** (village of) Maulbronn
*__die Medizin', -, -en__ the medicine
das **Meer, -(e)s, -e** the sea, ocean
(das) **Meersburg, -s** (town of) Meersburg
*__mehr__ more
mehrere several
die **Meile, -, -n** the mile
*__mein__ my
meist most
meistens mostly

der Meister, -s, - the master
die Melodei', -, -n the melody;
  (*obsolete and poetic*)
die Melodie', -, -en the melody
*der Mensch, -en, -en man,
  human being; *pl.* people
das Menuett', -s, -e the minuet
*merken to notice
*das (*or* der) Meter, -s, - the
  meter
mild mild
das Militär', -s the military,
  soldiers
*die Million', -, -en the million
der Millionär', -s, -e the millionaire
die Mineral'quelle, -, -n the
  mineral spring
das Mineral'wasser, -s, - the
  mineral water
die Miniatur', -, -en the miniature
das Ministe'rium, -s, Ministerien
  the ministry, government office
der Minnesänger, -s, - the minnesinger (*German lyric poet of
  the 12th or 13th century*)
*die Minu'te, -, -n the minute
mißtrauisch distrustful
*mit (+ *dat.*) with, by, at
mitleidig compassionate(ly),
  sympathetic(ally)
mit-nehmen, nahm mit, hat mit-
  genommen, er nimmt mit to
  take along
mit-spielen to join in the play
  with
*der Mittag, -(e)s, -e the midday,
  noon
ᵏdas Mittagessen, -s, - the midday
  meal, dinner
die Mitte, -, -n the middle,
  center
das Mittelalter, -s the Middle
  Ages

mittelalterlich medieval
der Mittelpunkt, -(e)s, -e the
  middle point, center
die Mitternacht, -, ⸗e the midnight
*der Mittwoch, -(e)s, -e Wednes-
  day
modern' modern
*mögen, mochte, hat gemocht, er
  mag to care for, like; may
möglich possible
*der Monat, -(e)s, -e the month
der Mönch, -es, -e the monk
*der Montag, -(e)s, -e Monday
*der Morgen, -s, - the morning;
  morgens in the morning
*morgen tomorrow
das Morgenland, -(e)s the
  Orient
das Morgenrot, -(e)s the roseate
  glow of early morning, aurora
morgenschön beautiful as the
  morning
die Mo'sel, - the Moselle (river)
müde tired
(das) München, -s (city of)
  Munich
der Mund, -(e)s, -e *or* ⸗er the
  mouth
das Muse'um, -s, die Muse'en
  the museum
die Musik', - the music
musika'lisch musical
das Musik'drama, -s, -dramen
  the music drama, opera
der Musiker, -s, - the musician
die Musik'stadt, -, ⸗e the city of
  music
*müssen, mußte, hat gemußt, er
  muß to be obliged, must
müßig idle
*die Mutter, -, ⸗ the mother
mütterlich motherly

N

*nach (+ *dat.*) toward, to, for, after, according to
der Nachbar, -s *or* -n, -n the neighbor
die Nachbarschaft, -, -en the neighborhood, vicinity
*nachdem' after
nach-denken, dachte nach, hat nachgedacht to reflect
*der Nachmittag, -(e)s, -e the afternoon
nächst next
*die Nacht, -, ⸗e the night
nah(e) near
die Nähe, -, -n the proximity
*der Name, -ns, -n the name
nämlich namely, that is to say
naß wet
die Nation', -, -en the nation
die National'galerie', -, -n the national gallery
*natür'lich natural; of course
der Nebel, -s, - the fog, mist
*neben (+ *dat.* or *acc.*) next to, beside
der Neckar, -s the Neckar (*river flowing through Heidelberg*)
das Neckartal, -(e)s the Neckar valley
der Neffe, -n, -n the nephew
*nehmen, nahm, hat genommen, er nimmt to take
*nein no
*nennen, nannte, hat genannt to name, call
*neu new
der Neubau, -es, -e *or* -ten the building in course of erection; die Neubauten (*m. pl.*) the new buildings
neugewählt newly elected
neugierig curious
das Neujahr, -(e)s, -e New Year

*neun nine
neunzehn nineteen
(das) Neuyork, -s New York
*nicht not
*nichts nothing, not anything
*nie never
nieder-legen to lay down
(das) Niedersachsen, -s Lower Saxony
niedrig low
niemals at no time, never
*niemand no one
nimmersatt never satisfied, insatiable
nit dialectical for nicht
*noch still, yet; nor
(das) Nordamerika, -s North America
der Norddeutsche Lloyd the North German Lloyd
(das) Norddeutschland, -s Northern Germany
der Norden, -s the north
nördlich north
der Nordpol, -(e)s the North Pole
(das) Nord'rhein-Westfalen, -s North Westphalia
die Nordsee, - the North Sea
das Nordufer, -s, - the north shore
der Nordwesten, -s the northwest
nordwestlich northwest
die Not, -, ⸗e the need, distress
die Note, -, -n the note, report, mark
nötig necessary
der November, - *or* -s, - November
*nun now; well
*nur only
(das) Nürnberg, -s (city of) Nuremberg
Nürnberger Nuremberg (*adj.*)

O

*ob if, whether
oben above, up above
(das) Oberammergau, -s (village of) Oberammergau
der Oberrhein, -s the upper Rhine
*obgleich′ although
der Obstbaum, -(e)s, ꞊e the fruit-tree
*oder or
die Oder, - the Oder (river)
*offen open
der Offizier′, -(e)s, -e the officer
öffnen to open
sich öffnen to open (oneself)
*oft often
*ohne (+ acc. or inf. with zu) without
der Okto′ber, - or -s, - October
*der Onkel, -s, - the uncle
die Oper, -, -n the opera
das Opernhaus, -es, ꞊er the opera house
der Ort, -(e)s, -e or ꞊er the place, locality
(das) Ostdeutschland, -s East Germany
der Osten, -s the east
(das) Osterreich, -s Austria
österreichisch Austrian
östlich east
die Ostsee, - the Baltic Sea
der Ostsektor, -s, -en the east sector
der Ostteil, -(e)s, -e the eastern part
der Ozean, -s, -e the ocean

P

*das Paar, -(e)s, -e the pair, couple
packen to pack

*das Paket′, -(e)s, -e the package
der Palast′, -es, ꞊e the palace
die Palme, -, -n the palm tree
die Para′de, -, -n the parade
(das) Paris′ (city of) Paris
*der Park, -(e)s, -e the park
die Parkstraße, - Park Street
das Parlament′, -(e)s, -e the parliament
der Paß, Passes, Pässe the pass
der Passagier′, -(e)s, -e the passenger
passen to fit
passie′ren (sein) to pass
das Passions′spiel, -(e)s, -e the Passion Play
der Pastor, -s, -en the pastor
die Pein, - the pain, torment
die Person′, -, -en the person
die Pest, -, -en the plague
die Pfeife, -, -n the pipe
der Pfennig, -(e)s, -e the pfennig (100 pfennigs = 1 mark)
*das Pferd, -(e)s, -e the horse
pflanzen to plant
die Pha′se, -, -n the phase
der Philoso′phenweg, -(e)s Philosopher's Walk (in Heidelberg)
*der Platz, -es, ꞊e the place, room, seat; square
plaudern to chat
*plötzlich sudden(ly)
(das) Polen, -s Poland
die Polizei′, -, -en the police
die Post, -, -en the post, mail; mail-coach
das Postgeld, -(e)s, -er the postage
(das) Potsdam, -s (city of) Potsdam
(das) Prag, -s (city of) Prague
*der Preis, -es, -e the price
(das) Preußen, -s Prussia
primitiv′ primitive

der Prinz, -en, -en   the prince
pro   per
*der Profes'sor, -s, die Profes-
so'ren   the professor
protestan'tisch   Protestant
das Prozent', -s, -e   the percent
prüfen   to examine
die Prüfung, -, -en   the examination
der Punkt, -(e)s, -e   the point
pünktlich   punctual(ly),
prompt(ly)

Q

das (or der) Quadrat'kilometer,
-s, -   the square kilometer
die Quadrat'meile, -, -n   the
square mile
die Qual, -, -en   the torment,
torture

R

sich rächen   to avenge oneself
der Rand, -es, ²er   the edge,
brink
das Rathaus, -es, ²er   the city
hall
*rauchen   to smoke
der Raucher, -s, -   the smoker
der Raum, -(e)s, ²e   space, room,
place
rauschen   to rustle, roar
*die Rechnung, -, -en   the bill
*recht   right; rechts   to the right,
on the right side
reduzie'ren   to reduce
reflektie'ren   to reflect
die Reformation', -   the Reformation
regelmäßig   regularly, always
der Regen, -s, -   the rain
*der Regenschirm, -(e)s, -e   the
umbrella
regieren   to govern, rule, manage

*regnen   to rain
*reich   rich
das Reich, -(e)s, -e   realm, empire; Reich
reichen   reach, give, hand
reichlich   plenty
die Reichsstadt, -, ²e   the imperial city
der Reichtum, -(e)s, ²er   the
wealth
rein   clean
*die Reise, -, -n   the journey, trip
*reisen (sein)   to travel
der Reisende, -n, -n   the traveler
die Reisetasche, -, -n   the traveling bag, suitcase
reiten, ritt, ist geritten (intr.) or
hat geritten (trans.)   to ride
(horseback)
die Reitschule, -, -n   the riding
school
das Relief,' -s, -s   the relief
(sculpture)
der Renaissancestil, -(e)s   the
Renaissance style
die Republik', -, -en   the republic
die Residenz', -, -en   the (royal)
residence
*das Restaurant', -s, -s   the res-
taurant
retten   to save
die Revolution', -, -en   the revolution
der Rhein, -(e)s   the Rhine
(river)
(die) Rheinland-Pfalz, -   the
Rhineland Palatinate
die Rheinreise, -, -n   the Rhine
journey
*richtig   right, correct
ringsum   round about, all around
das Rohmaterial, -s, -ien   the
raw material

das **Roko'ko**, -s   the rococo (*style*)
der **Rokokostil**, -(e)s   the rococo
style
romantisch   romantic
der **Römer**, -s, -   the Roman;
namϵ of the city hall in Frankfort
römisch   Roman
die **Rose**, -, -n   the rose
der **Rosengarten**, -s, ⸗   the rose
garden
das **Röslein**, -s, -   the little rose
rot (**roter** *and* **röter**)   red
(das) **Rothenburg ob der Tau-
ber**, -s   (city of) Rothenburg-
on-the-Tauber
der **Rucksack**, -s, ⸗e   the knapsack
rufen, rief, hat gerufen   to call;
exclaim
ruhen   to rest
*__ruhig__   quiet, calm
das **Ruhrgebiet**, -(e)s   the Ruhr
district
die **Rui'ne**, -, -n   the ruin
(das) **Rumä'nien**, -s   Rumania
der **Russe**, -n, -n   the Russian
(das) **Rußland**, -s   Russia

S

die **Sache**, -, -n   the thing,
matter, cause
(das) **Sachsen**, -s   Saxony
die **Sage**, -, -n   the legend
*__sagen__   to say
Salomo   Solomon
die **Salzach**, -   the Salzach (*river
flowing through Salzburg*)
(das) **Salzburg**, -s   (city of) Salzburg
der **Samstag**, -(e)s, -e   Saturday
die **Schachtel**, -, -n   the box
schaffen, schuf, hat geschaffen
to create
*__sich schämen__   to be ashamed

der **Schatten**, -s, -   the shadow,
shade
schauen   to look. gaze
der **Schauspieler**, -s, -   the actor
der **Schein**, -(e)s, -e   the light,
glow
*__scheinen, schien, hat geschienen__
to shine; seem
die **Schere**, -, -n   the scissors
der **Scherz**, -es, -e   the jest, joke
*__schicken__   to send
*__das Schiff__, -(e)s, -e   the ship, boat
der **Schiffer**, -s, -   the boatman
*__schlafen, schlief, hat geschlafen,
er schläft__   to sleep
schläfern; mich schläfert   I feel
sleepy
der **Schlafwagen**, -s, -   the sleeping car
das **Schlafzimmer**, -s, -   the bedroom
**schlagen, schlug, hat geschlagen,
er schlägt**   to strike; beat; sing
schlecht   bad; poor
**schleichen, schlich, ist ge-
schlichen**   to sneak, creep, steal
der **Schleier**, -s, -   the veil
(das) **Schleswig-Holstein**, -s
Schleswig-Holstein
**schließen, schloß, hat geschlossen,
er schließt**   to shut, conclude
schließlich   finally, at last
*__das Schloß__, -sses, ⸗sser   the castle,
the palace
das **Schlößchen**, -s, -   the small
castle
der **Schmerz**, -es, -en   the pain,
grief
der **Schnee**, -s   the snow
der **Schneeberg**, -(e)s, -e   the
snow-capped mountain
der **Schneider**, -s, -   the tailor
*__schnell__   quick, fast, rapid
der **Schnellzug**, -(e)s, ⸗e   the
fast train, express

*schon already
*schön beautiful
(das) Schönbrunn', -s Schönbrunn (*castle and gardens in Vienna*)
die Schönheit, - the beauty
der Schoß, -es, ⸗e the lap
der Schrei, -(e)s, -e the cry, scream
*schreiben, schrieb, hat geschrieben to write
der Schrein, -(e)s, -e the shrine, coffin
der Schriftsteller, -s, - the author, writer
der Schritt, -(e)s, -e the step, stride
schüchtern shy
*der Schuh, -(e)s, -e the shoe
die Schuld, -, -en the debt; guilt
schulden to owe
schuldig guilty
*die Schule, -, -n the school
*der Schüler, -s, - the pupil
*die Schülerin, -, -nen the pupil (*fem.*)
das Schuljahr, -(e)s, -e the school year
das Schulzimmer, -s, - the schoolroom
der Schutzmann, -(e)s, ⸗er *or* die Schutzleute the policeman
die Schwalbe, -, -n the swallow
das Schwalbenvolk, -(e)s the crowd of swallows
*schwarz black
das Schwarze Meer the Black Sea
der Schwarzwald, -(e)s the Black Forest
Schwarzwälder Black Forest (*adj.*)
das Schwarzwaldhaus, -es, ⸗er the Black Forest house

schweigen, schwieg, hat geschwiegen to be silent
die Schweiz, - Switzerland
Schweizer Swiss (*adj.*)
schwellen, schwoll, ist geschwollen, er schwillt to swell, rise
*schwer heavy; difficult
*die Schwester, -, -n the sister
schwirren to whir
*sechs six
*sechzehn sixteen
*sechzig sixty
der See, -s, -n the lake
die See, -, -n the sea, ocean
seekrank seasick
*sehen, sah, hat gesehen, er sieht to see
die Sehenswürdigkeit, -, -en the thing worth seeing, object of interest
*sehr very, very much
*sein, war, ist gewesen, er ist to be
*sein his, its
*seit (+ *dat.*) since; *conj.* since
seitab off to one side
seitdem since that time
*die Seite, -, -n the side; page
*die Sekun'de, -, -n the second
*selbst (selber) self; myself, yourself, *etc.*; even
*selten seldom, rare(ly)
das Semester, -s, - the university term, semester
das Semesterexamen, -s, -examina the term examination
der Septem'ber, - *or* -s, - September
*setzen to set, place; sich setzen to sit down
*sich himself, herself, *etc.*
*sicher certain(ly), sure(ly)
*sie she, they, it
*sieben seven
siebzehn seventeen

siebzig seventy
die Sinfonie', -, -n the symphony
*singen, sang, hat gesungen to sing
das Singen, -s the singing
der Sinn, -(e)s, -e mind, spirit, thought
der Sitz, -es, -e the seat
*sitzen, saß, hat gesessen to sit
*so so, therefore, as
sobald as soon
sogenannt so-called
*sogleich' (gleich) at once
der Sohn, -(e)s, -e the son
*solcher, solche, solches such
der Soldat', -en, -en the soldier
*sollen, sollte, hat gesollt shall, ought, to be to, is said to
*der Sommer, -s, - the summer
*sondern but
*der Sonnabend, -(e)s, -e Saturday
*die Sonne, -, -n the sun
der Sonnenuntergang, -(e)s, -e the sunset
*der Sonntag, -(e)s, -e Sunday
*sonst otherwise
die Sorge, -, -n the care, worry
spanisch Spanish
*spät late
spätgotisch late Gothic
spazie'ren to promenade
spazie'ren-gehen, ging spazieren, ist spazierengegangen to go for a walk
*der Spazier'gang, -(e)s, -e the walk; einen Spaziergang machen to take a walk
die Speisekarte, -, -n the bill of fare
speisen to dine, eat
das Spiel, -(e)s, -e the play
spielen to play
das Spital, -es, -er the hospital

der Spitalhof, -es, -e the courtyard of the hospital
die Sprache, -, -n the language, speech
*sprechen, sprach, hat gesprochen, er spricht to speak
die Spree, - the Spree (river flowing through Berlin)
springen, sprang, ist gesprungen spring, jump, leap; fly
die St. Jakobskirche, - the Church of St. Jacob (in Rothenburg-on-the-Tauber)
der Staat, -(e)s, -en the state
*die Stadt, -, -e the city
das Städtchen, -s, - the small town
der Stadtteil, -(e)s, -e the quarter, section (of a city)
der Stall, -es, -e the stall
stammen to stem from, date back to
stark strong; hard
statt-finden, fand statt, hat stattgefunden to take place
die Statue, -, -n the statue
stechen, stach, hat gestochen, er sticht to sting, prick
stecken to stick
*stehen, stand, hat gestanden to stand
steil steep]
*der Stein, -(e)s, -e the stone
die Stelle, -, -n the place
*stellen to place, set, put
die Stellung, -, -en the position
der Stephansdom, -(e)s the Cathedral of St. Stephen (in Vienna)
*sterben, starb, ist gestorben, er stirbt to die
der Stern, -(e)s, -e the star
das Sternlein, -s, - the little star
der Stil, -(e)s, -e the style
still still, silent

die Stille, - the silence, stillness
der Stoff, -(e)s, -e the material, cloth
stören to disturb
der Strand, -(e)s, -e the strand, shore
*die Straße, -, -n the street, road
*die Straßenbahn, -, -en the street car
*das Streichholz, -es, ⸗er the match
der Streit, -(e)s, e the quarrel; battle, combat
der Strom, -(e)s, ⸗e the stream, river
das Stück, -(e)s, -e the piece, part
*der Student', -en, -en the student
das Studen'tenhaus, -es, ⸗er the students' house
das Studen'tenleben, -s the student life
die Studie, -, -n the study, studies
*studie'ren, studierte, hat studiert to study
*der Stuhl, -(e)s, ⸗e the chair
*die Stunde, -, -n the hour
stürmisch stormy
(das) Stuttgart, -s (city of) Stuttgart
stützen to support, rest
suchen to seek, look for
(das) Südame'rika, -s South America
(das) Süddeutschland, -s Southern Germany
der Süden, -s the south
südlich southern
der Südosten, -s the southeast
der Südwesten, -s the southwest
die Suppe, -, -n the soup
süß sweet

T

Table d'hote regular dinner
*die Tafel, -, -n the blackboard
*der Tag, -(e)s, -e the day
tagelang day after day
die Tageszeit, -, -en the time of day
das Tal, -(e)s, ⸗er the dale, valley
die Tanne, -, -n the fir
der Tannenbaum, -(e)s, ⸗e the fir tree
der Tannenwald, -(e)s, ⸗er the fir-wood
*die Tante, -, -n the aunt
*die Tasche, -, -n the pocket
*die Tasse, -, -n the cup
die Tauber, - the Tauber (river on which Rothenburg is situated)
*tausend thousand
tausendmal a thousand times
der Tee, -s the tea
der Teil, -(e)s, -e the part
teilen to divide
teilweise partially
*teuer dear, expensive
das Thea'ter, -s, - the theatre
die Theologie', - theology
der Thüringer Wald, -(e)s the Thuringian Forest
tief deep
*das Tier, -(e)s, -e the animal
der Tiergarten, -s the Tiergarten (park in Berlin)
(das) Tirol, -s the Tyrol
*der Tisch, -es, -e the table
*die Tochter, -, ⸗ the daughter
das Töchterlein, -s, - the little daughter
der Tod, -es, -e the death
das Tor, -(e)s, -e the gateway, gate
tot dead
töten to kill

die Totenbahre, -, -n   the bier
der Tourist', -en, -en   the tourist
die Tradition', -, -nen   the tradition
träge   idle, lazy
tragen, trug, hat getragen, er
 trägt   to carry; wear
die Träne, -, -n   the tear
trauern   to mourn
der Traum, -(e)s, ⸗e   the dream
träumen   to dream
traurig   sad
*treffen, traf, hat getroffen, er
 trifft   to meet
treiben, trieb, hat getrieben   to
 drive, pursue; Wintersport treiben   to engage in winter sports
treten, trat, ist getreten, er tritt
 to step, walk
treulos   faithless
*trinken, trank, hat getrunken
 to drink
das Trinkgeld, -(e)s, -er   the tip
das Trio, -s, -s   the trio
der Tritt, -(e)s, -e   the step,
 stride
die Trommel, -, -n   the drum
trotzdem   nevertheless, in spite of
 that
die Tsche'choslowakei', -
 Czechoslovakia
*tun, tat, hat getan   to do
*die Tür, -, -en   the door
der Turm, -(e)s, ⸗e   the tower

U

*über (+ dat. or acc.)   over, at,
 above, concerning
überall   everywhere
überflüssig   superfluous
überhängend   overhanging
überlas'sen, überließ, hat über-
 lassen, er überläßt   to leave to
überle'gen   to think over, reflect

*übermorgen   day after tomorrow
übernach'ten   to spend the night
übrig   over, left
das Ufer, -s, -   the bank, shore
*die Uhr, -, -en   the watch, clock;
 o'clock
*um (+ acc.)   about, around, by,
 after, at, for; (+ inf. with zu)
 to, in order to
umgeben   surrounded
die Umge'bung, -, -en   the sur-
 roundings
umhül'len   to envelop
un'angenehm   disagreeable
un'bedeutend   insignificant, unimportant
unbewußt   unconscious
*und   and
(das) Ungarn, -s   Hungary
ungeduldig   impatient
*ungefähr   about, approximately
unhöflich   impolite
*die Universität', -, -en   the uni-
 versity
die Universitätsstadt, -, ⸗e   the
 university town
der Universitätsstudent, -en, -en
 the university student
un'praktisch   unpractical; impracticable
*unser   our
unten   below, downstairs
unter (+ dat. or acc.)   under,
 below, among
Unter den Linden   name of a
 street in Berlin
der Unterlaß; ohn' Unterlaß
 without cessation, incessantly
der Unterricht, -es   the instruction, lessons

V

*der Vater, -s, ⸗   the father
verarmen (sein)   to become poor

verdan'ken to owe to
die Verei'nigten Staaten the United States
verfol'gen to pursue
*verges'sen, vergaß, hat vergessen, er vergißt to forget
vergif'ten to poison
*verkau'fen to sell
verknüp'fen to connect
verlan'gen to demand
verlas'sen, verließ, hat verlassen, er verläßt to leave, desert
verleben to pass, spend (time)
verlie'ren, verlor, hat verloren to lose
verschie'den different
verschlin'gen, verschlang, hat verschlungen to swallow up, engulf
verschwin'den, verschwand, ist verschwunden to vanish
versin'ken, versank, ist versunken to sink down; in Leid versunken lost in sorrow
*verspre'chen, versprach, hat versprochen, er verspricht to promise
verste'hen, verstand, hat verstanden to understand
verzei'hen, verzieh, hat verziehen to forgive, pardon
*viel much; *pl.* many
*vielleicht' perhaps
*vier four
*das Viertel, -s, - the quarter
vierzehn fourteen
die Violi'ne, -, -n the violin
der Vogel, -s, = the bird
vogelsprachekund understanding the language of birds
das Volk, -(e)s, =er the people; nation
die Volksschule, -, -n the public school
voll full

vollkommen completely
vollständig complete(ly)
*von (+ dat.) from, of, by
*vor (+ dat. or acc.) before, in front of, from, for, ago
voraus in front, on ahead
vorbei' gone, over
vorbei'-fahren, fuhr vorbei, ist vorbeigefahren, er fährt vorbei to sail by
vorbei'-fliegen, flog vorbei, ist vorbeigeflogen to fly by
vorbei'-kommen, kam vorbei, ist vorbeigekommen to pass
*vorgestern day before yesterday
*der Vormittag, -(e)s, -e the forenoon
sich etwas vor-sprechen, sprach vor, hat vorgesprochen, er spricht vor to say something to oneself
der Vorteil, -(e)s, -e the advantage
vorüber along by, past

W

wachsen, wuchs, ist gewachsen, er wächst to grow
der Wagen, -s, - the wagon, carriage
wählen to elect
*wahr true
*während (+ gen.) during, while
*der Wald, -(e)s, =er the forest
waldig wooded
der Walnußbaum, -(e)s, =e the walnut tree
walten to rule, reign, hold sway
der Walzer, -s, - the waltz
*die Wand, -, =e the wall
die Wandergans, -, =e the wild goose
wandern (sein) to travel (on foot), wander

der **Wandersmann, -(e)s, die Wandersleute** the wanderer

*__wann__ when (*in questions*)

*__warm__ warm

*__warten__ to wait

das **Wartezimmer, -s, -** the waiting room

*__warum__ why

*__was__ what, whatever

waschen, wusch, hat gewaschen, er wäscht to wash

(das) **Washington, -s** (city of) Washington

das **Wasser, -s, -** the water

das **Wasserbecken, -s, -** the water basin

weder neither; **weder . . . noch** neither . . . nor

*der **Weg, -(e)s, -e** the way, road, path

wegen (+ *gen.*) on account of, because of

weg-reißen, riß weg, hat weggerissen to tear away

das **Weh, -s** woe; das **Weh und Ach** woe and alas, a cry of pain

wehen to blow, be wafted

die **Wehmut, -** sadness, melancholy

sich **wehren** to defend oneself

das **Weib, -(e)s, -er** the woman, wife

*die **Weihnacht(en), -, -** Christmas

der **Weihnachtsabend, -(e)s, -e** Christmas eve

*__weil__ because

*die **Weile, -** the while

*der **Wein, -(e)s, -e** the wine

der **Weinberg, -(e)s, -e** the vineyard

weinen to cry

weisen, wies, hat gewiesen to show, bestow

die **Weisheit, -, -en** the wisdom

*__weiß__ white

*__weit__ far, distant; **weiter** farther, further

weiter-fragen to continue to ask, to ask further

weiter-reisen (sein) to continue to travel, to go on

weiter-rauchen to continue to smoke

weiter-spielen to continue to play

weiter-zählen to continue to count

*__welcher, welche, welches__ which what, who

welken to wither, fade

die **Welle, -, -n** the wave

*die **Welt, -, -en** the world

der **Weltkrieg, -(e)s, -e** the world war

*__wenig__ little; *pl.* few

weniger less

*__wenn__ if, whenever, when

*__wer__ who, whoever

*__werden, wurde, ist geworden, er wird__ to become

*das **Werk, -(e)s, -e** the work

*__wert__ worth

wertvoll valuable

die **Weser, -** the Weser (*river flowing through Bremen*)

(das) **Westdeutschland, -s** West Germany

der **Westen, -s** the west

westlich west

*das **Wetter, -s, -** the weather

wichtig important

*__wie__ how, what; *conj.* as, such as, like

*__wieder__ again

wiederentdecken to discover again (*insep.*)

wiederher'-stellen to restore

wieder-kommen, kam wieder, ist wiedergekommen to come back, return

(das) Wien, -s Vienna

Wiener Viennese

die Wiese, -, -n the meadow

das Wiesental, -(e)s, ⸗er the fertile valley

*wieviel how much

wild wild

der Wind, -(e)s, -e the wind

*der Winter, -s, - the winter

der Wintersport, -(e)s, -e the winter sport

*wir we

wirklich real(ly)

*der Wirt, -(e)s, -e the innkeeper, host, landlord

die Wirtin, -, -nen innkeeper (*fem.*), hostess, landlady

das Wirtshaus, -es, ⸗er the inn, restaurant

*wissen, wußte, hat gewußt, er weiß to know

wittern to scent, get the wind of

*wo where

*die Woche, -, -n the week

*wohin where, whither

*wohnen to live, dwell

*die Wohnung, -, -en the dwelling, apartment, house

das Wohnzimmer, -s, - the living room

*wollen, wollte, hat gewollt, er will to will, wish, want; claim to

womit with what, wherewith

*das Wort, -(e)s, -e *or* ⸗er the word

wovon whereof, of what

wovor before what, of what

das Wunder, -s, - the wonder, miracle

wunderbar wonderful

das Wunderkind, -(e)s, -er the child prodigy

*sich wundern to be surprised

wundersam wonderful

wunderschön wondrously beautiful

wundervoll wonderful

*wünschen to wish

(das) Württemberg, -s Württemberg

(das) Württemberg-Baden, -s Württemberg-Baden

das Würzlein, -s, - the little root

Z

die Zahl, -, -en the number

*zählen to count

der Zauber, -s the charm, spell

die Zauberin, -, -nen the enchantress, witch

*zehn ten

*zeigen to show

*die Zeit, -, -en the time

die Zeitung, -, -en the newspaper

die Zelle, -, -n the cell

zerstö'ren to destroy

zerstreut' absent-minded

ziehen, zog, hat gezogen to draw, pull

*ziemlich rather, fairly, pretty

die Zigaret'te, -, -n the cigarette

die Zigar're, -, -n the cigar

*das Zimmer, -s, - the room

der Zoll, -(e)s, - the inch

die Zone, -, -n the zone

*zu (+ *dat.*) to, at, for, in, with; *adv.* too

zu-decken to cover

*zuerst' first, at first

*zufrie'den satisfied

*der Zug, -(e)s, ⸗e the train

die Zugspitze, - the Zugspitze

zünden to light, kindle

zurück' back

zurück'-bringen, brachte zurück, hat zurückgebracht to bring back

zurück'-kommen, kam zurück, ist zurückgekommen to come back

zurück'-schlagen, schlug zurück, hat zurückgeschlagen, er schlägt zurück to throw back, thrust back

zusammen together, jointly

zusammen-spielen to play together

der Zuschauer, -s, - the spectator

der Zuschauerraum, -(e)s, ⁼e the house (*opposite to the stage*), auditorium

*zwanzig twenty

zwar indeed, to be sure

*zwei two

zweigen to put forth new branches

zweimal two times, twice

zweit second; zu zweit for both of us

zweitens secondly

zweitgrößt second largest

der Zwerg, -(e)s, -e the dwarf

*zwischen (+ *dat.* or *acc.*) between

*zwölf twelve

ENGLISH-GERMAN VOCABULARY

A

a ein, eine, ein
about (*concerning*) über (+ *acc.*);
  (*approximately*) ungefähr
acquaintance der Bekannte, -n,
  -n; **an acquaintance** ein Bekannter, eines Bekannten, Bekannte
afraid: to be afraid of sich
  fürchten vor (+ *dat.*); Angst
  haben vor (+ *dat.*)
after (*prep.*) nach (+ *dat.*); (*conj.*)
  nachdem
again wieder; **again and again**
  immer wieder
ago vor (+ *dat.*); **a year ago** vor
  einem Jahr
air die Luft, -, ⸗e
already schon
all (*neut. sing.*) alles; (*pl.*) alle
almost beinah(e)
alone allein
also auch
although obgleich
always immer
America das Amērika, -s
American (*masc.*) der Amērikaner,
  -s, -; (*fem.*) die Amērikanerin, -,
  -nen
American (*adj.*) amērikanisch
an ein, eine, ein
and und
angry böse
animal das Tier, -(e)s, -e
another noch ein
answer die Antwort, -, -en
answer antworten, antwortete,
  hat geantwortet, er antwortet

anything: not anything nichts
apartment die Wohnung, -, -en
arrive ankommen, kam an, ist angekommen
as wie
ashamed: to be ashamed sich
  schämen
ask fragen; **to ask a question**
  eine Frage stellen; **to ask for**
  (*inquire*) fragen nach (+ *dat.*);
  to ask for (*request*) bitten um
  (+ *acc.*)
astonished erstaunt
at an (+ *dat.* or *acc.*); auf (+ *dat.*
  or *acc.*); **at the house of** bei
  (+ *dat.*); **at two o'clock** um
  zwei Uhr; **not at all** gar nicht
automobile das Auto, -s, -s *or*
  das Automobil, -(e)s, -e

B

bad: it is too bad es ist schade
be sein, war, ist gewesen, er ist
beautiful schön
because weil
become werden, wurde, ist geworden, er wird
bed das Bett, -(e)s, -en
beer das Bier, -(e)s, -e
before (*prep.*) vor (+ *dat.* or *acc.*);
  (*conj.*) ehe
begin anfangen, fing an, hat angefangen, er fängt an
behind hinter (+ *dat.* or *acc.*)
believe glauben (+ *dat. of person*)
belong gehören (+ *dat.*)
bench die Bank, -, ⸗e
beside neben (+ *dat.* or *acc.*)

big groß
bill die Rechnung, -, -en
black schwarz
blackboard die Tafel, -, -n
blue blau
book das Buch, -(e)s, ꞊er
born geboren
boy der Junge, -n, -n; der Knabe, -n, -n
breakfast das Frühstück, -s, -e
bread das Brot, -(e)s, -e
brother der Bruder, -s, ꞊
but aber, sondern; (*except*) außer (+ *dat.*)
butter die Butter, -
buy kaufen
by von (+ *dat.*); **by railroad** mit der Eisenbahn

C

call nennen, nannte, hat genannt; **to be called** heißen, hieß, hat geheißen
can können, konnte, hat gekonnt *or* hat können, er kann
car das Auto, -s, -s *or* das Automobil, -(e)s, -e
care for mögen, mochte, hat gemocht *or* hat mögen, er mag
castle das Schloß, -sses, ꞊sser
cat die Katze, -, -n
certain(ly) gewiß
chair der Stuhl, -(e)s, ꞊e
chalk die Kreide, -, -n
cheap billig
child das Kind, -(e)s, -er
city die Stadt, -, ꞊e
class die Klasse, -, -n
cold kalt
color die Farbe -, -n
come kommen, kam, ist gekommen
correct richtig
cost kosten

country das Land, -(e)s, ꞊er; **in the country** auf dem Land(e); **to the country** auf das Land
course: of course natürlich
cow die Kuh, -, ꞊e

D

dark dunkel
day der Tag, -(e)s, -e; **day before yesterday** vorgestern; **one day** eines Tages
die sterben, starb, ist gestorben, er stirbt
difficult schwer
diligent fleißig
dinner das Mittagessen, -s, -; **for dinner** zum Mittagessen
do tun, tat, hat getan
doctor der Doktor, -s, die Doktoren; (*physician*) der Arzt, -es, ꞊e
dog der Hund, -(e)s, -e
door die Tür, -, -en
down hinunter, herunter; **to go down town** in die Stadt gehen
dress das Kleid, -(e)s, -er
drink trinken, trank, hat getrunken
drive fahren, fuhr, ist gefahren, er fährt
during während (+ *gen.*)

E

early früh
eat essen, aß, hat gegessen, er ißt
egg das Ei, -(e)s, -er
eight acht
either entweder; auch
end das Ende, -s, -n; **at the end** am Ende
enough genug
Europe das Europa, -s
evening der Abend, -s, -e; **one evening** eines Abends
every jeder, jede, jedes

everything alles
expensive teuer
eye das Auge, -s, -n

F

fall fallen, fiel, ist gefallen, er fällt
fall der Herbst, -es, -e
family die Familie, -, -n
fast schnell
father der Vater, -s, ⁼
fear die Angst, -, ⁼e; **to have fear of** Angst haben vor (+ *dat.*)
feel fühlen; **to feel ashamed** sich schämen
few wenige; **a few** einige, ein paar
find finden, fand, hat gefunden
fire das Feuer, -s, -
first erst; **at first** zuerst
five fünf
flower die Blume, -, -n
follow folgen (sein) (+ *dat.*)
foot der Fuß, -es, ⁼e; **on foot** zu Fuß
for (*prep.*) für (+ *acc.*); (*conj.*) denn; (*since*) seit (+ *dat.*)
forest der Wald, -(e)s, ⁼er
forget vergessen, vergaß, hat vergessen, er vergißt
formerly früher
four vier
Fred Fritz
fresh frisch
Friday der Freitag, -(e)s, -e
friend (*masc.*) der Freund, -(e)s, -e; (*fem.*) die Freundin, -, -nen
from von (+ *dat.*)
front: in front of vor (+ *dat.* or *acc.*)

G

garden der Garten, -s, ⁼
gentleman der Herr, -n, -en

German deutsch; **in German** auf deutsch
Germany das Deutschland, e-
get werden, wurde, ist geworden, er wird; (*fetch*) holen; (*receive*) bekommen, bekam, hat bekommen
get up aufstehen, stand auf, ist aufgestanden
girl das Mädchen, -s, -
give geben, gab, hat gegeben, er gibt
go gehen, ging, ist gegangen; **going to be** werden, wurde, ist geworden, er wird
good gut
grandfather der Großvater, -s, ⁼
grandmother die Großmutter, -, ⁼
greatly sehr

H

hand die Hand, -, ⁼e
handbag die Tasche, -, -n
happy glücklich
hat der Hut, -(e)s, ⁼e
have haben, hatte, hat gehabt, er hat
he er
hear hören
heart das Herz, -ens, -en
help helfen, half, hat geholfen, er hilft (+ *dat.*)
her ihr; **of hers** von ihr
here hier
high hoch; **higher** höher; **highest** höchst, am höchsten
his sein
home nach Hause; **at home** zu Hause
horse das Pferd, -(e)s, -e
hour die Stunde, -, -n
house das Haus, -es, ⁼er

how wie; **how much** wieviel;
how are you? wie geht es
Ihnen?
hungry hungrig

I

I ich
if wenn, ob
in in (+ *dat.* or *acc.*)
innkeeper der Wirt, -(e)s, -e
instead anstatt (+ *gen.* or *inf.* with
zu)
interesting interessant; **much
that is interesting** viel Interessantes
into in (+ *acc.*)
it es; er, sie

J

journey die Reise, -, -n; **to go on a
journey** eine Reise machen

K

kilometer das (*or* der) Kilometer,
-s, -
kind: what kind of was für (ein)
king der König, -s, -e
knock klopfen
know (*a fact*) wissen, wußte, hat
gewußt, er weiß; (*be acquainted
with*) kennen, kannte, hat gekannt

L

lady die Dame, -, -n
large groß
last letzt
last (*verb*) dauern
late spät
lazy faul
learn lernen
leave abfahren, fuhr ab, ist abgefahren, er fährt ab
left link

lesson die Aufgabe, -, -n
letter der Brief, -(e)s, -e
lightning: there is lightning es
blitzt
like gern (+ *verb*); (*please*) gefallen, gefiel, hat gefallen, es gefällt (+ *dat.*)
little klein
live (*general existence*) leben; (*reside*) wohnen
living room das Wohnzimmer,
-s, -
long lang
look forward sich freuen auf (+
acc.)

M

maid das Dienstmädchen, -s, -
make machen
man der Mann, -(e)s, ⸗er
many viele
map die Karte, -, -n
match das Streichholz, -es, ⸗er
meat das Fleisch, -es
medicine die Medizin, -
meet begegnen (+ *dat.*); treffen,
traf, hat getroffen, er trifft
memorize auswendig lernen
meter das (*or* der) Meter, -s,
million die Million, -, -en
mine: of mine von mir
minute die Minute, -, -n
money das Geld, -(e)s, -er
month der Monat, -(e)s, -e
more mehr; **no more money**
kein Geld mehr; **a few more**
noch einige, noch ein paar
morning der Morgen, -s, -; **good
morning** guten Morgen; **this
morning** heute morgen
most meist; **most of all** am liebsten
mother die Mutter, -, ⸗
Mr. Herr

Mrs. Frau
much viel; **much that is new,** *etc.*
viel Neues, usw.
must müssen, mußte, hat gemußt
or hat müssen, er muß; **must not**
nicht dürfen, durfte nicht, hat
nicht gedurft *or* hat nicht dürfen,
er darf nicht
my mein, meine, mein

N

name der Name, -ns, -n; **his name
is** er heißt
name (*verb*) nennen, nannte, hat
genannt
need brauchen
never nie
new neu
night die Nacht, -, ⸗e
no nein; (*not any*) kein, keine, kein
not nicht
notebook das Heft, -(e)s, -e
nothing nichts
now jetzt, nun

O

o'clock Uhr
of (*generally rendered by the genitive*); von (+ *dat.*)
off ab; **take off** abnehmen,
nahm ab, hat abgenommen, er
nimmt ab
often oft
oh ach
old alt
on auf (+ *dat.* or *acc.*); an (+ *dat.*
or *acc.*)
once einmal; **at once** sogleich
one ein, eine, ein
only nur
open offen
open (*verb*) aufmachen, machte
auf, hat aufgemacht

or oder
order bestellen
other ander
our unser
out aus (+ *dat.*)
over: school is over die Schule ist
aus

P

package das Paket', -(e)s, -e
parents die Eltern
pay bezahlen
peasant der Bauer, -s *or* -n, -n
pen die Feder, -, -n
pencil der Bleistift, -(e)s, -e
people die Leute
picture das Bild, -(e)s, -er
place der Platz, -es, ⸗e
place (*verb*) stellen
please bitte; **to be pleased** sich
freuen
pocket die Tasche, -, -n
poet der Dichter, -s, -
poor arm
potato die Kartoffel, -, -n
prefer lieber (+ *given verb*)
professor der Profes'sor, -s, die
Professo'ren
promise versprechen, versprach,
hat versprochen, er verspricht
pupil der Schüler, -s, -; *fem.* die
Schülerin, -, -nen
put stellen

Q

question die Frage, -, -n
quick schnell

R

railroad die Eisenbahn, -, -en
rain regnen
raise aufheben, hob auf, hat aufgehoben
read lesen, las, hat gelesen, er liest

receive bekommen, bekam, hat bekommen
remain bleiben, blieb, ist geblieben
restaurant das Restaurant, -s, -s
rich reich
ride fahren, fuhr, ist gefahren, er fährt
right recht; **to be right** recht haben
room das Zimmer, -s, -
run laufen, lief, ist gelaufen, er läuft

S

same derselbe, dieselbe, dasselbe
satisfied zufrieden
Saturday der Samstag, -(e)s, -e *or* der Sonnabend, -s, -e
say sagen
school die Schule, -, -n; **to school** in die Schule *or* zur Schule
second die Sekunde, -, -n
seat; to take a seat sich setzen; Platz nehmen
see sehen, sah, hat gesehen, er sieht
sell verkaufen
send schicken (an + *acc.*)
seven sieben
seventh sieb(en)t
several einige; ein paar
shake hands die Hand geben
she sie; es
ship das Schiff, -(e)s, -e; der Dampfer, -s, -
short kurz
show zeigen
sick krank
since seit (+ *dat.*); *conj.* da
sing singen, sang, hat gesungen
sister die Schwester, -, -n
sit sitzen, saß, hat gesessen; **sit down** sich setzen

six sechs
sixty sechzig
sleep schlafen, schlief, hat geschlafen, er schläft
small klein
smile lächeln
smoke rauchen
so so; also
some manche
something etwas
son der Sohn, -(e)s, ⸗e
song das Lied, -(e)s, -er
sorry: I am sorry es tut mir leid
speak sprechen, sprach, hat gesprochen, er spricht
spring der Frühling, -s, -e
stamp die Briefmarke, -, -n
start out sich auf den Weg machen
station der Bahnhof, -s, ⸗e
stay bleiben, blieb, ist geblieben
steamer der Dampfer, -s, -
stone der Stein, -(e)s, -e
stop stehen bleiben, blieb stehen, ist stehen geblieben
story die Geschichte, -, -n
strange fremd
street die Straße, -, -n; **on this street** in dieser Straße
street car die Straßenbahn, -, -en
student der Student, -en, -en
study studieren, studierte, hat studiert
stupid dumm
such solch
summer der Sommer, -s, -
Sunday der Sonntag, -(e)s, -e
surprised erstaunt

T

table der Tisch, -es, -e
take nehmen, nahm, hat genommen, er nimmt; **take a walk** einen Spaziergang machen; **take a seat** sich setzen; **take a trip**

eine Reise machen; **take off** abnehmen, nahm ab, hat abgenommen, er nimmt ab

teacher der Lehrer, -s, -; *fem.* die Lehrerin, -, -nen

telephone telephonieren, telephonierte, hat telephoniert

tell sagen; (*a story*) erzählen

ten zehn

than als

that jener, jene, jenes; der, die, das; *conj.* daß

the der, die, das

their ihr

there da, dort; **there is, there are** es gibt (+ *acc.*); es ist, es sind

think denken, dachte, hat gedacht (an + *acc.*)

third dritt

thirty dreißig

this dieser, diese, dieses

three drei

thunder: there is thunder es donnert

ticket die Fahrkarte, -, -n

time die Zeit, -, -en; **what time** wieviel Uhr

to zu (+ *dat.*, *usually with persons*); nach (+ *dat.*, *with things*); (*with inf.*) zu

today heute

tomorrow morgen

too auch; **it is too bad** es ist schade

town: go down town in die Stadt gehen

train der Zug, -(e)s, ⸗e

travel reisen (sein)

tree der Baum, -(e)s, ⸗e

trip die Reise, -, -n; **take a trip** eine Reise machen

true wahr

Tuesday der Dienstag, -(e)s, -e

two zwei

U

umbrella der Regenschirm, -(e)s, -e

uncle der Onkel, -s, -

under unter (+ *dat.* or *acc.*)

usual gewöhnlich

university die Universität, -, -en; **at the university** (*of students*) auf der Universität; (*of professors*) an der Universität

V

vacation die Ferien (*pl.*)

vegetable das Gemüse, -s, -

very sehr

visit besuchen

W

wait warten (auf + *acc.*)

waiter der Kellner, -s, -

walk gehen, ging, ist gegangen; **take a walk** einen Spaziergang machen

wall die Wand, -, ⸗e

want wollen, wollte, hat gewollt *or* hat wollen, er will

warm warm

way der Weg, -(e)s, -e

we wir

weather das Wetter, -s, -

Wednesday der Mittwoch, -s, -e

week die Woche, -, -n; **a week ago** vor acht Tagen; **a week from today** heute über acht Tage

well (*adv.*) gut

well-known bekannt

what was; **what time** wieviel Uhr

when (*interrogative*) wann; (*definite event in past*) als; (*all other cases*) wenn

where wo; (*whither*) wohin

whether ob
which welcher, welche, welches
wide breit
will (*future*) werden (+ *verb*)
window das Fenster, -s, -
wine der Wein, -(e)s, -e
winter der Winter, -s, -
wish wünschen
with mit (+ *dat.*); **with it** damit
without ohne (+ *acc.* or *inf. with* zu)
who (*interrogative*) wer; (*relative*) der, die, das; welcher, welche, welches
whoever wer
woman die Frau, -, -en
work arbeiten

worth wert; **not worth anything** nichts wert
write schreiben, schrieb, hat geschrieben
wrong falsch

Y

year das Jahr, -(e)s, -e
yellow gelb
yesterday gestern
yet noch; **not yet** noch nicht
you (*fam. sing.*) du; (*fam. pl.*) ihr; (*conventional*) Sie
your (*fam. sing.*) dein; (*fam. pl.*) euer; (*conventional*) Ihr
young jung

GRAMMATICAL INDEX

(*The numbers refer to pages*)

aber, 37
adjectives, possessive, 42 f., 84 f.,
  235; declension of, 127 ff., 137 ff.,
  243 f.; comparison of, 162 ff.,
  244 f.; compound, 179
adverbial compounds, da (dar) +
  preposition, 120; wo (wor) +
  preposition, 146, 147
adverbs, 12, 22, 139, 162 ff.
alphabet, 1, 260 f.
als, 106, 165
als ob, als wenn, 209
articles, definite, 27, 44, 62, 67, 114,
  235; indefinite, 44, 81, 235; omission of indefinite article, 44; definite article as substitute for possessive adjective, 114

capitals, 6
cases, use of, 28
comparison, 162 ff., 244 f.
conditional, 207
conjunctions, coördinating, 104;
  subordinating, 104

denn, 105
derselbe, 197
der-words, 84f., 235
diminutives, -chen or -lein, 236

ein-words, 84 f., 235

future perfect, 95
future tense, 94

geboren, auxiliary with, 197
gibt, es gibt, 137

haben, present tense, 21; past tense,
  50 f.; past perfect, 59; present
  perfect, 59; auxiliary, 61

idioms, list of, 265 f.
imperative, 95 f.
indicative, in real conditions, 208;
  in indirect discourse, 216 f.
indirect discourse, 214 ff.
inseparable prefixes, 113 f.

kennen, 187
können, 187

leben, 44

man, 139
modal auxiliaries, 184 ff., 255, 257

nouns, gender, 11; declension of
  strong, 27 f., 67 ff., 236 ff.; weak,
  75 ff., 240 ff.; irregular, 76 f., 243;
  mixed, 76 f., 244; summary of
  rules, 77; compound, 178 f.
numerals, 173 ff., 248
nun, 105

passive, 195 ff., 256
past perfect, 59 ff.; use of, 62
past tense, 50 f.
possessive adjectives, 42 f., 84 f., 235
prepositional contractions, 120 f.
prepositions, 29, 176 f., 246 f.
present perfect, 59 ff.; use of, 62
pronouns, personal, 11, 119 f., 245;
  interrogative, 145 f., 246; indefinite relative, 147 f.; reflexive, 154
  f.; relative, 146 f., 246